General Conference of Lutherans

First general Conference of Lutherans in America

Held in Philadelphia, December 27-29, 1898

General Conference of Lutherans

First general Conference of Lutherans in America
Held in Philadelphia, December 27-29, 1898

ISBN/EAN: 9783337008321

Printed in Europe, USA, Canada, Australia, Japan

Cover: Foto ©Lupo / pixelio.de

More available books at **www.hansebooks.com**

GENERAL CONFERENCE OF LUTHERANS

IN AMERICA

HELD IN

PHILADELPHIA, DECEMBER 27-29, 1898

Proceedings, Essays and Debates

PUBLISHED CONJOINTLY BY

GEN'L COUNCIL PUBLICATION BOARD | LUTHERAN PUBLICATION SOCIETY
No. 1522 Arch Street | No. 1424 Arch Street

PHILADELPHIA:
1899

PREFACE.

Only with the publication of the proceedings and papers of the General Conference of 1898 can its significance be properly estimated. Such interest was elicited that there has been much premature discussion based upon the meagre press reports and the various impressions of participants and visitors. This volume enables the Convention to be carefully studied, and makes its appeal to future generations of Lutherans whom it will influence. Apart from their place in the Conference the papers are of themselves of permanent value.

The committee having sincerely endeavored to secure representatives of the various tendencies within their several bodies, if any element was not represented it was due to the declinature of some originally invited to respond.

Although the essayists were limited in the reading of their essays, no such restriction was placed upon the copy furnished for publication. The remarks after the essays, not being stenographically reported, were reproduced from memory, and, in some cases, more fully elaborated by some of the speakers, while, in the failure of others to do the same service, they are passed by. The discussions given are rather records of the matured opinions of the speakers than exact reproductions of what was said. While every one, therefore, is responsible for what is attributed to him no argument from silence can be just.

Neither for the settlement of any question, nor for indiscriminate discussion, was the Conference called and held. Its aim was simply to afford a faithful presentation of how the living, urgent doctrinal and practical problems of the hour are being met within the several General Bodies. Whether writers and speakers regarded themselves as the exponents of the prevalent positions in their own Bodies, or were correct in their assumptions, or simply uttered their individual convictions, must be judged by the intelligent reader. The strength of the Conference and the permanence of its influence are to be found in the clearness and distinctness of the testimony to the truth for which it afforded the opportunity, and the love of Christ, and of all who are Christ's, that pervaded it from its inception to its close.

HENRY E. JACOBS,
Chairman of Committee of Arrangements.

Philadelphia, April 20th, 1899.

TABLE OF CONTENTS.

INTRODUCTION.

OFFICIAL ACTION AND PRELIMINARY STATEMENT, 9-16.

OPENING SERVICE, 17-30.

OPENING ADDRESS, 30-34.

PROCEEDINGS OF THE CONFERENCE, 35-40.

ESSAYS AND REMARKS, 41-321.

    "OUR COMMON HISTORICAL ANTECEDENTS."

        First Essay by the Rev. Prof. E. J. Wolf, D.D., 41-62.
        Second Essay by the Rev. Prof. J. Nicum, D.D., 63-80.
        Remarks by the Rev. J. A. W. Haas, 80.
          "   "   "   E. T. Horn, D.D., 80.
          "   "   "   D. Earhart, 80.
          "   "   "   Prof. A. Spaeth, D.D., LL.D., 80-1.
          "   "   "   E. T. Horn, D.D., 81.

    "PRAYER: ITS DOCTRINE AND FORMS," by the Rev. E. T. Horn,
        D.D., 81-7.

        Remarks by the Rev. Prof. J. Nicum, D.D., 87-8.
          "   "   "   "   D. H. Bauslin, D.D., 88.
          "   "   "   "   E. J. Wolf, D.D., 88-9.
          "   "   "   G. F. Krotel, D.D., LL.D., 89-90.
          "   "   "   L. E. Albert, D.D., 90.
          "   "   "   Prof. A. Spaeth, D.D., LL.D., 90.
          "   "   "   "   J. Fry, D.D., 90.
          "   W. H. Staake, Esq., 90-3.
          "   Dr. G. G. Burnett, 93-4.
          "   Rev. E. T. Horn, D.D., 90.

ESSAYS AND REMARKS—Continued.

"Our Educational Institutions."
First Essay by the Rev. Prof. F. V. N. Painter, D.D., 94-104.
Second Essay by the Rev. Prof. S. A. Ort, D.D., LL.D., 105-115.
Remarks by the Rev. J. A. Seiss, D.D., LL.D., L.H.D., 115-16.

"The Scope and Limitation of Church Authority."
First Essay by the Rev. Prof. D. H. Bauslin, D.D., 116-132.
Second Essay by the Rev. G. F. Krotel, D.D., LL.D., 132-143.
Remarks by the Rev. J. A. W. Haas, 144.
" " " Chas. S. Albert, D.D., 144.
" " " J. C. Kunzman, 144-5.
" " " Prof. E. J. Wolf, D.D., 145-6.

"The Sacramental Idea in Lutheran Theology and Worship."
First Essay by the Rev. Prof. A. Spaeth, D.D., LL.D., 146-52.
Second Essay by the Rev. J. C. Koller, D.D., 152-61.
Remarks by the Rev. Prof. H. E. Jacobs, D.D., LL.D., 161-3.
" " " J. R. Groff, 163.
" " " Prof. A. Spaeth, D.D., LL.D., 163.

"Problems in Foreign Mission Work,"
by the Rev. George Scholl, D.D., 164-74.

"The Common Book,"
by the Rev. L. A. Fox, D.D., 174-84.
Remarks by the Rev. Prof. H. E. Jacobs, D.D., LL.D., 184.
" " " J. A. Seiss, D.D., LL.D., L.H.D., 184-6.

"Common Sunday-School Literature,"
by the Rev. L. L. Smith, 186-96.

"Lutheranism and Spirituality,"
by the Rev. E. K. Bell, D.D., 196-205.

"Deaconess Work."
Essay by the Rev. W. H. Dunbar, D.D., 205-16.

ESSAYS AND REMARKS—Continued.

"The Beginnings and Some Principles of the Deaconess Motherhouse."
  Essay by the Rev. W. A. Passavant, Jr., 216-27.
  Remarks by the Rev. Prof. A. Spaeth, D.D., LL D., 227.
    "   "   "   Frank P. Manhart, 227-9.
    "   "   "   W. H. Dunbar, D.D., 229.
    "   "   "   V. L. Conrad, Ph.D., 229-30.
    "   "   "   W. A. Passavant, Jr., 230.
    "   "   "   F. A. Kaehler, 230.

"The Lutheran Estimate of Ordination."
  First Essay by the Rev. J. A. W. Haas, 230-7.
  Second Essay by the Rev. J. R. Dimm, D.D., 237-46.
  Remarks by the Rev. Prof. E. J. Wolf, D. D., 246.
    "   "   "   J. A. Seiss, D.D., LL.D., L.H.D., 247.
    "   "   "   G. W. Enders, D.D., 248-9.
    "   "   "   E. T. Horn, D.D., 249.
    "   "   "   J. A. W. Haas, 250.
    "   "   "   J. R. Dimm, D.D., 250.

"The Standard of Ministerial Education."
  First Essay by the Rev. W. E. Parson, D.D., 250-62.
  Second Essay by the Rev. F. A. Kaehler, 262-9.
  Remarks by the Rev. Prof. J. R. Dimm, D.D., 269-70.
    "   "   "   "   J. Fry, D.D., 270.
    "   "   "   Geo. Scholl, D.D., 270.
    "   "   "   W. A. Passavant, Jr., 270-1.
    "   "   "   F. J. F. Schantz, D.D., 271.
    "   "   "   Chas. S. Albert, D.D., 271.
    "   "   "   G. F. Krotel, D.D., LL.D., 271.
    "   "   "   W. E. Parson, D.D., 271.
    "   "   "   F. A. Kaehler, 271.

"The Lutheran Church and Modern Religious Issues in Germany."
  Essay by the Rev. A. G. Voigt, D.D., 272-82.

ESSAYS AND REMARKS—CONCLUDED.

"THE LUTHERAN CHURCH AND MODERN RELIGIOUS ISSUES IN AMERICA."

Essay by the Rev. T. E. Schmauk, D.D., 283–97.

"THE PROBLEM OF CO-OPERATION."

Essay by the Rev. M. W. Hamma, D.D., 297–307.
Remarks by the Rev. L. E. Albert, D.D,, 307.
    "   "   "   Prof. F. V. N. Painter, D.D., 308.
    "   "   "   G. F. Krotel, D.D., LL.D., 308–9.
    "   "   "   S. W. Owen, D.D., 309.

"THE CHILD CATECHUMENATE."

Essay by the Rev. G. U. Wenner, D.D., 309–321.

REGISTER OF NAMES, 322–25.

INDEX OF PERSONS, 326.

INDEX OF SUBJECTS, 329.

GENERAL CONFERENCE OF LUTHERANS.

OFFICIAL ACTION
AND
PRELIMINARY STATEMENT.

The General Conference of Lutherans held in Philadelphia, Pa., December 27–29, 1898, has passed into history as an accomplished fact of more than ordinary interest and importance to Lutherans in this country. It was the First General Convention ever called together by the official action of three of the general bodies of the Lutheran Church in America.

The General Council, at its Twenty-fifth Convention, held at Easton, Pa., in 1895, where the General Synod was represented by a fraternal visitor and the United Synod of the South by a letter of fraternal greeting, passed the following resolution:

"*Resolved,* That this Council heartily approves and recommends the holding of a General Conference within the year 1896 whereby, in an unofficial way, there may be a reading of papers and a comparison of views, by members if possible, of all our General Bodies, and larger independent synods, on the various doctrinal, liturgical, educational and missionary interests (including that of Deaconesses) in which all are alike engaged."

In accordance with this resolution, the Rev. Prof. Henry E. Jacobs, D.D., LL. D., was appointed the Council's representative on the joint committee to make arrangements for the proposed Conference.

The General Synod, at its Thirty-eighth Convention, held at Mansfield, Ohio, in 1897, endorsed the above action of the General Council, and adopted the following resolution:

"That we approve the recommendation of the General Council that a General Conference be held, 'whereby, in an unofficial way, there may be a reading of papers and a comparison of views by members, if possible, of all our general bodies and larger independent synods, on the various doctrinal, liturgical, educational and missionary interests, in which all are alike engaged.' And that we approve the appointment of a committee in which Dr. Jacobs is to represent the General Council, Dr. Lund the United Norwegian Church, Dr. Horn the United Synod of the South and Dr. Owen the General Synod, to which all the arrangements for such a Conference shall be entrusted."

The Rev. S. W. Owen, D.D., of Hagerstown, Md., was appointed the General Synod's representative on the joint committee.

The United Synod of the South, at its Sixth Convention, held at Newberry, S. C., in 1898, adopted the following:

"*Resolved*, That we approve the recommendation of the joint committee for the holding of a General Conference or diet, and that Rev. H. F. Scheele be appointed to represent this body to co-operate with Dr. H. E. Jacobs and Dr. S. W. Owen in arranging for such diet."

At the Twenty-sixth Convention of the General Council, held at Erie, Pa., in 1897, the Rev. Dr. Jacobs reported with reference to the proposed General Conference, as follows:

"The undersigned appointed to arrange with representatives of the General Synod and the United Synod in the South, a General Conference, to be held in the year 1896, respectfully reports, that, although at one time the time and place of said meeting had been agreed upon, the Committee found it difficult to arrange the programme with any prospect of providing for attendance and discussions commensurate with the results that could be justly anticipated from such a gathering. It was best, therefore, to defer action until after the other General Bodies had formally approved the project. This has been done by the General Synod, and its representative, the Rev. Dr. S. W. Owen, has informed me of his readiness for a meeting to arrange preliminaries. As the representative of the United Synod, the Rev. Dr. Horn, is no longer a member of that Body, and the President of the United Synod doubts his authority without action of the General Body, to appoint a successor, the arrangements having been temporarily delayed in the expectation that the United Synod, at its approaching meeting, will provide for its representation. We would respectfully suggest that a small committee of laymen be appointed, with authority to add to their number representative laymen of the other bodies proposing to participate, for the purpose of gathering a fund for the necessary expenses of said Conference."

This report was adopted and a committee of laymen with power to add to their number, was appointed to provide a fund for the General Conference. Dr. Jacobs was continued as our member of the committee, with Dr. T. E. Schmauk, as alternate.

The joint committee thus constituted, issued the following preliminary statement, during the Summer of 1898:

The three general bodies representing the Evangelical Lutheran Church in this country, having taken action concerning the holding of a Free Conference in the near future, appointed each a representative to carry forward this project. Rev. Henry E. Jacobs, D.D., was appointed by the General Council; Rev. S. W. Owen, D.D., by the General Synod, and Rev. H. F. Scheele, D.D., by the United Synod of the South.

This committee met at the Blue Mountain House, Maryland, July 27, and organized, electing Dr. Jacobs, chairman, and Dr. Owen, secretary of the committee. They determined to ask the use of St. Matthew's and St. John's Churches, Philadelphia, Pa., in which to hold the sessions of Conference, and selected December 27-29, 1898, as the time. A program was also arranged. In order to pay the traveling expenses of the essayists and other necessary expenses of the committee it was estimated that $400 would be needed. Of this amount Dr. Scheele assumed, for the United Synod of the South, $75, and the General Council assumed $165, leaving $160 to be raised in the General Synod. The General Council, at its meeting in Erie, Pa., October 14-20,

1898, appointed a committee of laymen for the purpose of securing a fund for the necessary expenses of the Conference. The following persons constitute that committee: Messrs. William H. Hengerer, Buffalo, N. Y., chairman; William H. Staake, of Philadelphia, Pa., treasurer; Oliver Williams, Catasauqua, Pa., and Charles Schimmelfeng, Warren, Pa. On the part of the General Synod the following Finance Committee has been appointed: Messrs. J. G. C. Taddiken, New York City; W. C. Stoever, Philadelphia, Pa.; A. F. Fox, Washington, D. C., and W. F. A. Kemp, M. D., of Baltimore.

The program will doubtless be printed when finally arranged. Dr. W. S. Freas, of Baltimore, Md., and Dr. S. E. Ochsenford, of Selin's Grove, Pa., have been appointed secretaries of the Conference.

The proposed Conference being approved, not only with substantial unanimity, but with enthusiasm, by the three general bodies, it is to be hoped that, with the blessing of God, it will prove to be of great benefit to the Lutheran Church in the United States.

S. W. OWEN,
Secretary of Committee.

Subsequently the Chairman of the Joint Committee issued the following:

CALL OF THE CONVENTION.

The General Conference appointed by the joint action of the General Council, General Synod and the United Synod of the South, will convene in Philadelphia, December 27–29th, and be opened by Divine Service and a sermon by Rev. Joseph A. Seiss, D.D., LL. D., in St. John's church, Rev. E. E. Sibole, D.D., pastor, Tuesday, December 27th, at 10 A. M.

The sessions of the Conference will be held on Tuesday, December 27th, in St. John's church and on the succeedings days in St Matthew's church, Broad and Mt. Vernon streets, Rev. Wm. M. Baum, D.D., pastor.

HENRY E. JACOBS,
Chairman of Comml'tee.

PROCEEDINGS OF GENERAL CONFERENCE. 13

This was followed by the announcement by the secretary of the Committee of the

PROGRAM.

TUESDAY MORNING, December 27th, 1898. 10 A. M., divine service, with a sermon by Rev. J. A. Seiss, D.D., LL.D.

After service the conference will convene. The members of the committee will preside in rotation, and conduct the conference according to the rules, for which they are responsible to the bodies that appointed them. Rev. W. S. Freas, D.D., of Baltimore, Md., and Rev. S. E. Ochsenford, D.D., of Selin's Grove, Pa., will be the secretaries. Mr. Wm. H. Staake, of Philadelphia, Pa., has been appointed treasurer.

The opening address will be made by the chairman of the committee, Rev. Henry E. Jacobs, D.D., and the rules under which the conference shall proceed will be read.

TUESDAY, 2 P. M., Rev. H. E. Jacobs, D.D., presiding. Topic: "Our Common Historical Antecedents." First paper, Rev. E. J. Wolf, D.D. Second paper, Rev. J. Nicum, D.D. 3:30, topic: "The Doctrine and Forms of Prayer," Rev. E. T. Horn, D.D. 4:15, topic: "The Child Catechumenate," Rev. G. U. Wenner, D.D.

TUESDAY, 8 P. M., topic: "Our Educational Institutions." 1. Rev. F. V. N. Painter, D.D. 2. Rev. S. A. Ort, D.D., LL.D.

WEDNESDAY, 9 A. M., Rev. S. W. Owen, D.D., presiding. Topic: "The Scope and Limitation of Church Authority." 1. Rev. D. H. Bauslin, D.D. 2. Rev. G. F. Krotel, D.D., LL.D. 10:25, topic: "The Sacramental Idea in Lutheran Theology and Worship.' 1. Rev. A. Spaeth, D.D. 2. Rev. J. C. Koller, D.D. 11:30, topic: "Problems in Foreign Mission Work," Rev. Geo. Scholl, D.D.

WEDNESDAY, 2 P. M., topic: "The Common Book," Rev. L. A. Fox, D.D.; topic: "Common Sunday-school Literature," Rev. L. L. Smith. 3 P. M., topic: "Lutheranism and Spirituality," Rev. E. K. Bell, D.D. 3:30, topic: "Deaconess Work." 1. Rev. W. H. Dunbar, D.D. 2. Rev. W. A. Passavant, Jr.

THURSDAY, 9 A. M., Rev. H. F. Scheele, presiding. Topic: "Lutheran Estimate of Ordination." 1. Rev. J. A. W. Haas.

2. Rev. J. R. Dimm, D.D. 10:30, topic: "Standards of Ministerial Education." 1. Rev. W. E. Parson, D.D. 2. Rev. F. A. Kaehler.

THURSDAY, 2 P.M., topic: "The Lutheran Church and Modern Religious Issues." 1. In Germany, Rev. A. C. Voigt, D.D. 2. In America. Rev. T. E. Schmauk, D.D. 3 P.M., topic: "The Problem of Co-operation," Rev. M.W. Hamma, D.D.

RULES.

The following rules have been adopted by the committee to be observed in the Conference of Lutherans to be held in Philadelphia, December 27 to 29, 1898:

1. All members of the three general bodies that have authorized the calling of the Conference to have the privilege of participating in its proceedings.

2. The Committee of Arrangements, being responsible to the general bodies that appointed them for the conduct of the Conference, will decide all questions that may arise, and will preside over the proceedings.

3. All essayists shall be limited to thirty minutes, and this rule shall be strictly enforced.

4. No speech in the discussion shall exceed ten minutes; nor shall any speaker be recognized a second time in the discussion of any one topic while the privilege of the floor is claimed by others who have not spoken. The essayist shall, in all cases, have the privilege of closing the discussion on his own paper

5. No vote to be taken on any of the topics under discussion, and all propositions and motions made in Conference shall be submitted to the committee, which, at its discretion, may refer them back to the Conference for decision.

6. All papers read to be at the disposal of the committee for publication.

The members of the committee are Rev. Henry E. Jacobs, D.D., General Council; Rev. S. W. Owen, D.D, General Synod; Rev. H. F. Scheele, D.D., United Synod of the South.

S. W. OWEN,
Secretary of Committee.

These announcements were followed by another statement, issued by the secretary of the committee, as follows:

We desire to again call the attention of the Church to the importance of making contribution toward the necessary expenses of the Conference to be held in Philadelphia, Pa., Dec. 27 to 29, 1898.

The Committee of Arrangements determined to try to secure a sufficient amount of money to pay the traveling expenses of the essayists. To do this would, in the judgment of the committee, require at least $400. Each representative of the three general bodies assumed a certain portion of the total amount. A committee on finance was appointed, consisting of four brethren in the General Council and four in the General Synod. The members of this committee, on the part of the General Council, are Messrs. William H. Hengerer, Buffalo, N. Y., chairman; W. H. Staake, Philadelphia, Pa., treasurer; Oliver Williams, Catasauqua, Pa.; and Charles Schimmelfeng, Warren, Pa. On the part of the General Synod the following brethren have been named: Messrs. J. G. C. Taddiken, No. 332 West Forty-sixth Street, New York City; William C. Stoever, No. 727 Walnut Street, Philadelphia, Pa.; Dr. W. F. A. Kemp, No. 305 North Green Street, Baltimore, Md.; and Albert F. Fox, Columbia National Bank, Washington, D. C.

All friends of the Conference in the General Synod are earnestly solicited to contribute toward these necessary expenses. Contributions can be sent to either of the above-named brethren, or to me, and the same will be paid over to the treasurer.

Pastors are requested to bring this matter to the attention of their congregations. It is feared that $400 will hardly cover the expenses.

A most cordial invitation is extended to all ministers and laymen to attend this Conference. A whole-hearted welcome awaits them.

It will be a most auspicious event in the history of the Lutheran Church in this country. It has been endorsed and ordered by the three general bodies represented. We believe it is of "the Lord's doing," and, with His blessing, the result will, no doubt, be "marvelous in our eyes."

S. W. OWEN,
Secretary of Committee.

We present in this connection, a statement by the Chairman of the committee on

THE AIM OF THE CONFERENCE.

Arrangements have at last been made for the holding of the General Conference provided for by the resolution of the General Council at Easton in 1895, and subsequently approved by the General Synod and United Synod of the South. It can scarcely be called a "Free Conference," as its privileges will be accorded only members of those bodies that have united in its convocation, and its proceedings will be conducted according to rules laid down by the committee whose members are responsible, each to his own body, for the character of the deliberations. No resolutions on any topic discussed can be passed, nor can any proposition be entertained unless the committee have first approved it. It differs from the Diets of 1877 and 1878, by being an officially recognized and ordered meeting, while they were entirely individual matters.

The Conference is intended to prepare the way for a better understanding and a more harmonious co-operation among the Lutherans in the bodies named. It will provide for doctrinal discussions: but not for these exclusively, provision being made also, as the General Council directed, for the consideration of practical questions. A number of papers will be read and opportunity be given for a brief interchange of opinion upon them. . . . It has been the feeling of the committee that in case this Conference be approved by the general judgment of the Church, the way will be prepared for other conferences at other places in which a still wider scope of representation will be provided for. . . . In determining the details, the committee has acted with entire unanimity. They have endeavored to carry out the instructions they have received from their general bodies. The holding of the Conference is by the unanimous action of these bodies. The committee has not been in haste in fulfilling its instructions. The time has passed for considering the expediency of the proposition. The Church, therefore, expects the heartiest co-operation of all in this project that has been so long in prospect.

ST. JOHN'S EVANGELICAL LUTHERAN CHURCH,
Race Street below Sixth, Philadelphia, Pa.
Rev. E. E. SIBOLE, D. D., Pastor.

THE OPENING SERVICE.

The General Conference of Lutherans, representing the General Synod, General Council and United Synod of the South, was opened in St. John's Evangelical Lutheran Church, Race street, below Sixth street, Philadelphia, Pa., on Tuesday, December 27, 1898, at 10 A.M., with Divine Service, in presence of a respectable number of Lutherans, clerical and lay, who had come from various parts of the country to be present at the opening service of this important convention. St. John's is the oldest English congregation in the country, having been organized in 1806, and has had only three pastors,—the Rev. Phillip F. Mayer, D.D., 1806-1858; the Rev. Joseph A. Seiss, D.D., LL.D., L.H.D., 1858-1875; and the Rev. Edward E. Sibole, D.D., who has been serving the congregation since April 22, 1875. In the opening service of the Conference, the Rev. S. E. Ochsenford, D.D., of Selin's Grove, Pa., conducted the liturgical service, and the Rev. Dr. Jos. A. Seiss, of Philadelphia, preached the sermon, based on Ephesians 4: 1-6. Following is the sermon:

THE UNITY OF THE CHURCH.

Grace unto you, and peace from God our Father, and from our Lord Jesus Christ.

DEARLY BELOVED, FATHERS, BRETHREN, AND FRIENDS:

In discharging the duty assigned me for the opening of this marked Convention, I invite your attention to the first part of the fourth chapter of Paul's Epistle to the Ephesians, where the great Apostle writes:

"I therefore, the prisoner of the Lord, beseech you that ye walk worthy of the vocation wherewith ye have been called, with all lowliness and meekness, with longsuffering, forbearing one another in love; endeavoring to keep the unity of the Spirit in the bond of peace. There is one body, and one Spirit, even as ye are called in one hope of your calling; one Lord, one faith, one Baptism, one God and Father of all, who is above all, and through all, and in all."—EPH. 4: 1-6.

Two leading topics are here presented to our contemplation: *The True Unity of the Church,* and *What that Unity Demands of Us.*

God help us to apprehend them aright, and to profit by the truth!

The Church is the community of saints, inclusive of all true Christians, of all nations and ages. This Church is here described as one,—"*one body;*" and it becomes us to inquire wherein this oneness consists. The question is very important; and to reach a proper answer, it may be justly said:

The Unity of the Church is not territorial—not national; for the Church of Christ is not limited to any one country or continent. It extends beyond all geographical boundaries, and exists in widely separated sections of the earth.

Neither does the Unity of the Church consist in uniformity of ceremonies or external regulations, whether liturgical, legislative, or executive. There is, indeed, that which constitutes its being, and which does not admit of change; but there is still much that may be externally variant. There have been, and are, many genuine Christians, under differing forms of outward government and administration; and it is quite agreed that traditions, rites, or orders instituted by men, need not be everywhere the same. Under many names, conditions, and denominational and territorial organizations, the Church of Christ has existed, and still exists,—not always and everywhere in the same perfection and efficiency, but in sufficient integrity to beget and nourish children of God.

Neither does the Unity of the Church consist in perfect identity of thought, expression, and details of interpretation and belief.

Differences of this kind have existed within the Church in every age, not excepting the first. There is an essential faith, which is everywhere and always the same; but different minds approach it from different directions, view it from different standpoints, and see it in different lights. It was so among the apostles themselves, and will be so while the present condition of human nature remains. Nor are differences of this kind to be rashly condemned. They may even be useful, and serve to bring out more clearly the many-sidedness of God's truth. Paul and James supplement each other; and Paul's controversy with Peter helped to the settlement of a great question. The clashings of theological thought often disturb the Church's peace, but without destroying its unity, or imperiling its being. Storms help to clear the atmosphere; and perfect coincidence of view, while not essential to the Church's oneness, is liable to breed stagnation and death.

Nor does the Unity of the Church consist in undisturbed affection, practical harmony, and unbroken accord between the various members or sections. Brothers in the same family are brothers, whether they quarrel or agree. Real Christians are joint partakers of the same divine nature, and so are members of the body of Christ, whether they acknowledge one another or not. They may refuse outward inter-communion; but in so far as they are Christians at all, there remains an inward oneness in Christ in spite of all personal and party alienations. Paul and Barnabas disagreed, even to a somewhat violent parting asunder; but they still were efficient apostolic members and servants of the one true Church of Christ, and perhaps more efficient and useful because of the separation. Indeed, nothing dependent on man, or man's endeavors, enters into the essential Unity of the Church.

These statements I take to be clear and incontrovertible.

We come, then, to the more positive answer to our question, in which the text furnishes an ample guide.

It is here to be noted, first of all, that the apostle presents the Unity of the Church as "*the Unity of the Spirit.*" This is not always rightly perceived. He does not mean a mere man-made agreement, or a common spiritual accord depending on the mutual consent of man; but a unity originating with, and constituted by, the Holy Ghost,—a unity of which the Spirit of God is the potent factor,—a unity which external conditions, arrangements, or diversities do not make or destroy. The Church does not first come into being, and then form itself into a spiritual corporation by human wisdom and endeavor. All true Christians are "born of the Spirit," and thus come into the family of believers from the start. That which makes them Christians, at the same time makes them members of the one body, whatever else may be true of them. Having become members of the household of faith, they are from the first and always one with all believers in Christ, and nothing can augment the reality of that oneness, or more essentially differentiate them from all other people The external conditions, or the particular outward forms and surroundings in which spiritual is life generated, may be so different in different cases and communities as to conceal the visible tokens of the oneness, and yet the true oneness exist. Indeed, we can never surely know, from outward signs, who of the various outwardly professing Christians are of the true interior Church. There are certain external marks and notes shown in the preaching and confession of the Gospel, and the administration of the sacraments, by which we may know where the Church is; but just who of its visible members are inwardly and truly of the community of saints, these marks and notes do not and can not determine. We know no Church apart from these external marks and signs; for the internal, spiritual and invisible being of the Church is not separable from visible men and women, or from the use of outward means of grace through which its spiritual members are begotten. Nevertheless, the Church may be present in outward showing, while those who appear as members may be no real part of Christ's mystical body. The true Unity of the Church is, therefore, something much more inward and spiritual than the notes and marks by which its presence is externally indicated. It is mainly in the realm of the Holy Spirit, and of the Holy Spirit's work, that the Unity of the Church has its being.

And yet it is a substantial reality, and not a mere shadowy

dream. It has its own life and embodiment in certain particulars which the apostle here sets forth.

1. It is a unity of *spiritual corporation*. "There is one body." It is a real and true body—a society of living men, women and children, joined together, it may be, in outward fellowship, but more really in a mystic organism. The members are many, and the particular groups of members may be many, with all the earthly diversities of nation, language, clime, age, culture, and estate; but one family nevertheless, begotten of the one Holy Ghost, and built into the one spiritual edifice. "For as we have many members in one body, and all members have not the same office, so we, being many, are one body in Christ." Some have higher place and greater honor than others; but all together are one mystical corporation, one body.

2. The Unity of the Church is a oneness of *soul*, or *life*. There is "One Spirit," the Spirit of God, by which men are quickened into life to God and heaven. There may be many spirits by which people are influenced and animated; but there is only one Holy Spirit, and one life to that Spirit. All Christians have not the same gifts, or in the same degree; yet all are animated by one life, from one and the self-same Spirit. Children do not more really live the life they derive from their parents, than all true members of the Church live the one life from the one Spirit. And the Church is one, because it has this one soul, and lives this one generic life.

3. The Unity of the Church is furthermore a oneness of *hope*. "Even as ye are called in One Hope of your calling." The purpose of grace is one, even the recovery of sinners from death and condemnation to salvation and eternal life. There is no Gospel call but this; and there is no true answer to that call, except to this end. Varied and unspeakable are the blessings promised to the willing and obedient; but whether or not they are all definitely understood, or specifically contemplated, there is this one goal to which all true Christians look and aspire. And this one hope of their calling furnishes another feature of their oneness in Christ, the oneness of the Church.

4. But the Unity of the Church is likewise a unity of *headship*.

"One Lord." There be lords many; "but to us," saith the apostle, "there is one Lord Jesus Christ," who is "the Head over all things to the Church, which is His body." People greatly differ in their views of Christ. Some assign to Him a character, place, office and relation to His people, very diverse from what others hold and believe. But Christ is not so elastic as to be whatever men may make of Him. Some may apprehend Him with greater fullness and perfection of faith and understanding than others; but He is not God to one, God-man to another, and a mere superior creature to a third. So far as He is savingly apprehended by any, He is One, "the same yesterday, to-day, and for ever," identical in nature and office to the view of all entitled to be named by His name. The Church knows but one Lord Jesus, the Messiah of prophecy, the Son of the living God, sacrificed on Calvary for the sin of the world, risen from the dead, alive for evermore, exalted to the right hand of eternal Majesty, clothed with all power in heaven and earth; and who, having loved the Church, and given Himself for it, is ever with it, to direct, command, and help it by His Spirit, Word and Ordinances, till perfected, and brought into everlasting union with Himself. And as there is no Church where this Christ is not preached, accepted and honored as its living Head, so the Church is one by its acknowledgment of Him, and union with Him.

5. Hence also, the Unity of the Church is a unity of *belief*. With its One Lord, it has but "One faith," by which He is apprehended, confessed and confided in. Unity of faith is essential to "the Unity of the Spirit." And the Christian faith is a specific and definite faith,—a faith that takes account of what it believes, and holds firmly to it. The chief substance of the One Faith has its centre in adoring love of Christ. This sums up everything. There may be weaknesses and mistakes here or there, or even interminglings of superstition, much to be lamented, and by no means to be ignored, which still may not entirely disable saving faith, or totally exclude from the family of believers. A diseased man, or one mutilated in some non-vital part, is still a man, though without perfect physical manhood; and one can

be a true member of Christ, along with many imperfections, provided the soul duly understands and firmly and lovingly holds to the true Christ as its hope and salvation. But, from this there can be no let-down or abridgment without total loss of Christian standing. Every living man or woman who would be saved must believe on the Lord Jesus Christ. What saith the Scripture? "He that believeth not the Son shall not see life, but the wrath of God abideth on him." And as every true part of the Church must have this faith, the Church is one in the unchangeable oneness of its essential creed.

6. Still further, the Unity of the Church is a unity of *the official marking of its members.* "One Baptism." By Christ's own appointment and command, a vital part in the work of making disciples is, "baptizing them." According to Him there is no way of making disciples with Baptism omitted. Whatever else people may be or possess, they are not, and cannot be, regular Christians without Christian Baptism. Some may look upon it as a mere outward and empty ceremony; but all the great things of the covenant of salvation are connected with it, and signified and sealed by it. To reject Baptism is to reject the seal of the covenant. It is the divinely instituted act of initiation into the kingdom—one of the visible marks of the invisible Church. Many receive it outwardly who never reach approved citizenship, because deficient in other particulars; but, so far as concerns us, no one can be scripturally counted in with the proper Church of God who refuses washing in this heaven-ordained "laver of regeneration." Where Baptism into the Name of the Father, Son, and Holy Ghost goes, there the Church is; and where that is not, the Church is not. And by this one sacred Baptism and official marking of its members, the Unity of the Church is shown, and its external boundaries determined.

7. And yet once more, the Unity of the Church is a unity of *worship,* especially in the object of that worship. Its Liturgies have varied somewhat in different ages and nations, but never in essential substance, or in the supreme object of its adoration: "One God and Father of all, who is above all, and through all, and in all." Jesus differentiated the Church's worship from all

other worships, when He said to the woman of Samaria, "Ye worship ye know not what; we know what we worship,—the true worshippers worship the Father in spirit and in truth." And in this worship, the Church of Christ is ever one.

Sublime is the majesty and glory of Him whom the Church worships and adores.

"God!" Who can fathom the full meaning of that one little word?

And Father of all! What an unbounded paternity of almighty power and origination is thus expressed!

Who is above all! There be many great and high things in the universe,—many quite over-reaching our comprehension and highest thought,—but He whom the Church worships is above them all, their Creator, their Ruler, their eternal Originator and their Lord.

"*And through all!*"—confined to no place, in time or space, but present everywhere, in all the fullness of His unsearchable Being.

"*And in all!*" In the faith, the experiences, the assemblies, the hopes, and the hearts of all His people, and in the government and direction of all things, visible and invisible.

"*One God!*" One only; but a Tri-unity,—God the Father, God the Son, and God the Holy Ghost, as also recognized in this text; not three Gods, but one God; for the Godhead of the Father, and of the Son, and of the Holy Ghost, is all one, the glory equal, the majesty co-eternal. The Unity in Trinity, and the Trinity in Unity, is the One, revealed, true and only God. And in the sole and devout adoration and worship of this God, the Church's Unity has its crown and highest fullness.

Having thus briefly indicated the true Oneness of the Church, although without having at all exhausted the subject, we now come to note, *What this Unity demands of us.*

Here observe again, that the apostle contemplates the Church's Oneness as something created by the Holy Ghost, and not as a thing to be made, or brought about, by human activities or endeavors.

The thought is not that it devolves on us to work up the

Church into oneness. That is no more in our power than it is in the power of brothers to make themselves children of their father. The oneness is already presupposed as the basis and ground of the admonitions given. And on this ground alone do they have their applicability and force.

To what, then, would the Apostle have us direct our efforts, if not to the making of the Church a visible organic unity? The words are plain. The entreaty is, that we walk worthy of the vocation wherewith we have been called into this invisible Unity of the Spirit, and show that we are one with all believers in our behavior toward one another. What exists in spiritual fact, the Apostle would have us personally illustrate and exhibit in external walk, by diligent endeavor to keep the peace. Having been graciously brought into the sacred brotherhood of believers, the idea is that we scandalize our profession if we do not try to live in amity with one another. That may not always be feasable. In the present condition of humanity, offences will come. Hence the direction to *endeavor*, that is, to exert ourselves with earnestness, to have our spiritual oneness as Christians appear also in outward behavior and temper. Because the real Church is one body in Christ, it is our business to aim at showing it by external harmony and peace. Organic union is not the matter in point. The meaning is, that, having become brethren and fellow-citizens in the sublimest of spiritual unities, it is to be to us an inviolable bond and stimulus to do all we can to keep the peace.

And in order to succeed in this, the Apostle specifies certain qualities of temper and behavior to be observed and cultivated.

All lowliness is named. Nothing is more out of place, or more ruinous to the Church's quiet and prosperity, than an uplifted, pretentious and vain-glorious spirit. Where there is a proud vaunting of self or party, and the putting forth of an inflated loftiness which looks down upon others as unworthy of recognition, the bond of peace cannot hold. Differences and contentions are not always avoidable; but it will not do for Christians to be imperious and harsh in their judgments and condemnations, particularly as the error to be corrected may not all be on one side. There needs to be moderation and lowliness, as over against the claim of being the only model saints, with whose standards all must fully accord, or accept anathema.

Meekness is named. This does not refer so much to a soft and yielding disposition, and the bridling of a passionate nature, as to submissiveness under ill treatment, and the quiet commitment of ourselves into the hand of God, trusting to His good providence for our vindication. Much evil may be avoided by a meek and passive non-resistance, where not otherwise bound in conscience. "The wisdom from above is first *pure*"; and so is unyielding where plain duty and God's truth are in question; but, in all other cases, it is "peaceable, gentle, easy to be entreated, full of mercy and good fruits, without partiality, and without hypocrisy." Meekness is ever a valuable conservitor of the peace. It often abashes the evil eye, silences the taunting tongue, and refutes the shameful accusation; while proud and brassy self-assertion is sure to stir up resentment and trouble.

Long-suffering is named. Life is full of frictions, hurts and irritations; and if any one wishes to take offence, or find room for quarrel, he will be at no loss for opportunities. Human nature is also very quick to resent wrongs, whether real or supposed. But, if peace and fraternity are to be maintained, there must be patient overlooking of provocations and faults, suppression of harsh retaliation, and willingness to suffer for the time rather than go to war with one another. As Christians, we are supposed to have grace and self-control enough for this. There are instances in which sternness and severity are in place, and must be exercised; but, in all cases, it becomes us to entertain and show Christian charity, which suffereth long, is kind, and is not easily provoked.

Forbearing one another in love is named. At best, we are all full of imperfections. In many things we all offend. We cannot help it. But love is a great healer of wounds. It covers many sins. And as we would have others allow for our faults, infirmities, mistakes and indiscretions, and for love's sake not hold us to strict account; we must be heroic enough to forbear and forgive wherein they may not be up to what we might think due and proper. In one of our confessional books it is said: "In all families and states concord is nourished by mutual forbearance and kindness, and tranquillity cannot be retained unless men overlook and forgive one another's mistakes; so, according to St. Paul, to preserve harmony in the Church, there must be love and charity, bearing, as need be, with the rougher ways of brethren, and overlooking minor errors, lest the Church rend into factions and schisms, and from these enmity, bitterness and heresies arise. . . . Public harmony cannot continue in the Church unless pastors and people overlook and pass by many things." Beautiful words! and true as beautiful.

And all this the holy Apostle very earnestly entreats of us, as so befitting Christians, that our personal Christianity is in doubt if we do not strive to demean ourselves after this manner. The implication is, that perfect and uninterrupted harmony is hard to maintain, if at all attainable; that alienations will come; and that breaches of brotherly concord will occur; but the requirement is, for us to exert ourselves in honest endeavor, that the fault may not be ours.

Nor is there a more powerful argument to move and animate us in these efforts, than that which the Apostle here urges. If the Holy Ghost has really begotten us unto God—if we really have been incorporated into the one indivisible body of the renewed and sanctified, and become joint heirs with Jesus to the eternal inheritance—how utterly unworthy of the sublime honor, and how glaringly inconsistent with our oneness with all believers, to refuse amity and good feeling toward others, who, so far as we can judge or know, stand in the same heavenly relationship! Disdaining to regard any of God's children as our brethren here, how can we count ourselves members of His household, or fitted for that deeper fellowship with them in the great hereafter!

Where the true Christ is rejected, His plain truth put aside, and His sacred ordinances trampled under foot, we are under holy bonds to refuse Christian recognition and fraternity. Pertinacity in heresy and schism dare not be treated with indifference. But I pity the people who claim to be God's children, and profess to stand in the Unity of the Spirit with all believers, and yet will not agree to live in peace and charity with those who are quite as likely God's children as themselves. I can conceive of nothing more unseemly, or more vitiating to one's claim to be of the family of the regenerated and saved, than a zeal so Pharisaic and unsavory.

Most solemn, therefore, are these entreaties of the imprisoned apostle, and most binding upon all who would be consistent Christians. And membership in the community of saints, as well as the true morality of the Gospel, demands of us honest and diligent endeavor to conform to them, that "the bond of peace" may not be broken.

To what extent we ministers and members of the Church have been governed by these apostolic admonitions in the various differences and contentions that have existed among us, is a question that comes home to each for earnest and devout heart-searching. Professing and claiming to be one in Christ, bearing the same family name, acknowledging the same Confession, and agreeing in so many things, we may well ask ourselves, before God, Have we really so ordered our temper, behavior, words and writings, as to do all we might have done to "Keep the Unity of the Spirit in the bond of peace?" Happy he who has nothing with which to reproach himself in this respect!

But the past is past, and its records cannot be altered. The conditions which it has wrought are here, and with these we have to do. We have our several predilections, our separate places and associations, and our somewhat variant judgments of what is most wise and politic in the management of our common cause. We belong to different outward organizations, with their several particular histories, conditions and requirements. All this may be, and be for the best, in the outworking of the problems with which we have to deal. It may not be wise to encroach too much upon what is, lest we spoil and damage more than we conserve. But there is nothing in this to hinder confraternity in the spirit of the text. We can come together betimes as brethren of the same general household, and confer with each other on matters that concern the welfare of our common Zion. We can grasp each other's hands, hear each other speak, and compare together each other's thoughts and views; and so fit ourselves the better to realize and appreciate the truth. And is it not a matter of good omen, that this Convention has been called by the joint action of the three general bodies to which most of us belong. And if we are careful to exemplify the entreaties of the Great Apostle, to which I have referred, there surely is reason to anticipate from it much personal edification, and much valuable benefit to the Church. God be merciful to us, and so rule and guide us by His Holy Spirit, that our intercourse, sayings and doings may be to His praise, and tend to inaugurate a new era for our too much divided Church in this land!

The day on which we meet happens to be St. John's Day, and this church is named St. John's Church. Here is coincidence that may not be without significance—perhaps even prophetic. St. John was preëminently the apostle of love and sacred meditation. He leaned the closest on the Saviour's bosom. He most fully described the dignity and sublime mystery of our Saviour's person. And if his spirit should prove to be the spirit of this Convention, it cannot fail to be a lasting benefaction.

German philosophers have voiced a theory, that the history of the Church has three characteristic stages, answering to the history of the individual man: First, the period of sensations and outward growth and expansion; then the period of self-consciousness, discontent with restraining authority, and the assertion of personal freedom; and then the period of sober reflection, the balancing and adjustment of ideas, and the crowning of manhood in the calm and kindliness of peaceful age. And so they say the first stage of the Church's history was *Petrine*—the period of missionary activity, of growth, and of the external upbuilding of the Church, culminating in the early centuries, and extending to the time of the Reformation. Then came a second stage, which they call the *Pauline*—the era of mental awakening, of controversy within the Church, of revolt against the bondage of legalism, tradition and super-exalted institutional dictation, tending to enthrone private judgment, and begetting many conflicting divisions of thought and organization, unfortunately so plentifully developed in these later times. But this they claim is now about to be followed by an incoming third stage, which they name the *Johanine*—marked by the softening and reconciling power of love and charity, the doing away with gnarled prejudices, the harmonizing of convictions in deeper and clearer apprehensions of the truth as it is in Jesus, the summing up of theology in the Christ, and the settling down of Christendom into the calm and peace of a better understanding of what belongs to a true and loving Christianity. O for the realization of such a time and order! O that this Convention, initiated on this St. John's day, in this St. John's Church, may be the precursor of such a Johanine age for our Evangelical Lutheran Church in America! Amen. And Amen.

After the close of the service, the Rev. Prof. Henry E. Jacobs, D.D., LL.D., of Mt. Airy, Philadelphia, Chairman of the Committee of Arrangements, called the Conference to order and formally opened the Convention with the following appropriate address:

ADDRESS BY DR. JACOBS.

FATHERS AND BRETHREN:

We meet on historic ground. Within thirty miles, two hundred and fifty-nine years ago, while Germany was amidst the throes of the Thirty Years' War, and the fall of Gustavus Adolphus on the field of Lützen was a recent occurrence, a Lutheran pastor was faithfully preaching the Gospel. Nine miles from here in Delaware county two hundred and fifty years ago, Luther's Catechism was translated into the language of the surrounding Indians. Within twenty minutes, the streetcars will take you to the venerable *Gloria Dei* church, nearly two centuries old, whose walls witnessed the first Lutheran ordination service in America. As you tread its aisle, you may pause to read the inscription over the remains of Rudman, who was instrumental in inducting the first German Lutheran pastor ordained here into the ministry, and who eagerly responded to every call that came to preach the Gospel, whether in Swedish, English or Dutch; and of that man of like spirit, Dylander, who served so faithfully the Germans of Germantown and Lancaster as well as the people of his own nationality; and may gather inspiration from the example of men, who not only laid the foundations of our Church, but who did so with a catholicity that provided for all professing the Lutheran faith.

Hither one hundred and fifty-six years ago, Muhlenberg

came, and near Fifth and Arch Streets, barely two squares hence, began his work in this city. One hundred and fifty years ago, last summer, in this immediate neighborhood, the Swedish Provost with Muhlenberg and four other German pastors laid the foundation of the Synodical organization of the Lutheran Church of America. The Liturgy then adopted is almost completely identical with that which the Joint Committee representing our three Bodies approved thirteen years ago, in a well-known building on the south side of the square at the head of this street. Not far was the old church to which the Congress of the United States repeatedly repaired for public service, when this city was its capital; and the grave-yard, where in the terrible scourge of yellow fever, one hundred and five years ago, Dr. Helmuth proved himself a hero. Ninety-two years ago, this congregation of St. John's, in whose church we have assembled on St. John the Apostle's Day, was founded to proclaim the faith of our fathers, in the language of this city and country. Although it has now only its third pastor it stands to-day the oldest Lutheran congregation in the land, in which the English has been, from the beginning, the language of public worship. In St. Matthew's Church, whose congregation is but nine years younger, the First Free Lutheran Diet met twenty-one years ago, bringing together in public discussion, for the first time, those who had been separated since the crisis thirty-two years ago at Fort Wayne.

A careful review of the history of our Church in the East, since the Diets of 1877 and '78 were held, would enable us to trace the great service they rendered in moulding opinion and cultivating mutual esteem. Those meetings, however, were purely individual matters, and lacked any formal endorsement by Synod or General Bodies.

To-day we meet by authority of the General Council, General Synod and United Synod of the South. The credit for originating the negotiations belongs to the General Synod; that for proposing this Conference, to the General Council. We are here not for the purpose of projecting any plans for the ultimate unification of the Church. Our General Bodies have not authorized us to pass any resolutions or take any action on the questions we are to consider. Nor are we here for the purpose of reviewing the history of our years of separation and controversy, and attempting in a public discussion to justify or condemn the action or position of Synods or General Bodies at particular times. There are no advocates here either of the infallibility of Synods, or of the conviction, that while they are fallible, nevertheless, they have been preserved always from error. We are no less loyal to our Mother Synod, when we candidly criticize her past history, and trace tendencies that are inconsistent with her confessional position. We are not here as partisans, to array one Body against another, and to seek to triumph in public debate. Our purpose is not to gain an advantage over some rival, to endeavor to general-councilize the General Synod, or to general-synodize the General Council; or to prepare the way for some radical readjustment of existing church organizations. What Providence intends by this Conference, and whither it may lead, no one can tell; but we have simply followed as the way seemed of itself to open. The proposition was almost spontaneously suggested, and without argument has met unanimous approval, on the floor of our General Bodies.

We are here to treat of the great principles we profess to hold in common, to descend beneath the surface to the foundations upon which they rest, and then again to rise to a proper conception of their manifold relations and far-reaching consequences. As the faith of the Church is greater than its organization, questions concerning the faith itself overshadow in importance all that pertains to organization. It is of more importance that we should be able to confer concerning principles, than that we should be ready to confer concerning organization itself. With entire loyalty to our several Synods, we are here to recognize the fact that the lines of church organization, important as they are for the efficient administration of church work, are entirely inadequate to limit the interest which, as Christians and particularly as Lutheran Christians, we take in each other's life and progress. There is only one divinely-instituted Church, and that is the congregation of believers or "communion of saints." There is only one essential to the true unity of the Church, and that is, as the Augsburg Confession declares, "not that human traditions or rites and ceremonies be everywhere alike," *i. e.*, that all should be under the same government, and be regulated by the same rules of administration, but that "they agree concerning the doctrine of the Gospel and the administration of the sacraments." When our agreement within these spheres is established, our separation into diverse organizations may serve to increase our efficiency, instead of retarding it; while union in organization without such agreement will tend only to strife and confusion. We are here to speak with entire candor and in the spirit of Christian love concerning the faith that is dearer to us than life itself; to patiently answer all questions and to remove misapprehensions.

But as faith has manifold modes of expression, it would be wrong to limit our view to but one side. As we cannot properly treat of any article of faith without considering its relation to the entire system, so, to be just, we must examine the confessional principle as it emerges into expression in the practical work of the Church. We are here to help one another in ascertaining the peculiar work that Providence has appointed the Lutheran Church in this Western world; to realize our opportunities; and to soberly estimate our discouragements and difficulties. We are here not only to provoke one another to love and good works, as we proceed on our way on parallel lines, but, so far as we can, to afford each other all aid in bearing burdens and repelling opponents and removing obstacles, and advancing our Master's Kingdom. We are all benefited by that which promotes the true interests of any of our General Bodies; we are all injured by that which retards or dishonors any. In a word, we are here to learn to know each other better—to grow more deeply into the faith of the Augsburg Confession we all profess to be the standard of our teaching, and into the love of Christ which is the source of all hopes for this world and the next.

We are here not as officially approved representatives of our several bodies, but as individuals, who, apart from all relations to these Bodies, may speak, each one according to the faith that is in him.

We may be only at the beginning of a series of Conferences

like these. All important movements and institutions in the Kingdom of God mature slowly. Three days are entirely inadequate for satisfactory discussions. They can only prepare the way for what Providence has yet in store. The committee, in the program it submits, has attempted only to make a beginning. If it be unsatisfactory, there may be ample opportunity hereafter to embody all improvements in provision for future Conferences.

Much has been attained already in the cause which this Conference represents. For twenty years, General Synod, General Council and United Synod of the South have been co-operating successfully in the work of liturgical reform. More recently an agreement to prevent collisions and friction in the establishment of missions has been officially approved by all these Bodies,—which if consistently maintained and administered through its Joint Board of Arbitration, will practically unite the several Bodies into one Confederation of Churches. For some years, our representatives in the great work of deaconesses have found an association for mutual encouragement profitable. Between our General Bodies there is an interchange of official visitors. All these relations the General Council has officially explained as follows: "The General Synod recognized the General Council as a Lutheran body by its invitation for co-operation. The General Council, in accepting the invitation and binding its representatives to the Fundamental Principles of Faith and Church Polity, regarded the General Synod's basis, properly interpreted, as not inconsistent with these principles, but held that the principles of the Council are necessary for the proper guardianship and defence of the Augsburg Confession, which the General Synod's basis professes to maintain."

We have come together, then, in the fear of God to meet the issues that our calling demands; and to learn, by a comparison of judgments, where we are and whither Providence directs us.

May He who has brought us together go before us with His most gracious favor, and follow us with His continual help, that all our deliberations and discussions, begun, continued and ended in Him, may glorify His holy Name, and advance His kingdom. AMEN.

PROCEEDINGS OF THE CONFERENCE.

FIRST SESSION.

St. John's Church, Philadelphia, Pa., }
Tuesday, December 27, 1898, 2 p.m. }

The Rev. Dr. Jacobs called the Convention to order and presided. The session was opened with prayer by the Rev. H. F. Scheele, of St. Joseph, Mo. According to previous appointment, the Rev. Drs. Wm. S. Freas, of Baltimore, Md., and S. E. Ochsenford, of Selin's Grove, Pa., acted as secretaries. The rules governing the Convention were read by the Rev. Dr. Freas.

The first subject considered was entitled: "Our Common Historical Antecedents." The first essay was read by the Rev. Prof. E. J. Wolf, D.D., of Gettysburg, Pa., and the second by the Rev. Prof. John Nicum, D.D., President of Wagner College, Rochester, N. Y.

Remarks were made by Revs. J. A. W. Haas, of New York City; E. T. Horn, D.D., of Reading, Pa.; D. Earhart, of Philadelphia; Prof. A. Spaeth, D.D., LL.D., of Mt. Airy; and Drs. Wolf and Nicum.

The second subject considered was that of "Prayer: Its Doctrine and Forms." The essayist was the Rev. Edward T. Horn, D.D., of Reading, Pa.

Remarks were made by Revs. J. Nicum, D.D., of Rochester, N. Y.; Prof. D. H. Bauslin, D.D., of Springfield, O.; Prof. E. J. Wolf, D D., of Gettysburg, Pa.; G. F. Krotel, D.D., LL.D., of East Orange, N. J.; L. E. Albert, D.D., of Germantown, Pa.;

Prof. Dr. A. Spaeth, of Mt. Airy; Prof. J. Fry, D.D , of Mt. Airy; W. H. Staake, Esq., of Philadelphia; Dr. G. G. Burnett, of San Francisco, Cal.; and Rev. Dr. Horn.

The Conference adjourned with prayer by the Rev. C. E. Hay, D.D., of Harrisburg, Pa.

SECOND SESSION.

St. John's Church,
Tuesday, December 27, 1898, 8 p.m.

The Rev. H. F. Scheele presided. The session opened with the Vesper Service, conducted by the Rev. E. E. Sibole, D.D., pastor of St. John's Church.

The topic for the evening session was "Our Educational Institutions." The first essay was read by the Rev. Prof. F. V. N. Painter, D.D., of Roanoke College, Salem, Va.; and the second by the Rev. Prof. S. A. Ort, D.D., LL.D., President of Wittenberg College and Seminary, Springfield, O.

Remarks were made by the Rev. Dr. Jos. A. Seiss, of Philadelphia.

The session was closed with the Vesper Service, conducted by the pastor of the church.

THIRD SESSION.

St. Matthew's Church, Philadelphia,
Wednesday, December 28, 1898, 9 a.m.

The Rev. S W. Owen, D.D., presided. The session was opened with prayer by the Rev. Prof. J. Fry, D.D , of Mt. Airy, Philadelphia.

The first subject considered was that of "The Scope and Limitation of Church Authority." The first essay was read by the Rev. Prof. D. H. Bauslin, D.D., of Wittenberg Seminary, Springfield, O., and the second by the Rev. G. F. Krotel, D.D., LL.D , of East Orange, N. J.

Remarks were made by Revs. J. A. W. Haas, of New York; Chas. S. Albert, D.D., of Philadelphia; J. C. Kunzman, of Pittsburg, Pa.; E. J. Wolf, D.D., of Gettysburg, Pa.; and Drs. Bauslin and Krotel concluded the reading of their papers.

The second subject on the program was entitled: "The Sacra-

ST. MATTHEW'S EVANGELICAL LUTHERAN CHURCH,
N. W. Cor. Broad and Mount Vernon Sts., Philadelphia, Pa.
Rev. W. M. BAUM, D.D., Pastor.

mental Idea in Lutheran Theology and Worship." The first paper on this subject was presented by the Rev. Prof. A. Spaeth, D.D., LL D , of the Theological Seminary at Mt. Airy, Philadelphia; and the second by the Rev. J. C. Koller, D.D., of Hanover, Pa.

Remarks were made by the Revs. Dr. Jacobs, of Mt. Airy; J. R. Groff, of Doylestown, Pa.; and Dr. Spaeth.

The third subject considered at this session was entitled: "Problems in Foreign Mission Work," and was presented by the Rev. Geo. Scholl, D.D., of Baltimore, Md.

The Conference adjourned with prayer by the Rev. Wm. M. Baum, Jr., of Canajoharie, N. Y.

FOURTH SESSION.

CHAPEL OF MARY J. DREXEL HOME,
Wednesday, December 28, 1898, 2 P.M.

The Rev. Dr. S. W. Owen presided. The session was opened with prayer by the Rev. Geo. C. F. Haas, of New York City.

The first subject presented was that of "Common Sunday-School Literature," by the Rev. L. L. Smith, of Strasburg, Va.

The second paper prepared by the Rev. L. A. Fox, D.D., of Salem, Va., on the subject,—"The Common Book," was read, in the absence of the author, by the Rev. Dr. Painter.

Remarks were made by Drs. Jacobs and Sciss.

The third essay, on the subject of "Lutheranism and Spirituality," was read by the Rev. E. K. Bell, D.D., editor of *The Lutheran World*, of Mansfield, O.

Remarks were made by the Rev. J. R. Groff, of Doylestown, Pa.

The fourth subject treated was that of "Deaconess Work." The first essayist was the Rev. W. H. Dunbar, D.D., of Baltimore, Md., and the second the Rev. W. A. Passavant, Jr., of Pittsburg, Pa.

Remarks were made by the Revs. Dr. A. Spaeth, of Mt. Airy; F. P. Manhart, of Baltimore; Dr. W. H. Dunbar, of Baltimore; Dr. V. L. Conrad, of Philadelphia; W. A. Passavant, Jr., of Pittsburg; and F. A. Kaehler, of Buffalo, N. Y.

The Conference adjourned with prayer by the Rev. A. S. Hartman, D.D., of Baltimore, Md.

FIFTH SESSION.

St. Matthew's Church,
Thursday, December 29, 1898, 9 A M.

The Rev. H. F. Scheele presided. The session was opened with prayer by the Rev. Luther Kuhlman, D.D., of Frederick, Md.

The first subject considered was "The Lutheran Estimate of Ordination." The first essay was read by the Rev. J. A. W. Haas, of New York, in place of the Rev. Dr. Weidner, of Chicago, who was prevented from being present. The second paper, on the same subject, was read by the Rev. Prof. J. R. Dimm, D.D , President of Susquehanna University, Selin's Grove, Pa.

Remarks were made by the Revs. Dr. E. J. Wolf, of Gettysburg; Dr. J. A. Seiss, of Philadelphia; Dr. G. W. Enders, of York, Pa.; Dr. A. Spaeth, of Mt. Airy; Dr. E. T. Horn, of Reading, Pa.; and concluding remarks by the Rev. Mr. Haas and Dr. Dimm.

The second subject treated was that of "The Standards of Ministerial Education." The first essay was read by the Rev. W. E. Parson, D.D., of Washington, D. C., and the second by the Rev. F. A. Kaehler, of Buffalo, N. Y.

Remarks were made by the Revs. Dr. J. R. Dimm, of Selin's Grove; Dr. J. Fry, of Mt. Airy; Dr. Geo Scholl, of Baltimore; W. A. Passavant, Jr., of Pittsburg; Dr. F. J. F. Schantz, of Myerstown; Dr. Chas. S. Albert, of Philadelphia; Dr. G. F. Krotel, of East Orange, N. J.; and by Dr. Parson and Rev. Mr. Kaehler.

Conference adjourned with prayer by the Rev. G. W. Enders, D.D., of York, Pa.

SIXTH SESSION.

St. Matthew's Church,
Thursday, December 29, 1898, 2 P.M.

The Rev. H. F. Scheele presided. The session was opened with prayer by the Rev. Prof. F. V. N. Painter, D.D., of Salem, Va.

The first subject considered was that of "The Lutheran Church and Modern Religious Issues." The first essay, prepared by the

MARY J. DREXEL HOME AND PHILADELPHIA MOTHER HOUSE OF DEACONESSES.

Rev. A. G. Voigt, D.D., of Wilmington, N. C., was read by the Rev. Dr. Horn, and viewed the subject from the German standpoint. The second essay, viewing the subject from the American standpoint, was read by the Rev. Theodore E. Schmauk, D.D., of Lebanon, Pa.

The second subject discussed was "The Problem of Co-operation," and was presented by the Rev. M. W. Hamma, D.D, of Washington, D. C.

Remarks were made by the Revs. Dr. L. E. Albert, of Germantown, Pa.; Dr. F. V. N. Painter, of Salem, Va.; Dr. G. F. Krotel, of East Orange, N. J.; and Dr. S. W. Owen, of Hagerstown, Md.

The third subject, which was to have been considered during the first session, to wit, "The Child Catechumenate," was presented by the Rev. G. U. Wenner, D.D., of New York City.

CONFERENCE BUSINESS.

After the conclusion of the Program, as above presented, Conference passed the following resolutions:

On motion of the Rev. Dr. Krotel, it was

Resolved, That we, as a Convention, make known to the three General Bodies, by whose authority this Convention was called, the desirability of holding another Convention of a similar character in the future.

On motion of the Rev. Dr. Chas. S. Albert, it was

Resolved, That a vote of thanks be tendered to the Committee of Arrangements for their work and the excellent Program prepared for this Convention.

On motion of the Rev. Dr. Jacobs, it was

Resolved, That the thanks of the Conference be tendered to the pastor and Congregation of St. John's Church, the pastor and congregation of St. Matthew's, and the authorities of the Mary J. Drexel Home, for the use of their buildings during the Convention.

On motion of the Rev. Dr. Owen, it was

Resolved, That the thanks of this Convention be tendered to the reporters for their excellent reports of the proceedings.

Resolved, That a vote of thanks be tendered to the Lutheran Social Union for the invitation to the reception to be tendered this (Thursday) evening by the said Union to the members of the Conference.

On motion of the Rev. Dr. Krotel, it was

Resolved, That the thanks of this Convention be tendered to all those who have contributed funds for the payment of the expenses of this Convention.

The Conference adjourned with the Apostles' Creed, the Lord's Prayer, and prayer by the Rev. Dr. Krotel.

RECEPTION BY THE SOCIAL UNION.

A reception was tendered on Thursday evening, December 29, 1898, by the Lutheran Social Union, at the Freeman Building, S. W. corner of 12th and Walnut streets, to the members of the General Conference of Lutherans. More than two hundred clergymen and laymen were present.

Mr. William J. Miller, president, was in the chair, and the Rev. Dr. Owen, offered prayer.

The following addresses were delivered:

Address of welcome by President Miller, in which he explained the object of the organization, referred to the influence of the General Conference on the Church, and welcomed the guests.

Address by Rev. Dr. Painter on "Right Emphasis."

Address by Rev. Dr. Bauslin on "A Lutheran Galaxy."

Address by Rev. Kuehler on "True Progress has its Strength in Conservatism."

Address by Rev. Passavant on "Laymen and Lay-women."

Address by Rev. Dr. Bell on "Aggressive Lutheranism."

During the evening music was furnished by Messrs. Geo. Ford and Frank van Roden. After the music and addresses, refreshments were served. The reception was enjoyed by all those present.

WM. S. FREAS,
S. E. OCHSENFORD,
Secretaries.

ESSAYS AND REMARKS.

OUR COMMON HISTORICAL ANTECEDENTS.
BY PROF. E. J. WOLF, D.D.

Gathered here as children of a common household, it behooves us to remember that we are not ecclesiastical foundlings. We share an undisputed and honorable parentage. Ours are the fathers, yea, we have one common father, even Muhlenberg, a most eminent and worthy patriarch, from whom we all in a direct line trace our lineage. He is the progenitor of the whole aggregate of Lutheranism represented here, except the Swedish portion of the General Council.

From this common fatherhood there descended to us a common heritage in the organization which received its initiative and permanence from Muhlenberg; in the devotion to "our evangelical doctrine, founded on the Apostles and set forth in our Symbolical Books," which he so emphatically protested; in his fixed purpose that "all the Evangelical Lutheran congregations might be united with one another;" and in his intense concern for the spiritual quickening of the congregation and the individual. Precious as was this legacy in which we all shared alike, neither of us has always fully estimated or properly guarded it. Our respective Synods have each in turn neglected their priceless heritage. They have all together deviated further from Muhlenberg than they ever deviated from each other. God forgive us that we have been degenerate sons of noble sires! Our unfaithfulness to the exalted ideals of the fathers brought untold suffering and unmeasured loss to our dear old Church. We do all now heartily repent of these our common derelictions, and join in the one desire and prayer that the whole Church may again realize its vital union with the original trunk in this country, that we may all return to the historic rock whence we are hewn and to the pit whence we are digged.

Muhlenberg and his co-laborers gave to Lutheranism in this country organic form, and the organism they created remains in its development to this day, and embraces these three bodies, and, we may add, the Joint Synod of Ohio. Whatever subdivisions or multiplications of organization have occurred in the lapse of a century, no branch represented here will admit its excision from the historic trunk. The first offshoot in the State of New York was designed simply to facilitate the common work. Not only did this first child adopt virtually the same constitution, but a minister could belong to both Ministeriums at the same time. The offshoot in North Carolina was of like character, for the Rev. Paul Henkel was a true son of the Mother Synod, as were the young pioneers who founded the Ohio Synod, though their action was not approved by the parent body. The Synod of Maryland and Virginia was not formed in order to detach the churches in those States from the Ministerium of Pennsylvania, but only to extend organized and efficient activity into those regions. It was a coalition of the Virginia Conference of the Synod of Pennsylvania with the congregations and ministers in Maryland, the mother and the daughter annually exchanging delegates until a very few years ago.

Separate organizations were effected in consideration of remote geographical isolation, and looking to the best interests of the Church, but with no idea of a total or permanent severance from the parent stock or from each other. Mother and children remained one communion, united by bonds of mutual sympathy and representation.

To guard against drifting apart, to forestall the division and alienation which was threatened by the Church's extension, the Mother Synod projected a new organic relation for the different portions in the formation of a General Synod, A.D. 1820, following in this a very general desire for some central bond between the Synods which should preserve their harmony, promote general conformity in church usages and uniformity in worship, and impart increased efficiency to all activities and movements in which concentration is indispensable to success. When the Mother Synod, still numerically larger than all the others, initiated this project "with extraordinary unanimity and the most hearty concord," it commanded a cordial response from the younger bodies—in fact the harmony, the homogeneity, the mutual affinity, which obtained between them made such a union as natural as the coalescence of adjacent drops of water.

There are of course always objectors. The voice of calumny is sure to attack a holy cause. The fatuous indolence of human nature breeds indifference, and invincible ignorance makes a formidable barrier to advancing Christianity, but for years the only opposition to the General Synod on principle came from the Henkels, and their antagonism was not unmixed with unworthy personal motives. The Ohio Synod was indeed at first deterred by an anonymous document which held up the bugaboos of a uniform Hymn Book and Liturgy, of a hierarchy, of ecclesiastical authority enforced by the law, of the encroachments of the English, but the attractions of a fraternal union overcame even these terrors, and had not the Pennsylvania Ministerium felt itself compelled "to desert the child it had brought into being,"—by a calumnious publication which diffused similar prejudices far and wide among the ignorant and narrow-minded within its fold, exciting serious alarm by the spectre of European Church despotism, the dangers and costs of theological seminaries, and the burden of "collections upon collections" which the poor farmers will have to pay—a current of prejudice and ignorance which the rural pastors made little effort to stem—there can be no doubt that the entire Church was sufficiently of one mind and heart to rally under this new banner set up by the mother Synod—the symbol of a united communion—the large, imposing, symmetrical tree, grown from the mustard seed planted by Muhlenberg.

Thus eighty years ago, although they had gotten farther and farther apart by geographical distances and want of communication, our churches knew of no friction or controversy on any subject pertaining to faith and worship; and to prevent the alienations and divisions which remote isolation and the varying development of new organizations might engender, they resolved upon forging a new bond of fraternal fellowship and union. No historian will challenge the statement that the founders of the General Synod had no other object than the closer union and the enlarged prosperity of the entire Church. It was meant to embrace the whole Lutheran household, to be "a joint Committee of the Special Synods," at a time when neither telescope nor microscope could have discovered any distinction among them.

And now when unhappy commotions excited solely by selfish and sordid considerations, constrained the author of the General Synod to recede for the time from official relations with it, this compulsory step implied no change of heart, no discovery of divergent or conflicting elements, no abatement of fraternal sympathy. The sundering of the outward bond did not sever inward ties. The majority simply and with great regret yielded against their convictions to the clamor of a minority. They were not dissatisfied with the object or character of the new organization, and their withdrawal was meant to continue only until the malcontents should see their own error and call for a reconsideration of the unreasonable action they had precipitated.

The leaders of the mother Synod continued, therefore, to cherish the friendliest feelings toward the General Synod, viewing it "as highly beneficial to the interests of the Church," and they strongly deplored "the peculiar circumstances" which enforced their separation, circumstances which the General Synod recognized "as excusing if not absolutely necessitating the attitude of the old Synod in its temporary recession."

With undiminished interest and affection the mother watched her children in their new relationship, nor were they in any measure estranged from her. Official expressions of the most cordial good feeling and confidence were frequently exchanged, and the hope was ever indulged and often voiced that the enforced separation might soon be ended. The general body henceforth led in promoting the common interests of Zion, it sounded the keynote for action, but the old Synod took a warm and active interest in every movement, cordially and nobly co-operating. The General Synod, on her part, heartily reciprocated this, examining its minutes, noting important Synodical action, publishing its statistics and commending its activity and liberality. Dr. Schmucker, in his "Retrospect" (1841), rejoicing in its prosperity, testifies strongly to its continued "substantial and increasing aid to every good work undertaken by this Synod, so that much of the credit which has been achieved, is justly due to their co-operation." Thus in spirit and in character there was still in the thirties and forties but one Lutheran Church, of which we are the common descendants.

The General Synod frequently assured the brethren of the Ministerium of its reciprocating "the ardent attachment of many in it," and placed on record its desire for the return of that body to "that union which they had been the principal instrument in establishing," its longing for the day when it could "see them unite their counsels and energies with ours." And in turn the Ministerium kept agitating the matter of reunion, especially in '39 and '40, but the old prejudice against English and other marks of progress still prevailed.

It was in fact only a portion of the Ministerium that had withdrawn—the portion east of the Susquehanna. "The peculiar circumstances" which compelled the separation did not exist west of the river, hence the churches and pastors of that section seceded from the parent body with its full consent and blessing, in order that they might retain their connection with the General Synod.

As an example of the Ministerium's fraternal coöperation with the General Synod, we may instance the theological seminary founded by the latter body. When final measures for its establishment had been taken at Frederick in 1825, and S. S. Schmucker had been elected professor, the solicitation of funds was next in order, and the first committee appointed for this purpose consisted of Drs. Lochman, Endress and Muhlenberg, and Rev. Demme for the Synod of East Pennsylvania. And the extent of their interest is evidenced by the testimony of Dr. Schmucker, who, after canvassing Philadelphia for funds, reported that he found the members of the Lutheran churches there "a liberal, wealthy and generous people." Although they were excluded from the government of the institution—not being connected with the General Synod—the churches east of the Susquehanna gave to it their generous support and their constant patronage, a large proportion of their ministerial candidates being educated there.

From the ranks of the Mother Synod came in 1833 the second professor of the Institution in the person of C. P. Krauth, who also forthwith became the first president of the newly-founded College at Gettysburg, which school numbered in its first Board three eminent ministers of the Pennsylvania Ministerium. This coöperation grew with the growth of both these institutions, and when Franklin College was dissolved in 1850, its Lutheran Trustees who represented the Ministerium were, with the funds of the Franklin Professorship, transferred to Pennsylvania College, giving the Mother Synod a large membership in that corporation. And so mutually satisfactory was this relation that the College requested the Ministerium to provide the funds and to name the incumbent for a German professorship, a request with which the Synod heartily and promptly complied. Thus from the year 1855 the Ministerium had two professors in that College, one of whom served at the same time as the third member of the Faculty of the Seminary.

As in education so in the work of Foreign Missions there was the fullest, friendliest working in harmony. While the Ministerium had, in 1836, formed itself into "a Missionary Society for propagating the Gospel at home and ultimately to coöperate in sending it to the heathen world," there was organized a year later, immediately after the General Synod's Convention at Hagerstown, a general Foreign Missionary Society, forty-four delegates being present, besides those who were members of the Synod. A fair proportion of these forty-four came from the Ministerium. The first selection for the foreign field was C. F. Heyer, a student of Helmuth, and a man who had been closely identified with the General Synod. His primary appointment came from the General Society, but declining to go under the auspices of the American Board, he offered himself to the Ministerium, which readily accepted his services and sent him to India, where he was soon reinforced by Walter Gunn, sent out by the General Society in 1843, and cordially welcomed as a fellow-worker by Heyer. The two societies adopted a plan of union in 1845, each remaining distinct, appointing and maintaining its own missionaries, but occupying the same district, "having but one interest and one aim in the foreign field, the joint Mission to be known as the American Lutheran Mission."

In Home Mission work there was not the same coöperation, it being long the practice of District Synods to manage Home Mission interests themselves. The policy of centralization was generally unpopular. For five years after the organization of the Home Missionary Society in 1845, only four out of the thirteen Synods within the General Synod contributed to it, and up to 1864 never one-half of them.

When the Publication Society was founded, the Ministerium had resumed its place in the general body, still the Society being a distinct organization special mention is made by the Society's historian and president, of the fact that many of that Synod's most prominent members were in hearty sympathy and coöperation with the movement. "Especially active and helpful were Rev. Benjamin Keller, our first and most successful financial agent, Drs. J. C. Baker, Charles W. Schaeffer, William J. Mann, C. A. Hay and others." This was in 1855.

Thus the most amicable relations were maintained, the Church in all those portions represented here being essentially one Church—our Church. No open quarrel or direct antagonism, no clash occurred in those days, excepting the breach which took place A. D. 1841 in the formation of the East Pennsylvania Synod, which proposed to occupy the same territory with the Old Synod. But no amount of divine grace, Christian charity, or human wisdom could prevent collisions where two bodies of the same character attempt a joint occupation of the same field.

So far from friction or antagonism being developed by the coöperation which we have sketched, it worked so well and proved so advantageous that it culminated in the organic reunion A. D., 1853, of the Ministerium with the General Synod, now embracing sixteen components, her return being greeted with a generous welcome and widespread jubilation.

Other Synods continued to be formed and to seek admission to the General Synod until it reached its maximum representative strength in 1860, when it embraced twenty-six Synods, spread over almost the entire country east of the Rockies; all the Synods which comprised to any extent the native Lutheran population; all the bodies sprung from Muhlenberg's work, excepting the Joint Ohio and Tennessee Synods, numbering two-thirds of the entire Lutheran membership—all now one organic body, as homogeneous and as harmonious as any other denomination in this country—our Church.

This organic oneness continued until the Synods south of the Potomac, owing to conditions which no one now voluntarily recalls, separated from the General Synod with which they had ever been of one mind and one heart. At York, in 1864, the General Synod itself repeated the blunder which had rent the body in 1823. The majority surrendered their deliberate and correct judgment to a clamoring minority. The action which refused admission to the Franckeans was reconsidered, and thus another rupture was threatened. Yet so strong was the feeling for a united Church that, in order to calm the excitement and preserve the integrity of the body, several energetic steps were taken which promised to insure this devoutly hoped-for consummation—steps so satisfactory to all that the President, Dr. Sprecher, congratulated one of the leading conservatives for having saved the General Synod. The Ministerium, accordingly, so far from terminating its connection, adopted the constitutional amendments which had been officially sent down to it and elected a delegation to the next Convention.

A parliamentary ruling caused a hitch in their participation (1866), yet such was the consciousness of substantial agreement and such the apprehensions of division, that neither party stood ready to assume the responsibility for schism. The General Synod requested the delegates of the Ministerium "to waive what may seem to them an irregular organization of this body," and repeatedly affirmed its readiness to receive them, while the delegates averred their perfect willingness to acquiesce in what they deemed an irregular organization, and their "readiness to take their seats in this body, equals among equals," if the General Synod would admit its parliamentary error. Whether their final separation occurred in the active voice or in the passive voice, is a question on which no impartial jury has as yet pronounced a verdict.

But a more vital matter than their outward association is the historic relation of these respective bodies to the Church's faith. To what extent have we common antecedents in the sphere of doctrine? How far have our bodies borne a common attitude toward that Confession which Luther drew from the Holy Scriptures, which Melanchthon reduced to a matchless formula, and which, along with the other Symbols, Muhlenberg made the foundation of all the congregations he organized. History replies that a common faith even more than the (virtually) common organization and activity has characterized these bodies. The good confession which the fathers so bravely witnessed in the face of the fanaticism and of the sects which had obtruded into our churches, has never been abandoned, corrupted or repudiated by any of them. There have been periods of forgetfulness, of indifference, of neglect, yea, even of slackness and looseness, but thanks to the indwelling Spirit of Christ, all of our bodies have been preserved from uttering one word inimical or adverse to the doctrines on which our Church is founded.

And these periods of laxity, neglect and ignorance of the Confession have been spread so completely over all our borders, that it is historically unsafe for either body to cast a stone at another. A monopoly of doctrinal indifference cannot be justly charged against any Lutheran body in this country. Formal Confessional subscription had disappeared from the mother Synod before she organized the General Synod. The same is true of the New York Synod. It was the same everywhere—they had all gone out of the way—the leaven had permeated the entire mass.

Das gemeinschaftliche Gesangbuch of 1817, zum Gebrauch der Lutherischen und Reformirten Gemeinden in Nord Amerika, published at the request of a majority of the preachers of both denominations, openly avowed in the preface of the first edition its aim "to break down the partition wall between Lutherans and Reformed, which is only based on prejudices." This Union Hymnal received the recommendation of the Synods of Pennsylvania, New York and North Carolina—the unqualified endorsement of our entire Church. Its chief merit to many lay in its tendency to establish the beautiful accord between the Lutheran and the Reformed hymns.

The projection of a theological seminary by the General Synod roused that body to the need of a standard of theological instruction, and as such a standard it set up the Augsburg Confession and the Catechisms of Luther "as a summary and just exhibition of the fundamental doctrines of the word of God." In 1829 it approved the Constitution for Synods which required a quasi-confessional subscription. In 1834 the same body published a German Hymnbook which calls forth the admiration of Dr. Spaeth, who pronounces it "a vast improvement on the Gemeinschaftliche." In 1835 it laid down the constitutional requirement for membership that "Synods must hold the essential doctrines of the Bible as they are taught in our Church." The initiative of returning formally to the symbols must without question be credited to the General Synod. The Agenda of the Ministerium in 1842, which became also the Liturgy of the General Synod, contained a form for the installation of a pastor, "in which for the first time, after a long pause, direct reference is again made [by the Ministerium] to the Confession of the Evangelical Lutheran Church." But it was only after another long pause, namely in 1852, that the Synod once more found occasion to allude to its Confessional status. And then the farthest it could go was to declare "that we have never renounced the Confessions of our Church, as a faithful exposition of the divine word." In April, 1853, in connection with the Report of a committee defining the sense of the phrase "the Confession of the Evangelical Lutheran Church," the Ministerium recognized that "The Evangelical Lutheran Church has of late arrived at clearer views of its doctrinal and other distinctive features," and acknowledged "the collective body of the Symbolical Books, as the historical and Confessional writings of the Evangelical Lutheran Church, and enjoined all the ministers and candidates . . . to make themselves better or more thoroughly acquainted with these venerable documents of the faith," but there is still not a word about their binding authority, and colorless as these resolutions were, Professor Schaeffer wrote: Some "may possibly regard them as quite stringent," while others "may find them to be a somewhat weak infusion, but still, perhaps, suited to a state of convalescence."

It thus appears that the Confessional history of the Ministerium is far from being an improvement on that of the General Synod, "during the years in which she was independent of it so far as organic union was concerned, but in close relations in all other respects." The Rev. Dr. Jacobs casts a clear light on the ratio of progress in this direction, namely, that "the movement advanced by a constant struggle in which the deteriorating process often seemed not only to be holding its own, but even to be able to obtain greater triumphs than ever." He also admits that "in many congregations of the General Synod the conservatism was almost equally as strong as in the older Synods which stood aloof." Gettysburg doubtless fluctuated, and by some it was denounced for being too conservative, while by others it was accused of laxness. The Franckeans had no more stomach for the General Synod than the Tennesseans. A full generation elapsed without any controversy respecting doctrine or worship between the two leading bodies, and even the organization of the Synod of East Pennsylvania had no pretext in doctrinal differences. Such grounds as the differences of language, the size of the old body, the oppressive nature of "the new or revised Constitution," are given as reasons which make a division desirable, but there is not a hint of any dissatisfaction with the Confessional status of the old body. On this point there was at that time substantial oneness in our Church.

While there was a constant growth of Confessional and Churchly sentiment—a deepening consciousness that the Church was not in doctrine and life what it ought to be—the steady tide toward a formal and hearty resumption of our distinctive faith did not set in until the signal for it was given by a Gettysburg professor in a sermon preached by him as President of the General Synod at Charleston, 1850. He described the Lutheran Church in this country as "in a state of reaction," as "retracing her steps," "acknowledging her error," "hunting among the records of the past for the faith of former days." "The desire for the symbols of our Church," he contended, "the attention that is paid to them, the admiration that has been expressed of them, the candor with which they are viewed, the expressed willingness on the part of many, only to dissent when it cannot be avoided, all indicate a new state of things—and are adapted to produce the conviction that the Church is disposed to renew her connection with the past, and in her future progress to walk under the guidance of the light which it has furnished. There is no fear of any doctrine which our Symbols contain, no unwillingness to give it a fair examination, and a predisposition, rather than the contrary, to receive and assent." These were brave and heroic words for that period, and they were followed by others still bolder, when he characterized the General Synod's form of subscription to be "such as to admit of the rejection of any doctrine or doctrines which the subscriber may not receive," holding that "a creed thus presented is no creed, that it is anything or nothing, that its subscription is a solemn farce."

When to head off this steadily growing reaction, another Gettysburg professor in company with several other eminent men ventured a recension of the Confession, eliminating the distinctive doctrines of the Church, and charging it with errors, the General Synod with one voice vindicated the soundness of the Confession by declaring it to be "in perfect consistence with the Scriptures," and superseded its equivocal subscription by a form, which according to the sworn testimony of a contemporary, the Rev. Dr. J. A. Brown, requires of Synods the "unequivocal and unconditional acceptance of the Augsburg Confession." Whether the Mother Synod's official acceptance of the Confession antedates or follows this action, there intervened at most but a few years, and those who were mainly influential in bringing her back to the faith, were almost to a man reared in the General Synod or trained at Gettysburg, which was ever regarded as the embodiment and exponent of General Synod sentiment. That was our Seminary then, and some of us from the three bodies here present know from what fountain we drank Lutheran theology twenty-five or thirty years ago.

That there was a doctrinal consensus of the General Synod and the Ministerium even at the time of the disruption appears,

1. From the fact that no imputation against the doctrinal soundness of either body appears in the proceedings at Fort Wayne.

2. From the formal invitation which the Ministerium after its withdrawal sent to a number of Synods adhering to the General Synod, asking them to unite in forming a new general body.

3. From the fact that the pen which drew the Fundamental Principles of Faith and Church Polity, wrote also, just a few years before, the Constitutional Amendment which now forms the General Synod's basis.

4. From the decree of the Supreme Court of Pennsylvania, which after judicially weighing "the arguments and opinions of celebrated and learned divines," the chosen champions of the contending parties in the Allentown case, decided that the difference in their Confessional subscriptions "is a difference of phraseology without any real difference in substance," "an attempted distinction" that "is incomprehensible to the judicial mind," the Hudibrastic distinction "'twixt tweedle dum and tweedle dee."

5. From the admissions made by eminent representatives of the Council and the General Synod at the Lutheran Diet in 1878.

The General Synod does not even now demand of its district Synods the acknowledgment of all the Symbolical Books, but it has never antagonized a doctrine or definition contained therein, and it was the testimony under oath of a most honorable living witness, Rev. Dr. Baum, that in the General Synod's interpretation of the Confession reference must be had to the other Symbolical Books, "that fidelity to the Lutheran Church binds us to make no interpretation of the Articles of the Augustana, which are at variance with the interpretations contained in the other books." And here, too, the learned and august tribunal referred to above ruled that "the distinction sought to be made does not exist in fact or substance."

It may be questioned too, whether each and all of these Symbols are now cited more frequently in the theological schools of one body than in those of the other.

Our respective bodies up to 1866 made use of common devotional manuals. A German Hymn book for the Evangelical Lutheran Church, published in 1849 by ecclesiastical authority, was the product of a joint committee appointed respectively by the Synod of Pennsylvania, of New York and of West Pennsylvania. "The friendly co-operation of other Synods" was solicited by the Mother Synod, and the two other bodies named cordially participated in the preparation and introduction of the new book, the West Pennsylvania representation on the Committee being Dr. S. S. Schmucker, Jacob Albert and A. G. Deininger.

A more Churchly and Confessional spirit breathes in this work, marking as it does "the first weak beginnings" of the revival of a true Lutheran consciousness. Dr. Spaeth calls it a cross "between the spirit of a sound historic Lutheranism and a constant yielding to the modern spirit which had been ruling our liturgical and hymnological literature for fifty years."

And so a common English hymnal was the aim of all using the English tongue. The New York collection of 1814, Arianizing, Pelagianizing, savoring of rationalism, ignoring the Trinity, casting other vital truths into the background, and wholly innocent of Lutheran doctrine, this travesty of Lutheranism was used in many of the Pennsylvania Synod churches, and in Albany and some rural districts of New York, as late as 1865. And so far was the General Synod from condemning it that when it published a Hymn Book in 1828 it so arranged its collection that "both books can be used together without inconvenience." This collection of the General Synod which well deserved such criticisms as "Methodistical," "sensational," "a deification of frames and feelings," appeared in 1841 in an enlarged edition in which "a reckless inconsistency in doctrine, temper, style and spirit runs riot," "low church and broad church mixed into an agreeable compound, presenting some of the worst qualities of both," and for eleven years this was the common hymnal of most of our English churches; though, as has well been said, it might have served for the hardshell Baptists or for a negro camp-meeting. The choice of English congregations lay between the New York collection, which a competent judge has pronounced "a cross of high Arianism and a mild loose form of old-style orthodoxy," and the General Synod's, which the same authority criticizes as "an agreeable mixture of Methodism, Presbyterianism, and a gentle tincture of our own faith." A somewhat improved edition of the latter appeared in 1850, but all our successive English hymnals were in those days only new and slightly modified editions of some predecessor—and this later one, charged with "Un-Lutheran, anti-Lutheran, Puritanic, Methodistic and Humanitarian leaven, was used until 1865 by almost the entire English Lutheran Church."

So we always had in like manner a common Liturgy—no one dreaming of anything else. Prior to the formation of the General Synod the Ministerium had its German Liturgy and the New York Synod its English order. When, in 1825, the General Synod first undertook to provide a Liturgy, neither of these Synods was connected with it, yet its Liturgical Committee, charged with the preparation of a Liturgy and a collection of prayers in English, was instructed to "adhere particularly to the New York Hymn Book and German Liturgy of Pennsylvania as their guides."

In 1831 a large "Editing Committee" was again directed to publish a liturgy in the English language, "having reference to the works of this kind now used in different parts of our Church."

In 1835 the Ministerium "endorsed and introduced" the New York Synod's last edition of the Liturgy as "the new Liturgy for its English congregations," and "requested the General Synod to do likewise for the sake of uniformity," whereupon the General Synod in 1837 directed a committee of seven clergymen to examine the Liturgy and prayers of the New York Synod, and if they found the last edition meeting the wants of the Church to have "said Liturgy and prayers appended to our Hymn Book."

In 1839 the Ministerium appointed a committee "to prepare a new edition of our Church Liturgy, in an improved and more complete form," and at the same time notified this action "to all the other Synods of the Church who used this Liturgy," and invited them fraternally to co-operate in this work—an invitation which the General Synod cordially accepted, authorizing its Committee on Liturgy "to co-operate with the Synod of Pennsylvania on the same subject in preparing a uniform Liturgy for the use of the Church." Thus arose the first Joint Committee on a Common Service, even the Synod of Ohio uniting.

The result, with a few changes, was adopted by the Ministerium in 1841, and the General Synod at its next convention in 1843 recommended it "as suitable for adoption among our German Churches generally."

At the same time ('41) the Ministerium appointed the use of the Liturgy of the Synod of New York in its English Churches, expressing the hope that "the General Synod will adopt said Liturgy, and uniformity in our churches be thus secured and promised." But the General Synod appointed a committee to furnish an English Liturgy, which at the next Convention reported its purpose "to translate the Liturgy of the Synod of Pennsylvania," for which it claimed the following advantages: (1) "It is more complete than the other English Liturgies. (2) It is in the strictest sense the Liturgy of the American Lutheran Church, inasmuch as it sprang from that portion of the Church which is the mother of us all, and which is still held in the highest reverence by the oldest congregations of our denomination. (3) If uniformity be desired, it will be reached by the adoption of these forms. Whether we attend German or English service, we hear the pastor as he stands before the altar, utter the same truths, address us in the same manner, and pour out the same prayer before the Hearer of prayer. (4) No other Liturgy can have the same historical associations. (5) As a large portion of the Church, namely, the Synods of Pennsylvania, New York and Ohio, as well as the General Synod, have already adopted the German Liturgy, it appears to be evidently necessary, or at least highly desirable, that not merely a work resembling this, but rather, if it is possible, the very same work should be published in the English language." The signatures to this memorable report are Charles Philip Krauth, B. Kurtz, W. M. Reynolds, Ezra Keller, J. G. Morris, C. A. Smith. And their advocacy in the Preface of "a Common Liturgy," of "common forms," of "uniformity in the public worship," of "the use of one Liturgy throughout a whole Church," as conducive to "order," as serving "to give character to a Church," as presenting "a summary expose of its doctrines," as begetting a homelike feeling when one visits "distant divisions of their own household of faith," makes seasonable and profitable reading a half century after its first publication.

The Ministerium was, of course, gratified with this translation of its German Agenda, and though faulting somewhat the English rendering, recommended it for the use of its congregations, and resolved, "That we rejoice that our brethren of the General Synod have translated our Liturgy into the English language, . . . and that we hope that this may be the means of promoting greater harmony, and of strengthening the fraternal relations between us and them, and the entire Church." This was in 1849.

This review of our liturgical history clearly evinces a conscious and cordial unity between our several bodies. All the liturgical development from 1839 to 1860 was a joint work of the Ministerium and the General Synod, with which the former always stood in close, if not organic, relations, and our worship was ever so ordered as "to promote greater harmony and strengthen fraternal feeling." The relations of the New York Synod and the Ministerium were always characterized on this point "by reciprocity and friendly harmonious co-operation," and the General Synod was ever marked by "an unmistakable tendency to have an understanding with the Ministerium on liturgical matters, to use and recommend its work."

From the earliest years of the General Synod we discover throughout our Church a revival of the spirit of Muhlenberg, who fervently prayed that "all the Evangelical Lutheran Churches might be united with one another," and prophesied that this would be realized were all to "use the same order of Service, the same Hymn Book, and in good and evil days would show an active sympathy and fraternally correspond with one another." How completely in accord with this was the resolution of the General Synod in 1843 when it declared that "uniformity in public worship is highly desirable, and the introduction of a good Liturgy is well calculated to accomplish this object."

The uniform Catechism which Muhlenberg had so earnestly desired never materialized, because of the unhappy practice of publishing individual and private editions, but whatever the merits or demerits of these numerous publications, they were pretty much all, until a generation ago, marked by an ignoring or dilution of Lutheran doctrine. In the General Synod there was long in use a German edition approved by the Synod of West Pennsylvania, which was virtually a reprint (1845) of the "Old Catechism of the Ministerium, with nearly the same Addenda, including the Augsburg Confession." Mayer's English Catechism, in 1816, in which the distinctive doctrines of the Church were not prominent, was reissued almost *verbatim* by the General Synod in 1825, with sundry foot notes, modifying, somewhat, the doctrine of the text.

Furthermore, in our periodical literature our antecedents are the same. The *Observer* was, in its earlier decades, the paper of the whole English portion of the Church, and, while teeming with reports of revivals, it also stoutly defended our distinctive usages, catechization and confirmation over against the incoming waves of "new measures." Along with rejoicings over awakened congregations, it warned against "all methods not strictly in accordance with the Gospel," "devices of human wisdom," "mechanical contrivances for saving souls," and deprecated "the departure from our biblical usages." Even Editor Kurtz sounded the alarm against "the man-made religion of the day." In its first volume (1830) it quotes the Symbolical Books as authoritative in the Lutheran Church, and it numbered among its frequent contributors the Schaeffers, John N. Hoffman and others whose names stand for Lutheran loyalty. In the crisis of 1864–1866 its editors were so conservative that on the decisive question at Fort Wayne one of them sided with the Pennsylvania delegation, and the other two declined to vote.

The *Evangelical Review* was founded at Gettysburg in 1849 "to promote proper union and co-operation in the Lutheran

Church of this country." Recognizing the emergence of diversities of view along with the revival of a Lutheran consciousness, and, apprehensive that conflicting elements were in great danger of having their sympathies entirely alienated from one another, its projectors proposed the *Review* as a remedy or preventive. Here "all parts of the Church should meet each other as upon neutral ground and hold friendly intercourse and exchange opinions with each other." "Here," the introduction proceeds, "they will find that they have much in common—a common origin, a common history, common sympathies, and many common tendencies, religious principles and usages." Acknowledging the modifications which a part of the Church had undergone, referring probably to the Ohio and Tennessee Synods, it expressed the belief that "the Church is still essentially one, and has a common substratum of doctrinal and religious character which only requires to be properly developed in order to bring us together in that oneness of faith which has always so strongly characterized the Lutheran Church." The editor knows of "no tendency to the absolute separation of different sections from each other." Notwithstanding different views and violent collisions, "we have never yet formed a 'New Lutheran' or an 'Old Lutheran,' a 'Radical' or a 'Conservative' Lutheran Church." "No part of the Church has ever yet formally announced its rejection of the Augsburg Confession or the Shorter Catechism, or, in short, of any of our Symbolical Books." "Nor has there yet been any serious attempt to set up any other doctrinal basis as a substitute for them, or anything like a denial of the Lutheran character of those who receive them. Nothing was then known that could "prevent us from growing up into one body," and grounds of hope were seen for the "ultimate union of all parts of the Lutheran Church, both in doctrinal views and external organization." What was needed was that "we should both know ourselves and know each other, as Lutherans." All parts of the Church were to have a hearing, "for it is only by the comparison of opposite views that we are harmonized in feelings and united in action." "If, therefore, the most opposite views should be expressed in this *Review* we shall by no means despair of reconciling them or of finally bringing together, in the unity of our common faith, the different parties that advance them."

This journal avowed its position as "Lutheran in the broadest and in the strictest sense of the term," "consecrated especially to the interests, to the history, to the theology, to the literature of the Lutheran Church. And, as a necessary result of this, it belongs to no particular school or party in the Lutheran Church." The discussions and controversies expected in its pages were viewed as "the necessary means for the establishment of peace and union among us."

Published at Gettysburg, the *Review* became the drum-beat for pronounced Lutheran views. Its second editor, C. Philip Krauth, who had the hardihood to translate Schmid's Dogmatik, declared "unequivocally in behalf of the study, the thorough study, of this theology; we would have it thrown over our Church with a liberal hand, we would have all our ministers acquainted with the Symbolical Books; we would have them all versed in the distinctive theology of the Church. We would have introduced into our theological schools the study of the Symbols, and didactic and polemic theology so administered as to bring before the view pure, unadulterated Lutheranism. The gain to our ministry and to our Church would be immense, if this course were adopted." He notes "the increasing desire to become acquainted with the doctrines of the Church," and recognizes the demand for the Symbolical Books as symptomatic of the fact that "the time has passed away in which we are to assume every phase which may be presented to us, to glory that we are like everybody, and, consequently, are nothing in ourselves, living only by the breath of others."

A contributor, Y. S. R., in January, 1851, urges that the Theological Seminary "should teach the doctrines of the Church as contained in her Symbols." If eclectic doctrines are taught, or those of other churches not in harmony with our Symbols, "it follows necessarily that the Seminary becomes the greatest enemy of the Church, which it professes to uphold."

With the continued good understanding and fraternal accord, with this community of doctrine, worship and literature, it naturally and actually follows that to a marked degree sameness of usage and practice, spirit and life obtained in the different bodies. Conditions were strikingly similar, if not actually identical. Pastors and people crossed synodical bounds, and transferred their membership without discovering any material difference or variation. Many evils, drawbacks, difficulties, burdens, were common to both bodies, though perhaps not in the same degree, nor always contemporaneously. An unprogressive, stolid element had to be dealt with in all parts of the Church. The transition from German to English was stubbornly resisted in Maryland and Virginia as well as in Pennsylvania. We came to be generally and correctly designated as the slow Lutherans, and though beyond question the General Synod was the more progressive body, all were slow enough. As the Old Synod was more predominantly German, its preachers and people were more effectually held back and aloof from the movements and measures which fostered the growth of other denominations, and enriched them with those of our own blood and faith. There, preëminently, several generations grew up without any proper education, a corrupt dialect being the medium of social intercourse, while the language of schools, books, periodicals and courts was unintelligible to young and old alike.

And when the fever of fanaticism followed the torpor of formalism, this again was not confined to one body. "Peculiar seasons of refreshment" are recorded within the bounds of the Mother Synod as in the General Synod,—east of the Susquehanna as well as west,—south of the Potomac as well as north. Even the Henkels did not escape the contagion, and the Ministerium will not disown such names as Helmuth, Ruthrauff, Gerhard, Keller, Schaeffer, Hoffman, Sahm and Baker. So also the opposition to those "New Measures" was quite as pronounced in the General Synod as in the Mother body. The question among the cooler and more deliberate heads was, in the words of Heyer, "Whether to adhere to the old European Church order, or in some respects pursue the same measures adopted by other denominations by which we are surrounded, if we wish to maintain the number and efficiency of our congregations."

Such then is our ancestral descent—a Church which though for a time divided into separate folds, yet always maintained cordial reciprocal relations, contemplated organic unity, and was up to 1866 to all intents one Church, one in doctrine, education, worship and life. The idea that the General Synod stands for a particular type of Lutheranism was hatched from the exigencies of controversy. And of a piece with it, is the claim that the American Synods now a part of the General Council stood in the past for sound doctrine and orthodox measures.

I do not affirm that there was no difference, nor do I forget that there was often heard in the land the voice of the self-elected champion, who imagines himself the incarnation of his school or party, and who with Pharisaic self-sufficiency fulminates wholesale anathemas against the other side; but it is the verdict of history that there never was a gulf fixed separating the true Lutherans from the bastards; there never were two flocks, the one made up of white sheep, the other of black.

Our historic antecedents were exactly the reverse of this. Under Muhlenberg and his co-laborers there burst forth in the desert a stream of blessing. Growing in volume and in breadth, this stream gradually assumed a devious and crooked course, meandering sluggishly around the cliffs and headlands in its path, but at last it cut for itself again by dint of its inherent strength a straight and rectilinear channel, which it has steadily followed for half a century. The current has not been always and everywhere equally swift, equally deep or equally clear. There have been ebbs and floods, eddies and rapids. Obstructions have not been wanting here and there, and occasional storms have in places troubled or muddied the broad expanse; but it has been everywhere and always the same water, the same historic glorious stream, the same river of life, bearing in its bosom the unsearchable riches of grace and truth and salvation for mankind.

OUR COMMON HISTORIC ANTECEDENTS.

BY PROF. J. NICUM, D.D.

Webster defines "antecedents" as "the earlier events of one's life, previous principles, conduct, course, history;" the *Standard Dictionary*, as "the facts, circumstances, etc., collectively, that have gone before in the history of any person or thing." Our subject may, therefore, be more fully stated thus: a delineation of the principles of faith and church-life which characterized the establishment of the Lutheran Church in this country, and the history of its early and later development. Up to the beginning of the present century the development of the Church was "common" to all parts of the Church. There were, indeed, two Synods, but there was no alienation, no strife. This division of the Church was not on doctrinal grounds, but for geographical reasons simply. The relations between the Synods then existing, the Mother Synod and the New York Ministerium, were of a most cordial nature, and all the Lutheran ministers and churches in this country were either members of these two bodies, or were in close relation with them. This harmonious and blessed relation of all parts of the Lutheran Church was brought about, under God, chiefly by the labors of the Rev. Dr. Henry Melchior Muhlenberg and his co-workers, notably Dr. Kunze. Wherever Muhlenberg built, and his field of labor extended from New York and Rhinebeck in the north to Charleston and Savannah in the south, he built upon the solid and tried foundation of the Unaltered Augsburg Confession and the other Symbolical Books of the Lutheran Church. The Lutheran Church in America during the latter half of the eighteenth century, in all her life and manifestations, bore the imprint of the healthy and evangelical confessionalism of Muhlenberg.

As this General Conference has been called for a "comparison of views on various doctrinal, liturgical, educational, and missionary interests" (Min. Gen. Council, 1895, p. 17), permit me to present a brief account of Our Common Historical Antecedents, especially with reference to the doctrinal interest. We will *first* view the *doctrinal position* of Lutheran pastors and churches in this country up to the nineteenth century.

I. The first Lutherans who settled here in larger numbers were the *Swedes*. They began to arrive in 1638. In 1639 the Rev. Reorus Torkillus came as pastor of the colonists. Among the instructions which the governor received from the Swedish government was the following: "Care shall be taken that divine service be zealously performed according to the Unaltered Augsburg Confession and the ceremonies of the Swedish Church." And these Swedes have not been without influence upon the early history of the Ministerium of Pennsylvania.

About ten years after the settlement of the Swedes on the Delaware *Dutch Lutheran Churches* were established along the Hudson, in New York and Albany. The Constitution of the Lutheran Church in Holland binds all preachers to teach according to the rule of the Divine Word, and forbids them to depart from either the doctrine or the mode of expression "of our Symbolical Books, viz., the Unaltered Augsburg Confession of Faith, its Apology, the Smalcald Articles, and the Formula of Concord, together with the two Catechisms of Luther." The Consistory at Amsterdam made it obligatory upon all Lutheran pastors in Holland to preach annually at least one sermon on the Augsburg Confession, and held to strict account all who, in any wise, departed from this standard. Though not one of the descendants of the Dutch Lutheran churches in New York or Albany is to-day a member of one of our Lutheran churches, still the influence of these Dutch churches has not been lost. It shows itself, *e. g.*, in the Constitution for congregations prepared by Muhlenberg. In a petition presented to the Council at New Amsterdam (New York) the Lutheran congregation styles itself, "The united members of the Augsburg Confession," and begs that the doctrine of the Unaltered Augsburg Confession be tolerated. Similar statements occur repeatedly in the history of the Dutch Lutheran churches. In 1728, after having been deceived by a clerical impostor, the Church at Hackensack resolved "in future to recognize none as a Lutheran preacher unless he came to us with testimonials of a Lutheran Consistory in Europe, or of the Swedish pastors in Pennsylvania, stating that he heartily receives the Unaltered Augsburg Confession of Faith." The Consistory of Trinity Church in London is requested to send them a minister who would "preach the Word of God in its purity, according to the Unaltered Augsburg Confession, and all the other Symbolical Books of our Lutheran Church."[1] The deed to the parcel of land which, in 1727, was granted to the Lutheran Church at *Loonenburg*, near Albany, N. Y., states, that in the church edifice to be erected upon this ground the Gospel must always be preached according to the "unalterable" Augsburg Confession.[2]

Not less faithful to the confessions were the *immigrants from southwestern Germany*, who began to pour into New York in 1708 and the following years. They were mostly served by the pastors of the Dutch churches. What they required of their ministers is shown in the petition of Trinity Church, in the city of New York, to Governor Clinton, in which they claim title to the glebe at *Newburg* given to the Lutherans by Queen Anne. The call cited in that petition,—and it is similar to the form of vocation issued by the other churches—states that the pastor "minister unto us as well in preaching the Holy Gospel purely, according to the Holy Scriptures and the Symbolical Books of our Lutheran Church, as in administering the sacraments according to Christ's institution, and practicing the usual ceremonies of the fellow-believers of the Unalterable Augsburg Confession"[3] In the call which, in 1731, the German Lutheran churches in *New Jersey*, sent to Hamburg for a pastor, they specified that such minister "in *ritualibus* conform to the liturgy of the Dutch churches of the Unaltered Augsburg Confession as published in Amsterdam" (1689).[4] We may also refer to the famous *New Rhinebeck* and *Sharon* church case, where the deed to the real estate required the "teaching of the doctrines of the Augsburg Confession of Faith and the other standards of the Lutheran Church."[5] These churches had united with the Franckean Synod which had published a confession of its own, repudiating

[1] Graebner, 179.   [2] Hartwick Mem., 197.
[3] Documentary History, III. 590 ff.
[4] Graebner, 231.   [5] 1 Sandford Chancery, 439.

5

in fact the Augsburg Confession. It is well to remember that large numbers of these Lutheran settlers along the Hudson, and in Schoharie immigrated to eastern Pennsylvania, forming the nucleus of a number of our oldest churches in the so-called Pennsylvania-German counties.

And what may we expect from the *Salzburg Settlements* in *Georgia?* From people who for conscience's and truth's sake left their homes in midwinter and sought refuge in the New World, where they could have the preaching of the Word of God in accordance with the confessions of the Evangelical Lutheran Church? In accepting the aid offered by the King of England, the Salzburg refugees made it a condition, "that they should be protected in the free exercise of their holy religion as contained in the Augsburg Confession and the other Symbolical Books of the Evangelical Lutheran Church."[1] And the confessional position of their pastors, Boltzius and Gronau, is well known.

Essentially the same conservative spirit and fidelity to the Lutheran Confessions we find among the settlements in *North* and *South Carolina*. When in 1776, St. John's Church in Charleston sent a call to Europe for a pastor, which call was signed by all the church officers and the contributing members, they specified what kind of man they wanted, to wit: "one able and willing to propagate the Gospel according to the foundations of the holy Apostles and Prophets, and to administer the holy Sacraments agreeably to the articles of our Unaltered Augustana."[2] The Constitution of *St. John's Church* in *Cabarrus Co., N. C.*, adopted in 1782, required of the pastor that he confess himself with heart and mouth to the Symbolical Books of our Evangelical Church. It prescribes the order of church service, including a brief catechetical exercise after the sermon and the Liturgy in use in St. James' chapel, in London.[3]

We now come to consider the doctrinal position of the man who is called the *patriarch* of the Lutheran Church in this country. In his certificate of ordination, which among others bears the signature of the celebrated Deyling, it is stated that Muhlen-

[1] Mann, "Lutheranism in America," 117. [2] Bernheim, 218 f.
[3] Ib., 252 ff.

berg solemnly promised that he would always conform in his teaching and in the administration of the Sacraments "according to the rule of faith as laid down in the writings of the Prophets and Apostles, the sum of which is contained in the Apostles', Nicene and Athanasian Creeds, in the Augsburg Confession of 1530, laid before Emperor Charles V, in the Apology of the same, in Dr. Luther's Larger and Smaller Catechism, in the articles subscribed to in the Smalcald Convention and in the Formula of Concord, written 1576 on disputed points of doctrine." When at the first synodical meeting of the Ministerium of Pennsylvania, *John Nicolaus Kurtz* was ordained, and the confessional requirements of subsequent ordinations was similar to his, he not only solemnly promised that neither publicly nor privately he would ever teach anything except what was in accordance with the Word of God and the Symbolical Books of the Evangelical Lutheran Church, and to that end he would make them the subject of his diligent study, but he also promised that in the public service and in the administration of the Sacraments he would introduce no ceremonies other than those approved by the Synod, neither use any other Agenda but the one sanctioned by them.[1] At the same convention, in a letter of the *Tulpehocken* Church, credit is given to Muhlenberg and his associates on account of their steadfastness in the doctrines of the Unaltered Augsburg Confession, which among them was at that time violently attacked.[2] At the laying of the corner-stone of *St. Michael's Church*, in 1743, it was publicly declared by Muhlenberg "that in it shall be taught the Evangelical Lutheran doctrines, as contained in the Unaltered Augsburg Confession and all the other Symbolical Books."[3] At the direction of Muhlenberg, a clause was inserted into the deed of the church at *Barren Hill* to the effect that the Church shall be forever devoted to the dissemination of the doctrine of the Evangelical Lutheran Church, "according to the Unaltered Augsburg Confession."[4] When, in 1748, in connection with the organization of the Ministerium of Pennsylvania, *St. Michael's* Church in Philadelphia was dedicated, he reminded the congregation of the fact "that the foundations of this church

[1] Jubilee Mem., 21. [2] Ib., 22. [3] Hall. Nachr., 288. [4] Ib., 864, 1182.

were laid with the view that in this building the Evangelical Lutheran doctrines as laid down in the Prophets and Apostles, in the Unaltered Augsburg Confession, and in all the other Symbolical Books should be taught." Such declarations were made at all corner-stone layings and church dedications. When, in 1762, Muhlenberg prepared a *constitution* for St. Michael's Church in Philadelphia, he inserted a clause which required the pastor to strictly adhere in all his teaching to the Unaltered Augsburg Confession, and this constitution has served as a model for many similar documents. In view of what has since occurred in the Church, this repeated mention and emphasizing of the *Unaltered* Augsburg Confession does almost seem to have also a prophetic meaning, for nowhere in the wide world has the changing and amending of this venerable document been oftener attempted as in Pennsylvania and New York.

The *Church Service* and *Agenda* adopted in 1748 by the Ministerium of Pennsylvania, under the leadership of Muhlenberg, breathe throughout the spirit of healthy Lutheranism. In the formula of distribution in the Lord's Supper Muhlenberg and his associates use language in such strict conformity to the words of the Tenth Article of the Augsburg Confession of 1530 and the Smaller Catechism of Luther, as is not even found in the communion service arranged by Luther, Bugenhagen or any of the strictest Lutheran theologians of the Reformation period. It was so worded, as Muhlenberg himself says, as a testimony against some malicious persons who charged him and his colleagues with lack of fidelity to the Confessions because they had come from Halle.

And we find more than a simple external or formal adherence to the Confessions. Muhlenberg and his colleagues faithfully and conscientiously conformed their *pastoral ministrations* to the principles laid down in the Confessions. That in the Holy Supper all communicants partake of the true body and blood of Christ they firmly believed. Hence their great care in the examination of the persons who desired to come to the Lord's Table. Whenever they could make it possible they spent several days in having the persons desiring to commune appear before them in order to hold a private and searching conversation with them. No more conscientious men ever graced the ministerial office than they. How zealous they were in the establishment and maintenance of *church-schools*, in which the children for a period of from six to eight years were taught Bible history, church hymns, catechism and Lutheran doctrine! And one examining the Pennsylvania Synod's Jubilee Memorial volume will be surprised at the large number of schools maintained in the different parishes, even after Muhlenberg's death. Many of them report as high as six, seven, eight and nine schools. Dr. Endress, of Easton, for years reports eleven, and Pastor Jaeger, of Hanover, even twelve schools. No less careful and conscientious do we find them in their work of *preparing the young people for their first communion*. Altar-fellowship was *unknown* to them. The thought of admitting, or of inviting persons to the Lord's Table in the Lutheran Church who were not Lutherans, but Zwinglians or Calvinists, would not only have been repulsive to Father Muhlenberg and his associates in the Pennsylvania Synod, but would have filled them with horror. In some localities the Lutherans built churches jointly with the Reformed, both being fellow-immigrants, but there were no union congregations, and the Reformed did not commune with the Lutherans, nor *vice versa*.

Muhlenberg and the founders of the Pennsylvania Synod did not practice *pulpit-fellowship*. And if there be any ground upon which pulpit-fellowship may be urged, it was the condition of affairs as it existed then, to wit: many settlements scattered far and wide, and few ministers of the gospel. Muhlenberg never exchanged pulpits with a minister of the German Reformed Church, although by history and circumstances closely connected, not even with the most prominent of their number, the founder of the German Reformed Church, the Rev. Michael Schlatter; and this is the more noteworthy from the fact, that Schlatter's wife was a daughter of one of the most influential families in St. Michael's (Muhlenberg's) Church in Philadelphia (Schleydorn). No church would permit any minister to preach in its pulpit, even if he claimed to be a Lutheran, unless first examined and recognized as a Lutheran minister by the Ministerium of Pennsylvania. Muhlenberg never accepted an invitation to preach to any but a Lutheran congregation, except in two instances, the one in Bucks County, Pa.,—if that may be called an exception—where German Lutherans requested him to preach to them. He held service in a Baptist meeting-house, and, upon request, explained the Lutheran doctrine of baptism. Once at Providence, when his feeble condition prevented him from going to the more distant Lutheran Church, he preached in the nearby Reformed Church (but to his congregation). Moreover, some point to the two cases, where ministers of other churches preached in the church of which Muhlenberg was at that time pastor. Thus the Rev. Richard Peters, of the Protestant Episcopal church, preached one Sunday afternoon in 1760, in Muhlenberg's church at New Providence. The circumstances were, however, peculiar. There were a number of settlers from Connecticut at the Trappe, and Muhlenberg, after holding services for his congregation in the morning, gave these English settlers an opporiunity of hearing Mr. Peters. The preaching of Whitefield in Zion's Church in Philadelphia, Pa., cannot properly be claimed as an instance of opening a Lutheran pulpit to a Methodist. The fact is that Zion's Church was not only the largest edifice of its kind in Philadelphia, but for some years in the country, and that because of its size it was selected for notable gatherings. When, therefore, Whitefield paid his last visit to Philadelphia, it was suggested that Zion's Church should be opened to him. By far the greater number of the thousands of attendants were English-speaking people. Preaching to the Independents, in Charleston, S. C., in 1774, admits of a similar explanation as Muhlenberg's preaching in the Baptist meeting-house in Bucks County, Pa. Some would call these exceptions or inconsistencies, but if they are such, they are exceptions that confirm and strengthen the rule, and if they seem inconsistencies, taking all the circumstances into consideration, they are such as to prove a higher consistency.

It is said that Muhlenberg favored *prayer-meetings*. Muhlenberg did not commence them where he did not find them in his churches, though he urged his people to have family worship; but where prayer-meetings existed he endeavored to keep control of them, lest they should degenerate into the noisy Methodistic meetings that were over-running the country like a prairie fire. The meetings in vogue in some of Muhlenberg's districts were not the strange wild-fire meetings, but they were of the character of the so-called pietistic conventicles of Spener and Francke, at which the German chorals were sung and passages of Scripture discussed, though in a more informal manner than at church service.

Notwithstanding all this Muhlenberg was, in 1761, *charged with heterodoxy* and infidelity to the Confessions by an ingrate named Raus, whose ocean passage Muhlenberg had paid twelve years before, thus saving the young man from being sold for his passage-money. In answer to this charge Muhlenberg says: "I have stated repeatedly, both orally and in writing, that in our evangelical system of doctrine, as it is found in our Symbolical Books, I discover no error, blemish or defect. I herewith challenge Satan and all his servile, lying spirits to prove aught against me where I have taught contrary to our Symbolical Books."

And now a few remarks on the doctrinal position of the *New York Ministerium*, founded in 1773 by the Rev. Fred. Aug. Chr. Muhlenberg, subsequently speaker of the first and third Congresses.

The *Constitution* upon which the New York Ministerium was founded, and which was in force until 1794, was the Ministerial Ordnung of the Pennsylvania Synod. Chapter V., Section 22, of this Constitution required every candidate and pastor to "preach the Word of God in accordance with our Symbolical Books," and Chapter VI., Section 2, provided for disciplinary measures against any one "teaching contrary to the Word of God and our Symbolical Books of faith."

In the second place, a "*Reverse*" was required of every minister who did not come from the Pennsylvania Ministerium, and of every candidate ordained.

On April 26, 1795, Georg Joseph Wichtermann is ordained at Albany by Dr. Kunze, assisted by the Rev. A. Braun, as pastor of the churches at East Camp and Tarbush. Before his ordination there was read to him, and signed by him in the presence of the congregation, a "Reverse," in which this passage occurs: "By these presents do I, in the most solemn manner, promise before God and my Chief Shepherd Jesus Christ, that, as long as mine eyes shall remain open, and as long as I shall discharge the duties of an Evangelical minister in America, I shall adhere to the doctrines of the Word of God, as explained in the Unaltered Augsburg Confession, and subject myself to the discipline of the reverend brethren in this State."

George Strebeck came of a Lutheran family. He had, however, joined the Methodists, and had occasionally preached in that denomination, but earnestly desired to return to the Lutheran Church. Dr. Kunze instructed him, and in 1794 he received license.

In the presence of the Ministerium the Reverse is read to him, which he signs. In the evening at public service in Christ Church, New York, the Reverse is read to him a second time; he again assents to it, and is thereupon licensed. In 1796 Strebeck is examined at Rhinebeck, and publicly ordained on Sunday, Sept. 25th. For the third time the "Reverse" is read to him, which he again signs. In it Strebeck declares "before God, my brethren in the ministry, and the entire congregation present," that "only so long will I discharge the duties of the ministerial office in the Evangelical Lutheran Church as my brethren, the Evangelical Lutheran Ministerium, find me in doctrine and life in agreement with the Word of God and the Symbolical Books of our Church." Others sign similar statements.

And not only were these "*Reverses*" required of ministers; they were also given by *congregations*. 1799 the Church at West Camp was received into Synodical connection. The Ministerium met at East Camp. The four representatives of the West Camp Church subscribed to a document in which they declared "that they will at all times submit to the action of the Ministerium, admit no minister, who is not a member of this Ministerium, into their pulpit," etc. June 9, 1800, the English Lutheran congregation in New York, founded three years before by Strebeck, asks for admission. The Ministerium lays down a number of conditions, which the representative of the church signs in its behalf. One of these reads: "That at no time we will admit any Lutheran minister into our Church who is not a member of the Evangelical Lutheran Ministerium."

And as to Altar-Fellowship, the practice had always been that such members of the congregation as desired to commune gave notice to the pastor by handing in their names on the day preceding the communion. These names the pastor then examined in the presence of the vestry (where every name could be passed upon) and read all the accepted names at preparatory service, thus altogether precluding an invitation to members of other denominations. But aside from this guarding of Lutheran altars, there is a resolution of the New York Ministerium not only discouraging any Altar Fellowship, *i. e*, communing of members of Lutheran churches at altars not Lutheran, but even authorizing disciplinary measures in the case of such members. In 1796 it was resolved at Rhinebeck, "That it be the general practice of the Evangelical (Lutheran) ministers in this State not to receive again a person who has communed in the church of another faith (denomination) into our churches, except upon the solemn declaration on the part of such person of future fidelity or constancy; and that, before such reception has taken place, persons standing in such relation are not to be recognized as members of the congregation." Pulpit or Altar-Fellowship with Episcopalians, Dutch Reformed, Presbyterians, or with any of the numerous denominations by which the churches of the New York Ministerium were surrounded, was unknown.

The "*Formula Juramenti*," which was required by the Consistory of Wernigerode of those it ordained and, among others, of Dr. Kunze, reads: "I swear unto God the Omniscient an oath into my soul that by the grace of God I will not only remain for myself faithful to the end to the true Lutheran Church books, to wit: the Unaltered Augsburg Confession of Faith, the Apology for the same, the Smalcald Articles, the two Catechisms of Luther, the contents of which books is specially summarized, briefly restated and clearly exhibited in the special Form of Concord, but that I will also teach and preach accordingly in the churches entrusted to my spiritual care." The other pastors had given similar pledges at their ordination.

The character of the churches which connected themselves with the Ministerium during the early period of its history was strictly confessional.

The Dutch churches of Hackensack, New York, Albany and Loonenburg, were established upon the constitution given to them by the Consistory of Amsterdam in Holland. This constitution provides, "that the minister shall not only conform in all his teachings, both public and private, to the Word of God as explained in the (severally mentioned) Symbolical Books of the Lutheran Church, but he shall likewise avoid all new phrases, according to the principle that he who changes the words changes the sense." [1]

One often quoted resolution, however, calls for an explanation. In 1797 the New York Ministerium resolved "not to recognize a newly established Lutheran Church, using the English language only, in any place where such Lutherans may partake of the services of the Episcopal Church, because of the intimate connection between the Episcopal Church and the Lutheran, the sameness of the doctrine and the great similarity of the discipline." This resolution cannot be justified in the light of the strictly Lutheran position the Ministerium held for ten years longer after the passage of this resolution. Still, it can be explained.

And if explained in the light of existing circumstances and of the statements of Dr. Kunze made at the time, it will be seen that the resolution was passed under a misapprehension, and under the influence of peculiar local conditions. In 1797 Strebeck, who had been Dr. Kunze's English assistant, organized an English Lutheran Church. Dr. Kunze was greatly displeased. He was not opposed to English preaching. There was no Lutheran pastor at the time who did as much for the English as did Dr. Kunze, but he desired his congregation to remain together and not separate on account of language. He severely denounced Strebeck's course. Synod met six weeks later. There

[1] Ch. Rev., VI. 188 ff.

that resolution was passed. Its framers seemed to think that it would prevent the organization of any more separate English Lutheran Churches. As soon, however, as Strebeck had gone over to the Episcopal Church (1804) the resolution was rescinded.

It is interesting to note how Dr. Kunze endeavors to justify the resolution. In the preface to Mr. L. Van Buskirk's sermons, which was written a few weeks after that action had been taken, Dr. Kunze seriously maintains that there is no essential difference between the two churches in matters of doctrine, and that there is a close resemblance in other respects. Dr. Kunze claims that the head of the Anglican Church is the Lutheran King of Hanover; and states that, before George I. of Hanover ascended the English throne, he had a commission appointed, consisting of representative men of the Lutheran and Anglican Churches, for the purpose of ascertaining whether there was any difference in doctrine between the two churches, as he would not accept a crown at the expense of his Lutheran faith and conviction. This commission reported that there was no essential difference in doctrine, and so he accepted the crown. Prof. Dr. G. Fritschel says of this attempt on the part of Dr. Kunze to justify that action: "It is clear from the justification of this exception, made with reference to the Episcopal Church and based upon an erroneous conception of the same, that the principle laid down in the Galesburg Rule was at that time maintained positively and decidedly."[1] So much is certain, that also during the seven years of the existence of this resolution there was neither pulpit nor altar-fellowship practiced with the Episcopal Church.

II. But now to the other side. The *deterioration* of the Church is also one of our Common Historic Antecedents. What a change within a few years! The breaking away from the faith of the fathers made itself first felt in the *South*. The South had no man strong enough to stem the tide of false liberalism, rationalism and Socinianism that was sweeping everything before it. The authority of Father Muhlenberg prevented the disciples of neology from publicly asserting their views in the Pennsylvania Synod.

[1] Kirchl. Zeitsch., XIII, 54.

But he had scarcely closed his eyes when radical changes were inaugurated. In New York the influence of Dr. Kunze was of a like character. As long as he lived the New York Ministerium did not depart from the confessional standards of the founders of the Lutheran Church in this country. But when in 1807 he departed this life, all is changed. Never was a change more sudden and more radical. Rationalism and Socinianism which had for so long a time been under constraint, now swept everything before it.

In 1787 the *Corpus Evangelicum* was organized in South Carolina. It consisted of five ministers and fifteen churches, and was an attempt to unite the Lutheran and German Reformed Churches. The majority in every congregation was to determine, if the Lutheran or the Reformed Liturgy and Catechism was to be used. In 1794 a conference of the Lutheran ministers in North Carolina *ordained* the Rev. *Robert Johnson Miller*, a licentiate of the Methodist Episcopal Church, as a Lutheran minister with the understanding that he should consider himself always bound to obey the rules, ordinances and customs of the Protestant Episcopal Church in America. This was followed by a fraternal union between the Synod of North Carolina and the Protestant Episcopal Convention of the same State. Thus, the leading spirit of the South at the beginning of this century, the Rev. *Gottlieb Shober*, was no Lutheran, but all his lifetime belonged to the *Moravian* Church.[1] He merely served the Lutheran Church as one of her ministers. In 1817 the North Carolina Synod approved a book, familiarly called "*Luther*," prepared by Rev. Shober, in which a union with the Episcopalians, Presbyterians, Methodists or Baptists is proposed, as among all these there is "nothing of importance to prevent a *cordial union*;"[2] Not less strange is the enumeration of the notorious Liturgy of the *New York Ministerium*—prepared under rationalistic influences—as a *Symbolical Book* of the North Carolina Synod.[3] In the *Pennsylvania Synod* neology first showed itself in an unmistakable manner in the adoption of a *new constitution* in 1792, which omitted the two references to the Symbolical Books that the old constitu-

---

[1] Bernheim, 411.   [2] "Luther," 210.   [3] "Luther," 172.

tion of Muhlenberg had contained. A new hymn book and liturgy suited to the vitiated taste of the times was published and used in the churches, and a union proposed with the German Reformed Church. Still, the Pennsylvania Ministerium has remained more conservative than its daughter, the *Ministerium of New York*. Soon after Dr. Kunze's death his excellent English *Hymn Book* and *Catechism* are supplanted by publications "adapted to the demands of the rising generation." In the so-called *Liturgy* or Agenda the efficacy of Baptism is denied; it is simply a "sign of purification." The Lord's Supper is no more than a "memorial of Christ's death." The words of distribution are those which were subsequently inserted into the Agenda of the United Church of Prussia. At the communion service the pastor welcomed all to this "feast of love." The guards which the fathers had placed about the altar are removed, and altar-fellowship is established. There is no longer any pledge of fidelity to the confessions on the part of ministers required. Ministers of all denominations are admitted to the pulpits, and the members of the Ministerium are at liberty to preach either Lutheran, Calvinistic or Zwinglian doctrines, and use Methodistic or any other measures if they prefer them. Catechization is neglected. The most notorious publication of that era was Dr. *Quitman's Catechism*. In it the doctrine of the Trinity is omitted. The death of Christ is referred to as simply a vindication of his teaching. Justifying faith is "an impressive sense of the glorious perfections of God, and a corresponding pious disposition arising from it." Faith in Christ is: "A firm belief in the divine authority of Jesus, and of his doctrine and promises, expressed by a sincere zeal to cherish Christian sentiments and dispositions." On page 48, question 29, of Justification and Eternal Life, it is stated, that "Justification and everlasting salvation are the *reward* that God has graciously promised to the true believers of Christ." It is further taught, that there is salvation without Christ, and that there are heathen in heaven. For proof he cites Rom. x: 14, "How then shall they call on Him in whom they have not believed," etc. It is not easy to understand, how a scholar of the standing of Quitman could deliberately print a statement like this, which is found in the appendix to the Catechism: "The friends of Luther ventured even in his lifetime to differ from him in some doctrinal points, and as the great Reformer was silent to these improvements by his friends, it appears as well from this circumstance, as from many expressions contained in his works, which were published by him in the latter part of his life, that he approved of these emendations." Quitman does not seem to have studied the life of Luther.

Thus we see that the *entire Church*, both North and South, with but few exceptions, had departed from the standards of the Reformation. The sentiment of the advanced leaders of the so-called American Lutheranism, as expressed by Dr. S. S. Schmucker, was: "The founders of the General Synod were men of enlarged, liberal, and scriptural views of the kingdom of Christ. They regarded it as the grand vocation of the American Church to reconstruct the framework of the Lutheran Church, assuming a more friendly attitude toward sister churches. This was the enlightened millennial attitude of the founders of the General Synod. In the Constitution they gave it power to form new confessions of faith and new catechisms suited to the progress of biblical light."[1] In another place he says: "The practice of binding the conscience of ministers and members to extended creeds . . . is, and must be, highly criminal."[2] In accordance with these sentiments, the Franckean Synod had published a revision of the Augsburg Confession, in which the original document is essentially changed.

Having disposed of the Symbolical Books, the leaders of this latitudinarian movement felt still the need of some confession, and they determined to supply the want. But they went about it in awkward manner. "The Definite Platform, Doctrinal and Disciplinarian, for Evangelical Lutheran District Synods," was, in September, 1855, sent to most of the more prominent members of the General Synod. It had been drawn up by Dr. Schmucker, after consultation with the radical Dr. Benjamin Kurtz; but the pamphlet did not bear the imprint of the author's name. Yet it was demanded that the Synods adopt, without further examina-

---

[1] Luth. Manual, dedic.   [2] Evangel. Rev., Oct., 1850.

tion, much less alteration, every article it contained, and swallow all its contents in one gulp. It was, moreover, recommended that the Synods should require every minister to subscribe his name to it, and if he refuse, to use disciplinary measures. In this platform, which claimed to be an American recension of the Augsburg Confession, the Augsburg Confession is charged with five distinct errors, and of the twenty-eight articles, eight are entirely omitted and twelve are materially changed.

But a reaction had already set in. This Platform opened the eyes of many more, and was almost universally repudiated by the Synods It powerfully strengthened the cause of conservative Lutheranism in the East.

III. We are met in this General Conference *for the purpose of reaching a better understanding and forming a closer union*. This can only be accomplished by a fuller appreciation of the confessions of our Church on the part of all who are here represented, and who long for such a union. We are aware that the return to the confessions and the cultivation of a healthy confessionalism among us will not remove all minor differences, which are the growth of time, individuality, education, and surroundings, but it certainly will bring about a unity in the faith, a unity in the spirit, and make possible a hearty coöperation (Augsb. Conf., Art. VIII.).

In conclusion we beg leave to submit a few *suggestions:*

1. True union is only possible upon the basis of the Divine Word.

2. We are Lutherans because we are convinced that our confessions depart in no respect from the teachings of the Word of God.

3. If this is the character of her confessions, it is the duty of all her ministers and churches to receive these confessions, and to receive them unreservedly. If, however, these confessions are repudiated or attacked in whole or in part the very foundation upon which the structure rests is undermined, and a united Lutheran Church is impossible.

4. The Lutheran Church in America was, without exception, built upon this foundation, and remained faithful to it for fully

one hundred and fifty years. In consequence there was union and coöperation over the entire Church.

5. Departing from the faith of the fathers and the entering of distrust and disharmony in the Church were related, as cause and effect.

6. The reaction against the baneful effects of neology did not result in mutual understanding and harmony; because it was not a return to the confessions of the Church, but an introduction of strange measures and views into the Lutheran Church which disparaged her doctrine, especially on the means of grace and the ministry.

7. During the past fifty years the Lutheran bodies represented in this General Conference have, with greater or less energy and success, striven to overcome the spirit of Pelagianism and Synergism, which has been dominant, and have come to a fuller appreciation of the doctrines of the Divine Word as taught in the confessions, with the happy result that we understand each other better to-day than ever before.

8. Only upon the basis of a healthy and evangelical confessionalism can a true union of the Lutheran Church be attained and maintained.

REMARKS.

Rev. J. A. W. HAAS said:—Is it correct to state that rationalism is a reaction against pietism? The general history of pietism, as we see it in Germany, shows that rationalism grew out of pietism. The immediate followers of our fathers here became rationalists. How then did pietism take a different course here?

Dr. HORN said:—The fact that Muhlenberg's Liturgy was replaced in 1786 by an inferior one, indicated that Mr. Haas was right.

Rev. D. EARHART said:—Did I understand Dr. Wolf to say that Rev. Dr. C. P. Krauth formulated the resolutions two years before they were adopted by the General Synod at York, Pa., in 1864? My recollection is that they were originally presented and adopted by the Pittsburg Synod in 1856 at its meeting in Zelienople, Pa.

Dr. SPAETH, in answer to Rev. D. Earhart's question as to the origin of the General Synod's confessional basis as prepared by Dr. Krauth, said that the resolutions of the Pittsburg Synod, prepared by

Dr. Krauth, were against the Definite Platform, and that from these the basis was formulated.

By Dr. Nicum:—When it is stated that the Hymn Book and Agenda of the Pennsylvania Synod published in 1786, one year before Muhlenberg's death, showed deterioration, it must be borne in mind that Muhlenberg was at that time feeble in body and had lost the vigor and strength of former days. And though a member of the committee which edited the book, he was no longer able to completely repress the spirit which was beginning to manifest itself in the Pennsylvania Synod. Still, he succeeded in giving the book more of a Lutheran character than otherwise it would have had.

PRAYER: ITS DOCTRINE AND FORMS.

BY EDWARD T. HORN, D.D.

By the accident of printing, the subject of this essay has been variously stated. I was asked to write on *Prayer: its Doctrine and Forms;* but in the first printed program of the Conference I saw my subject given, *The Doctrine and* MODES OF *Prayer;* and this has at last become, THE DOCTRINES *and Modes of Prayer.* The paper had been prepared before the printed program appeared. And I would prefer to seek and state the essential and real truth which underlies the fact of Prayer under all its forms, rather than to criticise the theories men have offered in explanation of it and enumerate the many modes of praying men have used.

Prayer is the human side of communion between man and God. This is obvious, and may seem hardly to deserve statement. But it is meant positively, as an assertion that there *is* communion between man and God; and that prayer is a generic name for man's part in it. Prayer is sometimes lauded as a *means of virtue.* It is said that it is good for us whether we obtain the things we ask for or not; whether it is heard or not; whether there is a God to whom it is addressed or not; for one thus praying comes to a recognition of his desire, and it is set in proper relation to moral and unworldly considerations, etc., etc. The old hymn says,

"Prayer is intended to convey
The blessings God designs to give."

Here it is defined as a *means of grace*, and it is intimated, I suppose, that it may become such by being a means of self-discipline. But these definitions are inadequate. It is the direct address of the spirit of man, of a man, to the Most High.

"He that cometh to God must believe that He is, and that He is a rewarder of them that seek after Him." (Heb. 11: 6.) Prayer rests on the fact of God's Being and Personality. "The eyes of the Lord are upon the righteous, and His ears are open to their cry. They cry and the Lord heareth." (Ps. 103: 15, 17.)

There could be no communion with God, if God did not first communicate Himself to us. Prayer is essentially *an answer*. Hence the significance of God's revelation of His Name, and the injunction not to take in vain that which has been given us for prayer, praise and thanksgiving. (The ancient Egyptian was warned not to forget the name of his god, for without knowing it he could not enter into life. So we could not pray if we did not know whom to address, and by what Name to call upon Him.) None pray to God now save those to whom He has in some wise and at some time come in His word. So it has been from the beginning. In a sense, prayer is natural, instinctive; but it is rather an outcry of pain, of grief, until we hear the Voice, to which we answer with a *prayer*. Hence the old custom of building an altar wherever God revealed Himself, and thinking a special worship due Him in connection with every such revelation. And hence the wisdom of fastening every petition on a word of God, and expecting an answer to our answer to His invitation or promise or revelation of grace.

Are the "prayers" of the heathen, then, no prayers? The ancient heathen offered sacrifices, and began every undertaking with sacred formulas, and exhibited many marks of religiousness. But in classic times, as well as now in heathendom, and among the worldly in Christendom, religious worship was a system of mechanical performances. Nearly all their rites were intended to ward off evil which vaguely imagined unseen powers might do. The purer aim and faith which seem to have underlain some observances, may have been a remnant of the tradition of primæval revelation. The Light that lighteth every man that cometh into the world sometimes spoke through conscience or in His providence in times and ways other than those in which He spake to the fathers by the prophets.

Prayer is rendered possible through the sin-offering made by our Lord Jesus Christ. Hence He calls Himself the *Door*, and bids us pray in His name. We would have been estranged from God and under His wrath but for the Lamb slain before the foundation of the world, but now we are from the beginning chosen in the Beloved. This sacrifice in the eternal Spirit made a way of access, which was symbolized and explicated by the Old Testament sacrifices. All the prayers of the Old Testament worship were based on Atonement made for sin. The Sin-offering was the basis and introduction to all worship, which culminated in the Peace-offerings, in which the worshipper eat and drank with God. It is in recognition of this that the Psalmist and we say, "Let the lifting up of my hands be as the evening sacrifice." Therefore, when the Church approaches its Maker, it is with confession of sin and absolution by the gospel of Christ's Atoning Death, and, therefore, our worship finds its centre and culmination in the celebration of and participation in our Lord's death for the remission of our sins.

All prayer is offered in the unity of the Body of Christ. As God for our sake treated Him as the one only sinner, so is He the one only Righteous One. We come in His Name, in His Name only can we come, *i. e.*, covered with His righteousness, as if we were He, to claim those things that are His, to prove that "all things are ours, and we are Christ's, and Christ is God's." Apart from Christ there is and can be no communion with God. We see God in the Face of His Son; we do not know Him apart from His Word; and in His Son we speak to Him.

Prayer takes many forms. We may embrace them under four designations, suggested by St. Paul. Prayer without ceasing (1 Thess. 5: 17); *The* Prayers, *i. e.*, the prayers of the Church (Acts 2: 42); *My* Prayers, *i. e.*, a man's own habitual prayers at stated times; and calling upon God in every time of need, occasional prayer, in every sense of that word.

St. Paul bade the Thessalonians pray without ceasing. He prayed for them exceedingly, night and day. He prayed at all seasons. He thanked God without ceasing. By this he does not mean that he was always on his knees, or, always abstaining from every other employment, was occupied with supplication. But he would have us always conscious of the immediate presence of God and of His open ear. A wish, a want, a longing, was no sooner felt and recognized than it was offered before Him, and no good thing could be received without instant acknowledgment. This consciousness and communion attended every action and thought. We ought to call upon God not only

" When in the hour of utmost need,
 We know not where to look for aid,"

but in *all our necessities*, in our little wants, as well as in great perils, always conscious of our helplessness, yet of our sufficiency in God. In Him, consciously, and by the act of our will, we should live and move and have our being.

It is said that those early converted and baptized remained in *the prayers*. That is, *the prayers of the Church*, the common prayers of the Body of Christ, of all its members with and for one another. St. Paul bids those who put on the whole armor of God to watch in all perseverance and supplication for all the saints. (Eph. 6: 18.) In the familiar passage in 1 Tim. (2: 1, 2) the rubric of such prayers is given: "I exhort, therefore, that, first of all, supplications, prayers, intercessions and giving of thanks be made for all men." In the earliest worship of the Church the celebration of the Holy Supper was a Eucharist, a thank-offering, in which the Body of believers, united with Christ their Head, gave God thanks for the blessings of Creation, and offered Bread and Wine as symbols of the things He had made and given to them for their maintenance and well-being, and offered themselves to God as those that had been bought with a price. Their thought is reflected in 2 Cor. 8: 5, "This they did not as we hoped, but first gave their own selves to the Lord, and unto us by the will of God." Their thanksgiving, their common prayer and their offering for the relief of the poor and the spread of the Gospel were united in one act; their *Eucharist* was a κοινωνία, a communion; and all these acts of communion with God were combined in one service.

It may briefly be said that that is not a Christian service of worship in the Church, which, without any consciousness of the unity of the whole body of believers in Christ in prayer, and without any thought of the varied needs of all believers, and of all Christ's wandering sheep, does not pray for all estates of men.

When the Church prays the prayers God has put into her heart, she is at one with her Head, who in the Holy of Holies presents her intercession as His own. Jesus and all of us pray one prayer. No prayer "in His Name" is presented apart from Him. The "intercession" by the Spirit, spoken of in Rom. 8: 26, 27, is not apart from and superadded to our Lord's intercession for us, spoken of in verse 34. The Spirit of God is in the world *in the Church*, through the means of grace which are the nucleus of the Church. The Spirit of God is not apart from the Eternal Son of God. The Spirit in the Church through the Word and Sacraments, stirs the hearts of God's faithful people to mutual love and fellowship with the Lord, and to common and mutual prayer; so that at the same time each is praying for all in union with the Son and the Holy Ghost, and each is sustained and assured by the prayers of all in the unity of the Son and the Holy Ghost.

I might say much more of the prayers of the Church. But only a few remarks are necessary. The Litany is historically and in its *rationale* a fair representative of the prayers of the Church. The participation of all by voice, under the guidance of a leader; the foundation of petition and hope upon the Godhead and work of our Saviour; the summary of every want in the appeal to God's mercy; all these are in every sense Christian. So the Collects, which are such wonderful monuments of the sincere piety that flowed on under all the corruption of imperfect and disturbed ages, are prayers suggested by and answered by the Word of God itself. The *Verba Testamenti* in the Holy Communion are a prayer in which we recite to our Lord His words of commandment and promise, and humbly claim their fulfilment. Our hymns also are prayers. Every hymn ought to be a prayer—an act of communion with God—and not an address to our fellow-men. The great prayer of the Church is the Lord's Prayer. In it we approach Him of whom our Lord said: *My Father and your Father*, and pray for the relief of our want in common with all our fellow-men. It is the prayer of Christ, in the only shape in which it can be said by those to whom sin clings.

Philemon and I Thess. 1: 2 show that Paul observed a *habit* of prayer. He "said his prayers." He speaks of *my* prayers, *every prayer of mine for you, our prayers*, and he prayed for his friends and converts by name. The Apostles of our Lord went up into the temple at the hour of prayer. Our Lord Jesus was wont to go apart to pray. And He has suffered us to know somewhat of the manner of His prayers. "I know that Thou hearest me always," He said. In the garden He said: If it be possible; nevertheless, not my will, but Thine. He repeated it; He struggled; He agonized. He prayed for His disciples by name: I have prayed for *thee*, He said to Peter, singling him out as fitted, after His prayer for him had been answered, to strengthen his brethren.

Our Lord used the Book of Psalms as a prayer-book. When He hung upon the cross, in the intensest hour of His life that wrung out its completest cry, His prayers were in the words of the Psalter. No doubt His soul was nourished by the same words of God, upon which His prayer was founded. It is apart from my object to deduce lessons; rather would I state principles; but may we not say that, as the Christian must never pray for himself exclusively, but always in the consciousness of the Body of Christ, so neither dare he be satisfied with a mere prayerful atmosphere (as, for instance, in the well-known story of Bengel, who is said to have gone to bed saying simply: "Lord, Thou knowest Thou and I are on the same old terms"), but should *say his prayers*, in them cast all his care upon the Lord, pray for others by name, make supplication with thanksgiving; and that in these prayers he may find great assistance in books of devotion and forms of prayer, above all in the example of our Lord, the Lord's Prayer, and the Lord's prayers, and the Psalter?

It should be remembered that a Christian man's own prayers are in a true sense prayers of the Church; they are the thanksgivings, petitions and supplications which he addresses to our heavenly Father *in his particular vocation and ministry* in the Church of Christ. A Christian prayer cannot be selfish, exclusive, forgetful of those God has given to us. A pastor, a parent, a ruler, for instance, in his closet, comes before God with the burden of his office, and prays for those God has given him. His prayers, therefore, belong to the organism of the prayers of the Church.

There is another form of prayer: we *are bidden call upon God in every time of need*. This refers to earthly, bodily need, but also to "all troubles and necessities whensoever they oppress us." Our Lord here also set us an example. It was His custom to go apart to pray before every especial act of His ministry. He prayed before the choice of the Twelve. He prayed at the close of His Galilean Ministry, upon the verge of conflict. He prayed when the Cup was at length to be drunk. So Paul says to Timothy that "every creature of God is to be received with thanksgiving; for it is sanctified by the Word of God and prayer." The Christian lives by the strength of the Son of God always, and always asks for and receives it; he knows God hears him always, and he calls upon Him for guidance, deliverance, and a happy issue to all his undertakings; and in life in every crisis, as well as at the hour of death, into His hands he commends his spirit.

REMARKS.

By Dr. NICUM: It is a most perplexing subject, and I refer to it in this Conference for the purpose of calling attention to it, to wit: The prayers of the lodges; how are they to be considered? Prayer in the name of Christ is not in harmony with the spirit and aim of the lodge. As the lodge is the great new temple into which shall be gathered all the nations, and as prayer in the name of Jesus is offensive to a Jew, a Mohammedan and a Hindoo, it can not be tolerated. If found in some inferior lodges it is out of place there, and has always been so declared by the supreme Lodge upon appeal. The presence of some of our church members in the lodge room and their actual participation in these pagan services is a difficult problem to deal with, owing chiefly to the prejudice which the money interest in the lodge creates. Still, it is our duty to study the matter in the fear of God, and in the light of the Word of God arrive at a conviction.

DR. BAUSLIN: Those prayers are not Christian prayers. There is a greater adherence to Evangelical prayer in the Lutheran Church than in any other denomination. We noted a perversion of prayer where a minister at a political convention went over the entire history of the achievements of a political party, as his prayer, which was applauded by the convention and noted in the daily press as an eloquent prayer. The forms of prayer in our common service have saved us from such perversion.

DR. WOLF said that he often felt that prayer was a supreme impertinence. He was confident that many who lead in public prayer have no idea of what they are doing, of the awful import of their action. What warrant has a creature like man to address the eternal throne, to ask for the notice, the attention, the audience of the Majesty on high, to whom worlds are but as the dust in the balance? We must ever shrink from approaching the Godhead, had not He in infinite condescension come down into the sphere of the creature and commanded us to enter into communion with Him, and in our helplessness direct our cry to His matchless grace.

He maintained also that undue stress was laid on the oral expression of prayer. Our words are nothing to God, who knows our heart's desire and our actual need. An inarticulate sigh, a look, a yearning appeals to our Heavenly Father.

> "Prayer is the soul's sincere desire
> Unuttered or expressed."

He instanced a pious lady who is in feeble health, and who by taking a drive on a recent pleasant afternoon and eating a light supper, had about used up the full measure of her limited strength. Then she felt the need of "Saying her prayers," and this effort proved too much for her exhausted condition and resulted in complete prostration, from which it required weeks to recover. It would be a serious reflection on our religion to claim that in such a case prayers must be articulated, expressed in forms of human speech.

In answer to Dr. Nicum's remarks about the Christless prayers of the lodges, I think it should be said that they are not distinctively Christian prayers at all, but so framed as not to antagonize the views of Jews and pagans. I was greatly pleased with the thoroughly sound and evangelical interpretation of prayer given in Dr. Horn's admirable paper, and I am disposed to feel that in the use of this important part of worship there is more conformity to these principles in the prayers heard in Lutheran churches than anywhere else in Christendom. There are so many lamentable paroxysms of prayer in our generation that it is refreshing to have our minds and hearts brought back to such sound principles as those enumerated in the paper just read. Let me give an example. Out in our State some months ago a political convention in one of our cities was opened with prayer by a minister selected for that purpose. In what he presented as a prayer the history of the party in the interest of which the convention was met, was said to have been given in more or less detail from Abraham Lincoln to William McKinley. Manifestly such business is a perversion and a reversal of the divine order.

But I believe that there are indications of improvement. The large number of prayer books for use in family worship now being issued would seem to indicate a revival of interest on this subject. Within the past year or two one bishop of the Methodist Episcopal Church has issued two such books. Another is published by Rev. Dr. Miller of this city, and editor of the Presbyterian Sunday-school Helps. Dr. Lyman Abbott has edited one such book, in which he has used several prayers of the venerable preacher who preached to us so admirably this morning. Rev. F. B. Meyer, of London, has another, and there are many others. These books, of course, are not published for fun, but to sell. They are put in print because there is a demand for them, we may be sure. Their appearance would seem to indicate a revived interest on the subject to which they all pertain.

Dr. KROTEL: As representatives of three General Bodies, it is a matter of gratification that we have made progress in this direction, in saying our prayers, if you wish. Formerly it was an offence to read a prayer out of a book, and yet these very people sang hymns, which were prayers, out of a book. That was praying in verse; I prefer to pray in prose. The Lord's Prayer is in prose. People have learned that they can pray those beautiful prayers which have come down through the centuries with heart and soul, and unite in one common service. Dr. Buckley, editor of the New York *Christian Advocate*, said that of all forms of service ours is the most Scriptural and that besides we maintain the right and practice of free prayers.

Dr. Luther E. Albert said: Whilst I frequently employ set prayers, I also use free prayers. He instanced the case of the Prince of Wales sending for a rector and asking that he lay aside the book of prayer and pray for him.

Dr. Spaeth: I also use free prayers, but I do not have the right to thrust aside the prayers of the Church and insert my own individual prayers into the public worship of the Church. The sermon is the place for individual presentations, and there, and not in the general prayer, is the place for my individual petitions.

Rev. Prof. J. Fry, D.D., said: While the paper read did not touch the matter of posture in prayer, the matter is worthy of our attention. It is to be regretted the custom of our fathers to rise up and stand during prayer in the public services on the Lord's day is being changed in some churches to kneeling, or more generally to remain sitting and simply bowing the head. It may seem a small matter, but there is a confessional principle involved in it. The early Christians stood during prayers on the Lord's day because it was the day of our Lord's resurrection, and at the Reformation this principle was recognized, and the posture of rising up and standing before the Lord was re-established, and it should be maintained and perpetuated as a matter of principle as well as of custom in Lutheran congregations.

Dr. Horn said that the brevity of his essay had not permitted reference to many subjects connected with Prayer. He asked whether it was not inconsistent with the sacredness, the reality, of prayer, to ask ministers to go through a mere form of prayer, which is not intended to be anything more than a form, at political conventions and literary performances. The decay of the custom of family prayer was adverted to. Loehe's *Samenkoerner des Gebets* was mentioned as a model of right prayers, in contrast with many books which cover unbelief under beautiful language.

William H. Staake, Esq., said: Mr. Chairman, I do not know if it is in order for me to speak in this Honorable Body, but, if I am in order, I would like to crave your attention for a moment to a subject which, to my mind, deserves the serious attention of every Christian minister, and every Christian layman, namely, the subject of greater regard for the name of Almighty.God, in the administration of judicial oaths, as well as in the appeal to Him for the protection of the Court and Commonwealth, in the opening of courts of justice.

I regard every oath as an appeal to Almighty God, upon the part of the person taking the oath, asking him to witness the truth of the statement the person is about to make, or the evidence he is about to give, and, being an appeal to Almighty God, such appeal is, in effect, a prayer, and should be made with due and proper reverence.

I regret to say, that in actual practice, especially before our minor judicial tribunals, but little respect, so far as reverence is concerned, is paid in the use of the Holy Name of God, in connection with the usual language of an oath.

Many of the officers of our Courts observe but little ceremony, and usually no reverence, when they administer the oath, either to witnesses, to members of the legal profession, or to officers who, in the usual transaction of the business of courts, may be called upon to assume an obligation, or give testimony.

During the past thirty years I can only remember one official of the Court,—a dear, gentle old man,—who, in his manner of administering an oath, gave constant testimony to his personal appreciation of the solemn act which was being performed by him. He would insist upon all persons in the Court room being seated; he would command a perfect silence, and then, with clear and distinct enunciation, in a most solemn and impressive manner, he would repeat the words of the oath which the person was about to take, and when he would come to the concluding portion, in which the name of Almighty God was used, he would raise his eyes, as if in prayer, towards Heaven, and repeat the great name of his Maker. This good old man,—who was universally respected by the members of my profession,—has been called to his reward. I wish that his example would be followed by all other officials in the Commonwealth occupying a similar position. I regret to say, Mr. Chairman, that in these practical days of ours, some of our courts have deemed it unnecessary to follow the tradition and custom of years, in the daily opening of the Court, by appealing to God to protect the Commonwealth and the Honorable Court, but have substituted, in the place thereof, a simple striking of the gavel, followed by the words: "In the name of the Commonwealth, this

Court stands open for business," followed by a few more raps of the gavel, and then the Court is considered open. I am happy to say, however, that the majority of our Courts still do appeal to God to preserve the Commonwealth and the Honorable Court, but the manner of the appeal might be made much more dignified, formal and reverential. In fact, so little attention is often paid to the use of a serious and reverential manner in the administration of an oath, that it has come to be a by-word, that the fee for the administration of the oath is often uttered in the same breath with the name of the great Jehovah, so that the uninitiated might think it was a necessary part of the language of the oath. The most solemn form of oath is that by the uplifted hand, in which the language is:

"I do solemnly swear, by Almighty God, the Searcher of all hearts, that the evidence I am about to give is the truth, the whole truth, and nothing but the truth, and so I shall answer to God at the Great Day."

The more usual form, however, is that of placing the hand upon the Bible, and simply saying "that the evidence (or the statement) is the truth, the whole truth, and nothing but the truth, so help me God."

The effect of this careless administration of oaths is apparent in the frequent cases of perjury. I know that some people say that a man who will tell a lie will perjure himself. I do not agree to the correctness of such a statement. On the contrary, I believe that there are many who might be guilty of falsehood, under some circumstances, who would hesitate to repeat the falsehood, and deliberately call upon Almighty God to witness the truth of the false statement. I do not know what is the cause,—whether it is because men are not so serious and reflective now as formerly, or whether it is due to a change of sentiment on the subject of conscientious scruples in the taking of an oath, or if for other reasons, but this I know, that twenty-five or thirty years ago you could go into any of our local courts and you would find, on a jury being impaneled and sworn, that on an average three, four, five, or often more of the jurors would demand to be affirmed, instead of sworn, while now, you often see—in fact it is the usual rule to see—the whole jury standing up and being sworn, the cases of those who ask to be affirmed being now very exceptional. I fear the cause of this is simple carelessness upon the part of men who have not taken the trouble to consider the subject at all. I do not believe it is due to an increased regard for the oath, and a decreased inclination to take an affirmation instead of a judicial oath, but, I repeat, I believe it is due to indifference or to a simple want of examination of the subject upon the part of those who have no time for such things in this busy, pushing, energetic, driving age of ours.

Here is a field of usefulness for the Church. Our pastors should impress upon their people that an oath is an appeal to Almighty God; that such an appeal is a prayer, and that, in the taking or the administration of an oath, there should be the same solemnity, the same dignity, the same reverence, as one would use in a spoken prayer.

G. G. BURNETT: Family prayer has always been recognized as a desirable and necessary part of the Christian life, but is it so in reality? In several years of traveling among our churches and congregations all over our land, it has been the privilege of the writer and his wife to be entertained in many homes of missionaries and pastors. We have expected to enjoy family worship, and in not a single instance have we been disappointed. The reading of the Bible and the subsequent prayer have been regarded as necessary as the morning meal. In one instance, a verse of Scripture would be read by the head of the family, followed in turn by each member in succession to the end of the chapter. Every morning the prayer would be made by each member of the family in turn; and the pleasure of hearing the mother of the flock and the children in their order conduct the prayer in their own language, was a rare treat, and an innovation recommended to all. That mother is able to conduct any gathering in church circles, while the children are being educated in spheres of action in the various church organizations into which they will naturally be called.

It is in the family gatherings of the laity to which especial attention is called. We have been entertained in very many of these, in the South and through the North from the Pacific to the eastern shores, and our conclusion, based on years of experience, is, that the family service ceases with the morning blessing of the food. Not only is this true of Lutheran households, but in other denominations. This is a sad commentary on the Christian home life. At this moment I do not recall three instances among the laity in which a full family service was held. Our clergy should, indeed, take this to heart. That our pastors are anxious that their people should perform such duties properly and reverently, none will question; but that they are remiss in penetrating into the home life, and ascertaining how these Christian duties and obligations are performed, is a fact.

A physician is the custodian of the physical ailments of his patients. Why do not our pastors solicit the confidence of their parishioners in their inner home life, and become the spiritual physicians and advisers in the conduct of the family service? Pulpit oratory and advice is excellent and timely, but of too general a character to strike at the root of the home delinquencies. The requirement needed is personal work. Individual advice and encouragement is needful and necessary, and pastors should feel no reluctance in tendering both. They will find such services warmly appreciated and followed, whereas timidity and fear of failure prevent the commencement of such service without some instruction. Let our ministers drop in at the morning meal of their various parishioners; they will surely be welcomed; let them call for the family Bible, and conduct service, and give a practical lesson to the family gathering, requesting its daily continuance, and great good will result therefrom.

Many grains of truth are absorbed by ministers in conference, and the seed thus planted will produce abundant fruit. The statements herein made of the absence of the family altar in Christian families will shock many of our clergy, but unfortunately it is the truth. Ministers in their pulpits look with complacency upon their work; and when one of their laymen opens a window to reveal the light from his standpoint, it jars disagreeably upon the equanimity of the former. It opens up a theme for thought and a field for action that will be well for our clergy to heed; and if the matter is honestly fathomed and properly treated, the blessings of God will rest upon the efforts of our clergy in the establishment and maintenance in their respective congregations of the family altar and family prayers.

OUR EDUCATIONAL INSTITUTIONS.

BY PROF. F. V. N. PAINTER, D.D.

In the widest sense, the subject before us includes all the schools through which the Church promotes the education of its youth. It might fairly lead to a consideration of our schools of every kind and every grade; and in each case, we might find something interesting or profitable to contemplate. But a limit has wisely been fixed for this discussion; and hence, for the sake of fuller treatment, which must yet be condensed and brief, this paper is restricted to a consideration of our colleges. Other schools, if mentioned at all, are mentioned only incidentally.

From the beginning the Lutheran Church has been active in

the work of education. The principles underlying the Lutheran Reformation of the sixteenth century, in contrast with those of Roman Catholicism, naturally and inevitably lead to the establishment of schools of every grade. These principles may be briefly stated as follows: 1. The Scriptures are the only infallible rule of faith and practice in religion; 2. Men are justified by faith alone; and 3. All believers are kings and priests unto God. These principles, first proclaimed by Luther and his co-adjutors, make the Lutheran Reformation the mother of popular education, and the friend of every department of learning.

The relation of these principles to education should be clearly apprehended. With the Scriptures as guide, every man is elevated to the freedom and dignity of ordering his own religious life. To the Protestant Christian, intelligence thus becomes a primal necessity. By its fundamental principles, the Lutheran Reformation contracted the obligation of placing every man in a position, through a study of the Bible, to save himself and lead a Christian life.

The operation of these principles is seen wherever the Lutheran Church exists. They led Luther to translate the Bible, to urge the establishment of primary and secondary schools, and to labor for the improvement of the universities. They have made Germany the school-mistress of the world. In every region where the Lutheran Church has been transplanted, we see an interest in education. The erection of a house of worship is quickly followed by the establishment of a school. During the last century, the great pioneer ministers of Pennsylvania were active in establishing parochial schools; and of the Salzburgers it is recorded that "no sooner did they take possession of the wilderness than a tabernacle was set up for the Lord. This was speedily followed by provision for the education of the children."

But the educational work of the Lutheran Church in this country does not show the prompt, uninterrupted, and vigorous growth that naturally springs from its principles. Various hindering causes intervened. The energies of our people, who were loyal to the cause of independence, were largely absorbed in the struggle of the American Revolution. The *Deutsches Seminar* in Philadelphia, founded by Dr. Kunze in 1773 under promising auspices, was broken up by the war. The principles of deism and infidelity, imported from England and France, in a measure paralyzed religious activity. But most potent of all these hindering influences was the unfortunate language dissension, which prevented the German and English-speaking elements of our Church from cordially uniting in educational work. As a result, the work of higher education has been belated among us, and our oldest College will have to wait many years yet before celebrating its centennial.

The tide of German immigration had set in strong as early as the first quarter of the eighteenth century. Before 1750 the Lutheran population of Pennsylvania is estimated at 60,000. Before the close of the century the Lutheran population must have been considerably more than 100,000. Yet the first College of the Lutheran Church—Pennsylvania College of Gettysburg—was not founded until 1832. Of the fifty colleges, including those for young women, credited to us in our Year Books, only four were established prior to 1850. Nearly all the rest have been established in the last three decades, and more than twenty since 1890. Our educational energies, long held back, seem suddenly to have burst forth like Arctic vegetation after the long winter.

This phenomenal activity is worth a moment's consideration. It is evident that special causes, apart from the general principles of the Church of the Reformation, have been at work. During the past three or four decades there has been extraordinary educational activity in our country at large, the influence of which has been felt in various parts of our Church. The great tide of Lutheran immigration has called for a rapid expansion of our educational facilities. There has been better synodical organization among our people, securing prompter and more efficient action than was possible at an earlier period. But apart from all these influences, differences of language and of synodical relations have especially contributed to the multiplication of colleges. Our fifty colleges represent four or five different languages and some twenty-five different Synods. With greater unity and homogeneousness, it is evident that fewer colleges would have been established.

The Lutheran Church in America has special reasons for activity in education. It cannot otherwise meet its grave responsibilities nor maintain a vigorous life. Without fostering education, it is untrue not only to its fundamental principles, but also to its history and traditions. The Lutheran Church was born in a university. It feels a just pride in its old-world institutions, and in its accumulated treasures of theology. But more than that; our Church is here placed in an atmosphere of intellectual freedom, where influence and progress must depend ultimately on the convincing power of the truth. To be without culture is to be without power. Without strong institutions of learning, we shall fail to make a deep impression on the intellectual and spiritual life of our country, which, as may be easily foreseen, is destined to play an important part in the divine drama of the world.

The Lutheran Church has a well-defined and noble educational ideal. It avoids Puritanic narrowness, secular incompleteness, and Roman Catholic asceticism and subjection to authority. It recognizes the validity of all man's faculties as divine gifts, and emphasizes the totality of life as a divine service. While laying stress on the supreme importance of moral and spiritual culture, it recognizes the claims of practical life. It begins with the consecration of baptism; and then, through uninterrupted training and culture from childhood, it aims at such a development of the physical, mental, and spiritual powers of man, as will realize the highest personal worthiness, and at the same time fit him, in the spirit of Christ, to render the greatest service to Church and State. Attaching special importance to the moral and spiritual element of education, the Church cannot give its unreserved endorsement to any system or institution in which this element of culture is neglected. For this reason, even in the presence of well-equipped secular institutions, it establishes and maintains its own colleges.

All our colleges make provision for the religious culture of the student. Apart from the daily exercises in chapel, instruction in the evidences of Christianity is frequently given. All the teaching is suffused with a Christian spirit, the field of knowledge being surveyed from the standpoint of evangelical truth. In recent years systematic biblical instruction has been introduced into many of our institutions. In some colleges, the doctrines of our Church, as embodied in the catechism, are made a required study. It is not difficult to find arguments, and even strong ones, in favor of such instruction. But in the colleges of the English-speaking part of our Church, it has generally been judged best not to make strictly denominational instruction a part of the required courses of study. Strictly sectarian teaching can hardly be regarded as forming an essential part of the liberal culture, which a college course is designed to give. Furthermore, none of our institutions are strong enough, as we shall see, to depend solely on Lutheran patronage; and hence, as a matter of practical wisdom, our English colleges aim only at the broad Christian culture that will commend them to the public at large. Instruction in the doctrines of our Church is generally provided; but it stands outside of the regular courses, and is left optional with the student.

The organic relation between our colleges and the Church is not everywhere the same. In the case of individual enterprises, the connection seems to be merely nominal. In some cases, the college is under the control of a self-perpetuating board of trustees, a large majority of whom are required by the charter to be members of the Lutheran Church. In other cases, one or more synods exercise control through the appointment of the governing board. Each of these two methods has its place and its advantages. The former method is the natural one, when institutions have originated independently of synodical action and are carried on without synodical support. The latter method brings the college into closer relation with the Church in its organized capacity, and is eminently proper where institutions are founded and maintained by synodical action.

It is now generally conceded that the young women of our country should have equal educational advantages with the young men. Hence, more than two-thirds of the colleges and universities of America are open to both sexes. In the West the system of co-education generally prevails, and nearly all our stronger institutions there admit women. But throughout our Church in the Atlantic States, co-education has not yet been cordially adopted, and the prevailing system is that of separate schools. Of the dozen colleges and seminaries for young women reported in our Year Books, only one is west of the Ohio River. The majority of these schools are within the bounds of the United Synod. With the limited resources at their command, they have accomplished surprising results, sending forth many noble, intelligent women. But none of these institutions are endowed. None of them have courses of study or standards of instruction equal to those of our best male or co-educational colleges. A really strong college for young women—one with sufficient means to enforce high standards—is really a desideratum in our Church. But those who hold that young women are incapable of high standards of education, or who believe that high culture unfits them for their work in life, have eminent reason to be satisfied with the existing condition of things in the Atlantic States.

The catalogues and published statistics of our colleges reveal some noteworthy facts. In many of our institutions, the standards of admission and graduation, as compared with representative colleges of our country, are very low. For lack of teaching force or under the inertia of educational conservatism, the courses of instruction in some colleges have not been expanded to keep pace with the development of science or to meet the new demands of modern life. None of our colleges are adequately endowed, and a large number are without any endowment at all. With only a few exceptions, they are deficient in buildings, libraries and scientific apparatus. Not one has dispensed with a preparatory department, and in most cases, the preparatory department constitutes numerically the larger part of the college. Of our fifty colleges, only five have more than one hundred students in the college classes. Nearly half of them have fewer than fifty students in the college department, and in not a few cases the number falls below twenty-five. In view of these facts, there are serious grounds for suspecting that many of our colleges, judged by proper standards, are colleges only in name.

Under the operation of the general and particular causes already considered, it seems that our Church has established too many colleges. With the existing standards in our country, which are being rapidly advanced, we have more colleges than we can properly equip and endow. The statistics, which seem to establish these truths, will hardly be found dry. According to the "Report of the Commissioner of Education" for 1895-96, the Methodists have eighty-seven colleges in this country, or one, on an average, for every 55,000 members. The Baptists have fifty colleges, or one for every 80,000 members. The Episcopalians have five colleges, or one for every 90,000 members. The Lutherans, according to our Year Books, have fifty colleges, or one for every 30,000 members. In other words, we are trying to do in the work of higher education nearly twice as much as the Methodists and three times as much as the Baptists and Episcopalians—denominations that are financially much stronger. At first sight this might be taken as a proof of the superior activity and devotion of our people; but an inquiry into the matter of equipment and endowment speedily dissipates this illusion.

Still following the statistics of the Commissioner of Education, we learn that the one hundred and eleven non-sectarian colleges and universities of our country have an average endowment of $582,000. The average endowment of Methodist colleges is $108,000; of Baptist colleges, $267,000; of Episcopal colleges, $315,000; of Congregational colleges, $330,000. After these magnificent figures, it costs an effort to state that the average endowment of our Lutheran colleges is only $18,000. Yet it would be unjust to express or imply any reflection on the liberality of our people. Our Lutheran population, now aggregating a church membership of a million and a half, is made up largely of recent immigration from Germany and Scandinavia. Our people, particularly in the South and West, have not yet acquired the abundant wealth from which munificent endowments come. In view of all these facts, is it not evident that we are trying to do more than we can accomplish with creditable efficiency?

The mistake of unduly multiplying colleges has been greatest in the South. The United Synod has only 40,000 members; yet within its territory there are no fewer than seven colleges, or one for every 6,000 members. Most of these colleges have no endowment; and the aggregate available endowment of the three strongest is less than $100,000. All of them, be it said to their honor, are doing good work; but it is done with inadequate equipment, and at the cost of heroic self-sacrifice. Their struggle for existence is maintained with great courage; but most of them, without a change of policy, are probably destined to succumb.

In this survey of our educational situation, which is not flattering in some of its features, let us not forget the invaluable service rendered to the Church by many of its struggling colleges. Whatever mistakes may have been made, the history of our colleges reveals a churchly devotion and faithful courage. Without the colleges founded in weakness four or five decades ago, our Church would have sustained immeasurable losses. For many years, as is well known, Pennsylvania College supplied the English-speaking part of our Church with ministers. The Church in Ohio and adjoining States owes a great debt to Wittenberg College. The two Synods of Virginia are composed almost entirely of graduates and former students of Roanoke College. The Synod of South Carolina is made up chiefly of graduates of Newberry College. In like manner it might be shown that all our older colleges have been invaluable to the Church in supplying it with ministers and intelligent laymen.

This study of our educational work would be an incomplete and thankless task if it stopped with a presentation of present defects and past mistakes. Fortunately it readily suggests some of the means by which our higher institutions of learning may be improved. Though nothing but the stress of necessity will probably lead to any considerable change, it is surely worth something to bring clearly before our minds some of the remedial measures that are needed.

1. First of all, has not the time arrived for insisting on higher standards for our colleges? With the marvellous growth of our Church in numbers, wealth and intelligence, we seem to be in a position, particularly in the East, to provide and require better

things. The college of fifty years ago, however useful in its day, does not meet the demands or satisfy the standards of the present. Institutions doing the work of high schools or academies ought not to be called colleges. A college worthy of the name can no longer be built up and maintained without large sums of money. Not a few enthusiastic educators, inspired by the achievements of half a century ago, undertake to found institutions without adequate backing in means and patronage. They forget the changed conditions that render success in such undertakings well-nigh impossible. The statistics of the Department of Education enable us to form a definite idea of what a college ought to be. The four hundred and eighty-four colleges and universities of this country have, on an average, twenty-five professors, one hundred and forty-two students in the academic department, scientific apparatus valued at $33,000, buildings and grounds worth $244,000, and an endowment fund of $228,000. These figures show us substantially what an average college ought to be in equipment, attendance and endowment. As we have seen, our institutions fall far short of this standard. It is a humiliating fact, and from this time on we should insist on greater things; and instead of multiplying weak and struggling colleges, we should henceforth strive, in our higher education, at least to approximate the average standard of our country. Otherwise our Church, whatever its heritage of history and doctrine, will stand shorn, in large measure, of its influence and power.

2. Again, our educational situation clearly shows the need of greater unity and co-operation in our Church. It is a happy omen that this need is coming to be generally felt. Our divisions and antagonisms, to say nothing of their offense to the supreme law of charity, are generally being recognized as sources of great weakness and waste. As we have seen, the undue multiplication of colleges in our Church was caused largely by doctrinal and linguistic differences. If this fatal policy is to be discontinued, if the unfortunate mistakes of the past are to be corrected, it must be through greater unity of feeling and action. The various parts of our Church must draw closer together. Under the lust for gold, men come together in great corporations,

in which individual opinions and interests are sacrificed for the general good. Under the influence of divine love and of devotion to Christ's kingdom, should we not unite more closely for the sake of greater power and efficiency in His work? Thus we should remove the reproach, as true to-day as it was nineteen hundred years ago, that "the children of this world are wiser than the children of light."

3. The method by which existing evils are to be corrected is *concentration*. We should cease trying to do more than we can do well. Fortunately, the application of this method is not so difficult as might at first be supposed. In the English-speaking part of our Church, there is a singular lack of separate preparatory schools. Within the bounds of the General Council, the General Synod, and the United Synod, with an aggregate membership of 568,000, our Year Book reports less than a half dozen academies or preparatory schools. Yet, as is evident from the preparatory departments maintained by our colleges, there is a real need for good secondary schools. Under these circumstances, would it not be wise for some of our weakest colleges, especially in the most crowded sections of our Church, to give up the work of higher education, and confine themselves to preparatory studies? Besides strengthening the central institution that might be selected, this course would relieve some of our struggling colleges of an almost intolerable burden, and fill a large want in our educational work. In other cases, the wasteful system of maintaining separate schools for the two sexes might be given up. Co-education is now the system of our country; and where separate schools are maintained in the same town or synod, a union might be advantageously effected, the weaker institution continuing its work as a preparatory school. There is, perhaps, no part of our Church in which this policy of concentration might not be profitably adopted; but it is especially needed in the South, where the union of any four or five colleges would not make one really strong institution.

4. Another important point, calling for special consideration, is the adequate endowment of our colleges. Our notable deficiency in this respect, as compared with the other colleges of our country, has been pointed out. But the urgent necessity of

liberal endowment can be fully understood, only when we bring before our minds the educational development and tendencies of our country. As every one knows, the educational progress of the past thirty or forty years has been wonderfully rapid. The state has been vigilant and untiring in improving its schools of every grade. Sooner or later the Michigan system, which proceeds in well-graded ascent from the primary school to the university, will be generally adopted. The state universities, especially in the South and West, are among the strongest and best equipped of our country. The non-sectarian and the strong denominational colleges are keeping pace with this rapid development. Unless our Lutheran institutions can likewise be developed and improved, we shall sooner or later lag far in the rear, and fail to command the respect and patronage of our laity. The importance of liberal endowment, as the only means of maintaining and developing our colleges, cannot be too strongly urged. With all earnestness it should be laid upon the minds and hearts of our men of wealth; for, without liberal endowment, our church colleges, under the stress of unequal competition with stronger institutions, will be compelled, sooner or later, to give up the struggle.

The concluding word of this paper is devoted to a beautiful ideal. Turning for a moment from the defects and difficulties of the present, we may find comfort and cheer in what, if it ever comes, will be the golden age of our Church in America. In that future day the narrow views and hampering conditions of the present will have disappeared. Our great Church, vastly increased in numbers and power, will have become conscious of its essential unity, and, earnestly rising to its responsibilities, will throw its united strength against ignorance and sin. Questions of anise and cummin will no longer interfere with its divine task of building up the kingdom of God. Our independent and often ill-considered efforts in education will have given place to a harmonious and well-ordered system; and rising above our schools and colleges, there will stand by some fair city, let us hope, a great Lutheran University, which, taking its place by the side of the strong and venerable institutions of the world, will be fearlessly open-hearted to all truth as a revelation of God.

OUR EDUCATIONAL INSTITUTIONS.

BY PROF. S. A. ORT, D.D., LL.D.

There are one hundred and thirty institutions of learning in the Lutheran Church of the United States. Of this number twenty-seven are theological seminaries, forty-three are colleges, twelve are young women's schools, and forty-eight are academies. These are our educational institutions. They exhibit the state of higher Christian education among Lutheran people in this country.

In dimension they are small, but nevertheless efficient. They furnish an intellectual development which is unsurpassed by larger schools, and afford an educational discipline peculiar to the small college. In schools of this order teacher and student come daily in contact with one another.

On this account the pupil gets from his instructor not only scholastic attainments, but specially that which books do not have and learning does not furnish. It is a something which is peculiar to the individual. It is termed sometimes magnetism, again, a spirit of enthusiasm, and still again, a positive characteristic of the teacher, a predominant element of his personality. Through daily association between instructor and student, such as can only be afforded in the small college, an acquisition of the best the teacher is, as well as has, is gained by the pupil.

. Although our schools are small, still they give a priceless education. At the same time it must be said that our institutions do their work under disadvantage. Usually they have small funds for the conduct of their operations. The amount of apparatus needed for the successful exhibition of scientific processes, is limited. The various appliances necessary for the right prosecution of educational work are, comparatively speaking, of inferior kind. Notwithstanding such like impediments, our schools are doing most useful service for Christian education and the practical concerns of the Redeemer's Kingdom.

If it be inquired, Of what service are these schools of ours to education, especially to higher education? it should be answered that they are making a most valuable contribution of mental and moral growth. Should the inquiry be pressed. Why might not all of them, with the exception of the theological, be closed, and the matter of literary and scientific culture be entrusted entirely to the care of the world schools? it must always be insisted that the best culture is a Christian, literary and scientific culture, that the truest education is a Christian education.

We often speak of higher Christian education; what does the expression mean? Evidently this: That truth in the kingdom of nature, as well as that of man, is viewed in its relation to every other truth, in the light of Christianity.

The State school, or the school of this world, views all truth in the light of natural reason. The education which it furnishes is non-Christian. It is heathen. In the progress of educational work, the Christian idea of the universe must be maintained. It is the only true idea of the natural world in its origin, progress and destiny. Who will uphold it? The Secular School? Assuredly not. Who then? Evidently the Christian institution; such an institution as is represented by our schools of higher learning. The Christian idea of man and of the natural world, both as they are in themselves and in their relations to each other, is the idea that must permeate education, if it shall be truly Christian. Who has this idea in its original fulness? The Christian school, the institutions of the Church of Jesus Christ. Being the possessors of it, their mission is, for one thing, to exhibit this idea in all its bearings, so that the education given the youths of any generation may be a knowledge of nature, man and God, an education eminently useful, because absolutely true. And this is a great service to education, to the promotion of that kind of education which conserves the truth in all things and preserves the consistent unity of human knowledge.

The school of this world is not qualified to do the work of the Christian College. The former cannot be a substitute for the latter. Our schools must hence be maintained for the sake of that better, truer education, which the Church of Christ alone can offer, although it be at the cost of a long continued, even desperate struggle for existence.

Furthermore, our institutions are serviceable to the cause of higher education in that they furnish opportunity to a large number of the youth in our churches to gain for themselves a sound intellectual culture. They bring, in a sense, to the doors of our people, educational advantages which otherwise they would not have, and make possible on the part of many young men and women in circumstances of poverty, the getting for themselves an advanced education. And surely this is a most valuable service. The youths in our congregations need to have the horizon of their intelligence broadened; they should be fitted to occupy positions of large responsibility; they should be filled with high aims and far-reaching purposes; they should in every way be qualified to perform the leading acts of Christian men and women in the great play of human life; they need education, higher education, the education which cultures mind, and heart, and soul. This is the education which our institutions offer the young men and women of our Church, and in so doing perform a service whose value cannot be ciphered in dollars and cents.

It is further to be observed that our schools of learning are most helpful to the Church, helpful to her in the doing of the vast work unto which she has been called and in the fulfillment of the mission to which she has been providentially appointed. The Lutheran Church occupies no mean place in the past history of 350 years. She holds a position of eminence among the record-making powers of to-day. Her vigorous growth and busy activity in the last years of the nineteenth century assure a development and progress in the coming hundred years unparalleled. She is destined to embrace by and by within her fold and under her influence many peoples of the earth. The field of her operations is wide as the world. The work which under God she is charged to do is not only that of making Christians, but of schooling them in the principles of our holy religion in such way that it will be seen everywhere that nature and grace are parts of one eternal plan, that they are not antagonistic, but in closest harmony, and that they stand together in perfect unity in the person of the God-man, Jesus Christ. It is a work of vast extent and loftiest reach, and can only be accomplished by laying under contribution every agency at command. The goal of human history, the destiny of man, unspeakable in its glory, will be attained only by the use of the powers of nature, enlivened, sanctified and inspired by the Divine. And this great and precious truth the Lutheran Church has always recognized. She has ever repudiated the heathen conception of nature and spirit in their relation to one another, and taught that in man they are bound together in an inseparable union; that human life, human history and human destiny involve the one in its fullness as truly as the other, and that hence science and religion, natural knowledge and faith, are in perpetual unison.

Accordingly, in the outset of her career, the Lutheran Church did not break with the learning of the ages. She began her course in a university. She appropriated the treasures of human wisdom and culture. She laid hold of the forms of thought furnished by man's reason, and by means of them gave a fresh expression of the eternal truths of Divine revelation. With her, intellectual culture became the embodiment of spiritual oppression. She expended the wealth of two literatures, the Greek and Roman, in formulating and expounding the fundamental principles of our holy religion. With the Word of God in one hand and human science in the other, she has gained for herself an enviable fame, and wields an influence in the realm of learning, supreme. In theology, philosophy and science she is to-day the teacher of the world. This commanding eminence she has reached through her fostering care of human learning in connection with the intuitions of an evangelical faith. Without the gymnasium and the university her past history would be far different from what it is. She would long since have vanished from view. She would scarcely have emerged from reformation scenes and passed beyond the struggles of the sixteenth century. Her career would have been a short and hasty course.

A true education and the Christian religion can never be divorced without inflicting on the body of Christ the deepest wounds. It would be a delusive opinion to suppose that in this country the Lutheran Church could meet the demands of her time, utilize in the best way her large opportunities and rise to the position of pre-eminence without being true to the genius of her ancestral history. She cannot flourish independent of the academy, the college, and the seminary. And she has not. Her schools to-day, modest though they be in appearance, are nevertheless proving themselves to be efficient agents in the promotion of her concerns, and powers whose influence is felt in every department of church endeavor and in the impression made on the external world. They are educating the leaders and chief actors of the coming generation. They are moulding the characters, and stimulating the minds and hearts of thousands of young men and women to higher aims. They are disseminating a better intelligence among our people. They are awakening the energies of our Church and prompting her to enlarged enterprise in the prosecution of those affairs which pertain to an aggressive Christianity. They are exhibiting the knowledge of a true Lutheranism and spreading it far and wide throughout our land. And with all this it must yet be said that these educational institutions, in the work they are doing and by the influence they wield, have made possible, and in large measure brought to pass, this convention in which are gathered many Lutherans from different bodies in the same Church, in peaceful conference.

These schools of ours, though small, are not to be despised. They are in the process of growth. They are advancing, slowly it may be, yet surely. Behind them is a great Church that will yet exalt them among the educational powers of the land. They deserve to be appreciated for what they are, for the service they render our Church to-day, and for the larger helpfulness they will furnish the cause of scientific and religious truth in the coming years.

Once more it should be noted that our educational schools, and especially those of theology, are serviceable to the interests of true religion in maintaining an evangelical Christianity and a pure Gospel. In our time much is said about broad religious views, liberal belief, the old faith outlived, creeds exploded, present-day religion minus the traditions of the Church, the theological teachings of Paul and the historic deeds of Christ, the simple exhibition of the Spirit of Jesus.

A new religious teaching is in fashion. It has much to say against dogma. It professes to exclude the philosophical element from the exhibitions of Divine truth. It puts away as worthless all formulated statements of belief, assuring us that no mould of the human understanding is sufficient to contain the Divine Word. Religious truth, truth contained in sacred books, is so many sided, and so over-reaching that the logical speech of man can never give it adequate expression. To accept hence the teaching and definite statement of the Christian mind concerning the eternal verities of a remedial scheme is a foolish mistake. It is an effectual barrier to right progress. It makes the moral and spiritual boundaries of human life quite narrow. It shuts out the spirit of heaven-born truth, ever aglow with freshness of a holy activity, and preserves only the deadness of the letter.

But for us human creatures knowledge of religious truth must have an authoritative source. This source is centered either in a divine revelation recorded in plain and fixed statement, or in the judgments of the scientific, literary or philosophical reason, or in the decisions of an infallible Church. The advancing liberalism of the day recognizes as supreme the second, namely, that of human reason. The Scriptures of the Old and New Testament, according to its judgment, are a book of alien parts, full of contradictions, inaccuracies and discrepancies, containing the religious opinions of the several authors, or those which were afloat in their respective times; crude, extravagant, over-statements, and under-statements of what is valid belief, and when taken together they form a medley of views from which it is the mission of modern scientific reason to extract the truth which will morally and religiously culture the race and save the world.

This is the new religion whose excellence some are enthusiastic to extol above the grandeur of the unchanged Bible and the old faith: a religion which repudiates the cardinal doctrines of evangelical Christianity while at the same time it retains their form. It believes in a God, but he is not the eternal triune God, whom our Scriptures, just as they read, reveal. He is an eternal existence whom the human mind imagines, but for whom it has no voucher save its own judgment: a deity who has no being anywhere, if these Scriptures are reliable, and they are, except in the brain of the new religionist; an ideal God whose only need for us mortals is to connect our religious ideas in order to effect the highest systematic unity in our spiritual knowledge.

Furthermore this new religion professes an earnest belief in the Christ, but he is not the Son of God, co-equal with the Father, and also the Son of Man. He is a subordinate being, divine as all men are divine, only in an inexpressibly higher degree, a veritable religious genius, who by his life has furnished to those since his day, the perfect model of the good and upright man. He is to be praised and honored as a hero, and taken as the pattern of the truly devout religious spirit, and that is about all. The old faith of God manifest in the flesh, justified in the spirit, seen of angels, preached unto the Gentiles, believed on in the world, received up into glory, is a Pauline dogmatism, which must be relegated to the shades of the Olympian gods.

Once more this new religion speaks glibly about justification and regeneration, but these are terms, in its use, of far different meaning from that taught by evangelical belief. Justification is no forensic act of God, but a consequence of well doing. Regeneration is not a work wrought in the human soul by the Holy Ghost, generating a new life, but a state which follows by consequence from moral living. Justification and regeneration are ethical results produced by an ethical cause. Or, to use the language of one of its ablest American expounders: "The dogma of justification, as a forensic act, springs out of the dogma of supernatural regeneration, and from the two arises the dogma of an atonement, in which the sufferings and righteousness of Christ take the place of our own righteousness and sufferings. Thus we build a theological block-house in defiance of ethical principles, and we pass righteousness backward and forward as though it were a commodity of the market." That is to say, the new religion rejects the atonement of a Christ who is our substitute, who suffered in our stead and in whose righteousness by faith we stand accounted just before God, repudiates a supernatural regeneration and hence Christ's lesson to Nicodemus, and affirms human redemption to be merely an ethical process. Such, as its advocates choose to call it, is a tendency of our time, a movement which seeking to put new wine into old bottles, in the end loses both bottles and wine.

This movement during some while has been making steady progress. It has found a welcome in many educational centres. It is supported vigorously by many religious teachers in high places. Entire schools have thrown themselves into the ranks of its advocates, while numerous religious journals, either in part or altogether, seek to promote its progress. It is a dangerous tendency, and, if unchecked, will finally undermine the foundation of our holy faith.

But it is pleasing to note that our schools, without exception, have given the new religion no place in their quarters. They have remained steadfast in the old doctrine, and to-day present an unbroken front against every foe of an evangelical Christianity. While here and there some are giving up well-tried belief and beginning to walk in new paths, our educational institutions continue in the old way, immovably grounded in the principles of a supernatural Christianity. Without hesitation they teach the old faith, the faith of Peter, of Paul, of Luther, and set forth with no uncertain sound the historical reality of those divine acts and movements so faultlessly exhibited in the sacred Word, and which constitute the recovery of a sinful race. These are the principles by which as exponents of higher Christian education they stand, and which they fix in the minds of young men and women who shortly will become centers of Christian influence in the busy world of mankind. By the loyalty to evangelical belief in the hearts of thousands of our youth which they secure, they are guarding the welfare of the Lutheran Church, not only in the present, but also for the future. They are making sure for a true Christianity, the pulpit and the pew in the twentieth century. They are rendering possible the leadership of the Lutheran Church in the movements of evangelical religion decades hence, and are preparing her, as of old she was prepared, to fight and win the battle of Apostolic Christianity in this country. Our educational institutions are truly bulwarks of the true faith and are giving a service in behalf of its interest, beyond estimate.

In addition it must be said that our divinity schools especially are centers of a true Lutheranism. They not only teach the fundamental doctrines of the Word of God, but they teach these doctrines as exhibited in that masterpiece of confessional statement, the Augustana. They are the conservators of the principles of the Reformation and of those distinctive apprehensions of the teachings of the Divine Word, which have ever distinguished the Lutheran Church from all bodies of Protestant belief on the one hand and, on the other, from the Roman faith. They heartily accept and enthusiastically teach a genuine Lutheranism. And this is a service to a pure Gospel of incalculable value. It assures the perpetuity and makes big with promise, the future of the Lutheran Church in this country.

Besides all this, the fact dare not be overlooked that our educational schools are ministers of good to the State. They are such not merely because they furnish an education to young men and women, but pre-eminently because they administer a Christian education and inculcate the cardinal truths of the religion of the Nazarene. No republic can endure whose citizens are infidels. It may flourish for the time being, but sooner or later it will perish. An education of the American youth of to-day that ignores or repudiates the principles of Christianity, endangers the perpetuity of our free institutions and is paving the way to their destruction. Free government cannot stand and endure on the principles of heathenism. The Christian colleges of to-day, the Church schools, are the hope of the Republic. They are preparing the salt that will preserve our nation in the coming generation. To the production of this most desirable result the institutions of the Lutheran Church are contributing no small aid. By their positive Christian teaching, by their earnest inculcation of the principles of the Gospel of Jesus Christ, and by their firm adherence to the truths of the inspired Word of God, they are preparing and sending forth thousands of youth to be stalwart and truly loyal citizens of a great republic.

Finally, in view of the most valuable service our schools are giving to higher education, to the Church, to evangelical

Christianity and to the State; what action in their case is imperative? I answer, They should be strengthened. How? In two ways. 1st. By money. They need larger endowments. They are in want of better equipments, both in apparatus and teaching force. Money can supply the need. The Lutheran people of this country are the possessors of large wealth. They have abundance of worldly goods. They can endow amply without delay every Lutheran college and seminary in the land. And it is their duty as a Christian people so to do. They owe it to the Christianity they have, to the Church of Jesus Christ of which they are members, to the Lutheranism of which they are loyal adherents, and to the institutions of civil and religious liberty which they enjoy, to exalt their educational institutions among the schools of the land, and amply qualify them to do the large and responsible work which, in the providence of God, they are charged to prosecute.

But 2nd. Our schools should be strengthened by more students. There are thousands, hundreds of thousands of Lutheran young men and women in America. Only a comparatively small number are in the schools of their Church. The vast majority are not in any college or academy of the land. Many of them should be in our institutions to-day, and if they were a far different condition, educationally taken, would prevail among us. Our schools would be in a highly flourishing state, all of them, and they would be sending forth an influence which would be felt in the highest circles of literary culture. Lutherans in America cannot afford to deprive their children of the benefits of higher education. By so doing they would prove themselves false to the genius of their church, indifferent to the best interest of the faith in which they have been reared, and wanting in the noblest type of patriotism. But I think better things of my people according to the faith. I believe the time is not far off when they will pour their hundreds of thousands into the treasuries of our schools, and crowd their halls with Lutheran students. But in the meanwhile prompt action is necessary. Our Church, in her school operations, must keep pace with the progressive march of the educational movements of the day. She dare not lag behind in the race for supremacy. She must begin without delay the improvement of her institutions. She must make them strong in order that she may retain her present energy, enlarge her borders and fulfill the worldwide mission for which she was brought into existence and has been kept in reserve unto this present hour. And lastly, as the outcome of all her educational movements, there should rise in the near future, before the gaze of the American Republic, a university, a genuine, great Lutheran university, which shall stand and flourish for the honor of our Church and for the glory of Him in whom are hid all treasures of wisdom and knowledge.

REMARKS.

Dr. Seiss said:—There are a few historical items that might be added to the statements contained in one of the papers just read. The institutions at Gettysburg have added greatly to the prosperity of the Church by the educational facilities there furnished; but there were earlier efforts made by our Church in this country for the promotion of higher education.

As early as 1769, at the instance of Dr. Kunze in this city, a society was formed, and contributions collected, for the establishment of a German-English school, designed particularly to prepare young men for the ministry. It was sanctioned by the Ministerium of Pennsylvania. Its curriculum was to embrace History, Mathematics, Latin, Greek, Hebrew, Elocution, etc. It was regularly opened in February, 1773, with arrangements for instruction in these several departments, and commenced with thirteen students. But in 1776 the Revolutionary War, with its attendant turbulence, compelled the closing of the school and ended a promising beginning.

Early in the present century another attempt in the same line was attempted in this city, in which Peter Muhlenberg was interested, along with other Lutherans. A plan for a classical school was sketched, a copy of which, I think, still exists, and some of the arrangements completed for carrying it into effect. But several causes interfered, and the intended institution failed to be established.

One of these hindering causes was the presence of the University of Pennsylvania, in which our pastors and people in this city were induced to take an interest, and which they helped to establish. And from those early times, even to the present, there has been considerable leaning upon this University on the part of our Church for the preliminary academic education of our candidates for the ministry. Lutherans have been among its directors and professors almost from its beginning, and many of our present clergy, as well as of preceding generations, were educated there.

In the State of New York, by the extensive gift of one of the founders of the Ministerium of Pennsylvania, a classical and theological school was established, nearly a score of years in advance of Pennsylvania College at Gettysburg. It was regularly opened in 1815, and has continued in operation to the present time. A goodly number of our ministers were educated at this institution, which is known as Hartwick Seminary.

Along with the interesting and valuable papers which have just been read, it seemed to me fitting that these items in the line of our Church's efforts in behalf of the higher education should also be stated.

THE SCOPE AND LIMITATIONS OF CHURCH AUTHORITY.

BY PROF. DAVID H. BAUSLIN, D.D.

It is an inadmissible assumption that true Christianity is nothing more than a set of doctrines arbitrarily demanding assent upon mere external grounds and assertions of authority, and that it coerces conviction and duty by the announcement of certain terrors and future inexorable events. This is to misstate the entire genius of the Christian religion. It may be asserted as indisputable, that in matters of religion the rejection of all authority outside of the individual is either a part and parcel of a philosophy which admits nothing but the objects of sense perception, and identifies all religion with superstition, or that, in some way, it is connected with and springs from an irreligious temper. In the subject of our discussion there are two extremes. There is the merely external view that would rest everything upon mere authority, giving no value to any proof but that of miracles, and reckoning men's judgments as to the truth and loftiness of doctrine as of no account. This is one extreme. The other is the rationalistic or mystical position, that nothing in religion is to be received except that which is discerned, and understood and accordingly recognized as true. The right position—that which is apostolic in its character and which was reaffirmed at the Reformation—is neither of these.

One of the theories regarding the origin of the Reformation— viz., that of Guizot—asserts that it was an insurrection against authority. It was an effort, in his judgment, to deliver the human reason from the bonds of what was mandatory; "an insurrection of the human mind against the absolute power of the spiritual order." It was not an accident, the result of some casual circumstance, nor simply an effort to purify the Church, or the assault of an Augustinian monk upon certain reprehensible practices of a Dominican. The comprehensive and most potent cause of that great movement was the dominant desire of the human mind for freedom. Free thought and inquiry are the legitimate product and the real intent of the movement. Such is Guizot's interpretation, and in entire harmony with this theory of the author of "Civilization in Europe," Romanists have always maintained that Luther's attack on the hierarchy in the sixteenth century broke up the foundations of faith in Western Europe, and that for this he deserves eternal infamy and perpetual maledictions.

On the other hand, there are those who reject the Christian revelation and deny all authority in the province of religious belief and administration, who maintain that Luther's chief merit consisted in that revolt against the authority of the pope, and which, in the judgment of Romanists, was his chief crime. The vindication of the right of private judgment is, in the opinion of such writers, the chief glory of Protestantism. Thus it comes that Catholic writers and the supporters of alleged free thought are practically agreed in attributing to Luther and Protestantism a large measure of responsibility for that form of modern unbelief which is distrustful of everthing supernatural. It has been maintained that free inquiry and revolt against authority were thus marks of the Reformation, and that therefore those who, as the result of the exercise of their right of private judgment in matters of religion, have lost their faith in Christianity, have a right to claim Luther as one of the great leaders in the movement which has terminated in their emancipation from all religious authority, and the abrogation of every species of supernaturalism.

It is, however, a gross perversion and an entire misrepresentation of the spirit of that epoch-marking movement to characterize the Reformation as a revolt against all authority in matters of religious belief and practice and a nullification of all standards in matters pertaining to man's higher nature and thought. It was a revolt against an arrogant hierarchy which claimed to be the permanent incarnation of Christ, the body of the Lord, the organ of the Holy Spirit, equally with Scripture, able to guide men to God, and assuming to be alone able to determine what was the Word of God. It was a rout of papal marplots, not in the name of freedom from all authority, but in the name of God. It was the assertion of an authority which was believed by devout and holy men to be true as over against an authority which had been found false, arbitrary and unethical. That great revolution was not a revolt against authority so much as a revolt against usurpation. The kind of authority which was now maintained by the reformed religion was a very different thing from that which had been exercised since the days of the consolidation of the hierarchy.

Let it be understood then that no right-thinking man is eager, in the exercise of Reformation principles, to claim intellectual freedom to such an extent as to abrogate *all* sorts of authority. There is such a diversity among responsible agents who have not merely private and free spheres of their own, that their mutual relations in society must be determined externally by some practicable standard of authority and felt to be binding on all. Thus there is authority, and the question as to its source and applications in whatever pertains to the high interests of religion is a living and momentous question.

The differences between the conceptions of ecclesiastical authority maintained by Romanism and Lutheran Protestantism, inhere fundamentally in the divergent conceptions of the two systems regarding the source of authority in religion. Catholic unity is limited to two things: (1) A recognition of the infallibility of the Church, and consequently of all doctrines upon which that infallibility is known to be stated; that is, which have been unquestionably defined by its legitimate organ, as a part of the deposit of faith, and therefore of universal obligation; and (2) acceptance of and submission to the supreme jurisdiction of the Roman see, and the authority, when lawfully exercised, of the local hierarchies that are in communion with it. It holds to a theory which affixes the attributes of unity, holiness, catholicity and apostolicity to the external, visible society of which the bishop of Rome is the chief; that the sons of the true Church belong to this society, and that accordingly the promises made in the New Testament to the Church and the privileges ascribed to it, are claimed for the hierarchy exclusively. The Church, says Bellarmin, is something as tangible as the Republic of Venice. The difference, the primal difference in the matter in hand, between Romanism and Protestantism, as has been admirably asserted by Luthardt, consists in opposite mental tendencies. "The opposite mental tendencies," says he, "are sometimes designated as authority and liberty. Catholicism represents authority; Protestantism represents liberty. The former advocates legitimacy; the latter the rights of historical progress. The former, says Protestant controversy, is stagnation; the latter, says Romish controversy, is the spirit of revolution, though revolution has ever had her seat in Romish lands."

In Romanism the standard of truth is something objective, universal and independent of all private thought or will. Accordingly authority is made to be everything and freedom nothing. It is not mediated at all by man's actual life, by the thinking and working of single minds; is in no sense living or concrete, but altogether mechanical, rigid and fixed. It looks upon the episcopate as the continuation of the apostolate, in which by virtue of succession there inhere the gifts or deposits of truth and grace and authority. It regards the acceptance of a certain amount of information for which man has no inward aptitude in the reason, upon the authority of the Church, as possessing the merit of evangelical faith. It is an episcopal hierarchy which has successively claimed the right to govern and teach the world in the place of Christ. Its system of doctrines has been constructed, accordingly, in obedience to one test, viz., its adaptability for holding mankind in subjection to external ecclesiastical authority. In the Latin Church we see the old Roman genius for rulership, the capacity to exercise authority characteristic of the great empire of the Cæsars.

When we pass to the region of Protestantism we are confronted by a radically different conception. Lutheranism revived and reasserted two fundamental and long obscured truths, viz., the material and formal principles of the Reformation. At once it stood for the religion of freedom, as over against the religion of mere objective authority; for the religion of personal conviction and inward experience as over against the religion of outward institutions, sacramental observances and mere obedience to authority. When the principle of church authority represented by the hierarchy as the *ecclesia docens* was repudiated by Luther in the interest of reform, the appeal was taken to the Bible as the word of God. Up to that time, in the long course of theological development, no attempt had been made to determine the relation of the Bible to the authority of the Church. The voice of the *ecclesia* had been regarded as final in all matters relating to the faith, and a practical infallibility was attributed to its decisions. When that authority began to be questioned and was finally set aside, it became necessary to find another source of authority to which all men could resort when in search of that absolute truth which God had communicated to men.

Luther's revolt was against a Church that had intrenched itself behind the arrogant assumption that the Bible was only a "deposit" in the hands of the hierarchy, and that to it alone belonged the right of determining what was the meaning of the divine revelation. He asserted the universal priesthood of believers, which meant that if the laity had faith, the spirit and mind of Christ, that they too were entitled to interpret the Scriptures. It was the affirmation of the right of private judgment, and as such was the first emphatic protest against the old appeal of Irenæus to tradition, the priority of which was guaranteed by the episcopate, or against the claim of Augustine regarding the divine prerogatives of the episcopate to teach infallible truth. In the face of the graduated system of ecclesiasticism in which the clergy represented the bishops, and the bishops represented the pope, and the pope represented God, Luther asserted the rights of the individual conscience and proclaimed the privilege of private interpretation, against all external authority. He asserted the principle which abolished all artificial castes, whether in church or state—a principle according to which every man became a priest standing in immediate relation to God, owning no other or higher allegiance than the will of God, clearly expressed in the divine word, would sanction. He asserted the potent contradiction of the theory upon which the authority of the papal hierarchy reposed. He denied the Church to be a mysterious and supreme entity, existing apart from the people and possessing a deposit of supernatural trusts which it alone was authorized to administer.

Thus I say that the truly Protestant view regarding the scope and administration of purely ecclesiastical authority inheres in the truly Protestant view as to the source of authority in religion itself. When men came to look upon the Church as the association of believers, as an institution for the dispensation of the means of grace, as our incomparable Augustana expresses it as nothing other than "the congregation of believers," then the axe was laid at the root of the tree, and the human mind was made free from the yoke of external authority, and the restoration of the Scriptures to their legitimate supremacy as the only infallible rule of faith and practice was made possible.

In accordance with these fundamental truths of all vital Protestantism, Lutheranism has arrived at certain conclusions which have been set forth in the accredited writings of the Church, and from which our view of the scope and limitations of Church authority may be easily inferred, and upon the basis of which our church government must always rest.

1. The headship of Christ, the recognition of which has given great assistance in the attempt to define the limits of the power belonging to the Church. The Lord Jesus Christ, the Head and Ruler of the Church, has given such power as is necessary for the government of His Church, not to any one man, nor to any order of men, but to the Church itself, that is to say, to the whole body of believers. The long history of the papacy had taught

the world how possible it is to convert Christ's donation of authority to the true Church into an instrument of cruel oppression. There are quarters in which one is almost afraid to mention church authority, or the " power of the keys," lest he should suggest a claim to exercise tyrannical dominion over man's faith. But this recognition of the Headship of Christ, which is the source from which all lawful church authority flows, is at the same time the effectual antidote to all the tyrannical dominion which Church rulers have corruptly asserted. Christ is not a dead or absent Lord, who has delegated His power to some vicar, or body of vicars. He is the Church's living and ever-present King; and the power bestowed by Him on the faithful and their officers is strictly ministerial. This most fruitful principle of the ministerial quality of church power flows directly from the sole Lordship of Christ.

2. This power, while given to the entire body of believers throughout the world, and which is called the Church, is also given to, and may be exercised by, those smaller bodies of believers which we call congregations. While the Augsburg Confession speaks of "the Church," it unmistakably recognizes the fact that "the Church" presents itself to us in the form of churches, and claims that these churches have certain rights and duties of which it speaks. The conception of a Christian congregation implies the presence and exercise of the ministry of the gospel; that is to say, a Christian congregation can be said to exist properly only when the gospel is preached and the sacraments properly administered. True, the congregation governs itself under the supreme Headship of Christ, and according to His Word; nevertheless, it does so through the instrumentality of men especially appointed to administer this power by preaching the Gospel and administering the sacraments. The keys were not given to Peter and his alleged successors, but to the whole Church which has power to ordain ministers, and to whom the people ought to render obedience as long as they confine themselves to the ministry of the Word, and whom they may likewise depose when they are proven unworthy.

3. These churches must not forget and live in defiance of or

neglect the "Church" of which they form a part. The confessors of our Church aimed at living in "unity and concord"—"in the one Christian Church." They express the desire that all "may be brought back to one true accordant religion." They speak of the "Church Catholic" as distinguished from the "Romish Church." They speak of the "true unity of the Church," and endeavor to inculcate and point out what will be promotive thereof. The Augsburg Confession, while it recognizes and vindicates the rights of the "Churches," nowhere advocated their isolation and independence, and in the very fact of the presentation of that great Confession, which Dr. Schaff pronounced "the most Churchly, the most Catholic, the most conservative creed of Protestantism," do we find, at the very beginning of the Lutheran Church, a desire for the co-operation of the "Churches" in promoting the "true unity of the Church." Thus it is easy to infer from what has been stated in the best accredited writings of our Church, that the power of judging in certain matters resides with the Church, all things, of course, being decided according to the Holy Scriptures and in subjection thereunto, and that the judgments of Councils or Synods, properly set forth, are the judgments of the Church. Thus, too, while the congregation governs itself, it is to remember that it is not the whole Church, but merely a part of it, and that it should be content to live in fellowship and communion with other congregations holding the same faith, and strive to promote the unity of the Church according to the wholesome principle that "unto the true unity of the Church, it is sufficient to agree concerning the doctrine of the Gospel and the administration of the sacraments. Nor is it necessary that human traditions, rites or ceremonies instituted by men should be alike everywhere."

Thus do the confessional writings of the Lutheran Church guard the rights of the individual believer and of the congregation; point out the true way of unity and co-operation, for such as hold fast to the same apprehension of the truths of the gospel, and in some measure outline the scope and limitations of church authority.

The principles I have thus stated as based upon the confessional writings of our Church apply to the authority of the Church in relation at once to doctrine, worship and discipline.

1. The Church has authority to teach. The Head of the Church having promised the Spirit to lead His people into the whole truth, there is reason to trust not only that they shall be kept from falling into fatal error, but that from age to age they shall be led forward into a more perfect knowledge of the truth once for all delivered unto the saints. In matters of faith great deference is, therefore, due to the deliberate judgment of the Church. But authority in this high function belongs to the Church only as the interpreter of God's written Word. She must be able to adduce the warrant of Holy Scripture for the every article of her teaching, else it has no claim to be received as the Word of God. Whenever the teaching of the Church contradicts or goes beyond the teachings of Christ, it may be rejected in all good conscience.

2. The Church has authority to see that the worship of God is duly celebrated. In this also, as in teaching, her authority is limited to the function of interpreting and giving effect to the directions given by Christ. Her commission is to make disciples of all nations, and then to "teach them to observe all things whatsoever Christ commanded." She has no power to frame new and mandatory ordinances of worship. She may construct liturgies and hymn books for the decent, orderly, historical and edifying conduct of the ordinances once for all appointed by the Lord; but further than that her commission does not warrant her to go. The Church is wise in recommending such adjuncts of well-ordered and becoming worship; but if she presumes to lay down inflexible laws regarding the service of God, which go beyond or contradict the appointments made by Christ in the Scriptures, the people are not bound to obey.

3. The Church has authority to exercise discipline. To the Church, to the body of believers, has been given the "power of the keys," and the Church in its own constituted ways, has the warrant to open and shut, to bind and loose—to admit into and to exclude from its communion. But here also authority is limited. The "power of the keys," as we have seen, is strictly ministerial,

and when through the ignorance or malice of those to whom it has fallen to judge his case, a man is unjustly cast out of the communion of the Church, the unrighteous sentence will not be ratified in heaven. In every case there lies open to conscience the right of appeal from the judgment of men to the judgment of God.

I have passed over thus hastily these three functions of the Church in the legitimate exercise of its authority, and come to the most important phase of our subject.

4. It comes within the scope and limitations of the Church's authority to impose certain restrictions upon its accredited and authorized teachers.

A very high and sacred function is assigned by the Head of the Church to His truth, the belief of which is said to be the condition and effectual agency of sanctification and attainment of eternal life. We are, therefore, warranted in assuming that a basis of theological opinions, made up of the great truths and doctrines of the Bible, unmixed with fatal misbeliefs, set forth in plain language, is necessary to the best interests of the Church, and to a not inconsiderable extent, to the religious life of the individual. And since religion as embodied in church life is largely communistic, having very large interests common to the whole body, a recognized consensus of belief is a condition requisite to the unity and welfare of the whole body. In religion and morals we have no possible solution for the problems of the present, save as it is furnished by the one light that comes to us from the far-off sunrise of Judea. But this we can do and should do, to so shape our studies of the Christian past as to give them a more vital hold upon the difficulties of the present. Our holding fast to the treasures and light of the past need not make us unmindful of the law of adaptability in the present. One of the best accredited scholars of our Church Dr. Henry Jacobs, has said—*vide* Preface to "Elements of Religion"—"The matter remains permanent, but the form changes not only with the language, but with the age, the currents of thought and the diverse classes of errors and attacks that succeed one another with great rapidity. We must speak the language of the time and place where Providence has placed us."

The great apostle to the Gentiles anticipated a growth of Christian theology and ethics beyond the elementary principles. He gave an example of such development, normal as far as it went, for all subsequent times, but not precluding a further advance in the same direction. He was resolved not to know anything among the Corinthians except Christ and Him crucified, and his declared purpose has been held up a myriad of times as an example and warning to the teachers of religion against meddling with anything but what is alleged to be the "simple gospel," and as a solemn admonition against the delusions and dangers of church creeds and standards of belief, to which accredited teachers of the Church are expected to express their assent. But it is forgotten that St. Paul goes on to say that he had dealt with the converts at Corinth as babes in the faith, and not as full-grown believers, among which latter class he had a wisdom to impart, a philosophy or theology, a more full and rounded exposition of Christian doctrine, to impart.

A firm grasp of the great central truth of redemption by Christ crucified, resurgent, and reigning, will dispose a man to take a fair view,—neither blindly conservative nor rashly hospitable,—of modifications of religious thought, and of amendments either in form or contents of the accredited symbols of the Church. Accordingly that the Church should insist upon her public teachers being held responsible to her apprehension of the truth of the gospel as expressed in her creeds, is not to be interpreted as any desire to stagnate the intellect of the Church.

Free thinking in religion is not necessarily lawless thinking. There is always a place for the Church's authority in the education and direction of both opinion and conduct, even though it shall never again sway men's minds as it did from the tenth to the sixteenth century. According to some men's individualistic standards of thinking Luther unchained an unruly spirit when he began to assert the right of "private judgment." But such always forget that he and his coadjutors sought to restrain private judgment within the bounds of a reasonable liberty. To assert the right of private judgment is not to assert the right of putting out upon religious seas without chart or compass to guide us on "our dim and perilous way."

Liberty is conceived by some men as the right to think and do as one pleases. There can be no broader definition than this, and probably no man on earth enjoys such liberty. Possibly during that brief period in which the first man stood alone he enjoyed the liberty of thinking and doing as he pleased, and this because he thought and pleased to do right. And it may be that his helpmeet so long as she was thus minded imposed no felt restrictions upon him; but it is certain that the social organism into which men are now born does lay rightful restraints upon every man's liberty:

> "Yet know withal,
> Since thy original lapse, true liberty
> Is lost, which always with right reason dwells."

There is no such thing as lawless liberty; a liberty which does not acknowledge its limitations, and any attempt to break over such proper restrictions is regarded by all right-minded men as perilous alike to life, property and sound morals.

We cannot believe what we please because always limited by the laws of thought and evidence. No man liveth unto himself in the trades, the schools or in the learned professions. We cannot divorce liberty from history and law, for this is to break up both continuity and order, to hush the music of the spheres and to institute chaos. To divest liberty of certain reigning principles is to institute anarchy among men. There can be no absolute liberty until each soul has a world unto itself, and even then it will forever hold that "true liberty always with right reason dwells."

In the present unsettled condition of the public mind there is no danger of such a preaching and teaching of authority in the Church as may give rise to a suspicion that the faith of the Church rests upon nothing deeper than authority.

In view of these principles I come to say that the Church has the right to impose certain confessional limitations upon her authorized teachers. The Reformation guaranteed to every man the right to take the Word of God as the only infallible rule of faith and practice, and to apply that standard as the test of the truth. Every man with the Bible in his hand may, at his own peril, decide for himself what that Bible teaches, and therefore what he ought to believe and what he ought to do. If as a result of his reading and study, aided by such helps as he may have at his command, he becomes a Roman Catholic or a Protestant, or decides in favor of any one of the denominations of Protestantism, or if he concludes his inquiries with the result of his having become an agnostic, or an atheist, nevertheless he should be entirely free from any sort of coercion, such as was attempted upon our Lutheran fathers in the New Netherlands in the seventeenth century; or that of the grim Puritan snatching the prayer-book from the hand of the churchman and the stiff churchman compelling the Puritan to read it; or of the founders of Massachusetts Bay driving out the Quakers and forcing Roger Williams to betake himself to the woods, where for fourteen weeks he knew not "what bread or bed did mean." Luther, employing the right of private judgment with entire freedom, freely conceded it to others, for he it was who said: "The pen, not the fire, is to put down heretics. The hangmen are not doctors of theology. This is not the place for force. Not the sword, but the Word, fits for this battle."

But although this right of private judgment is as sacred and inalienable as the right to life or liberty, nevertheless it has its wholesome and necessary denominational limitations. In one denomination the chief bond of union may be a ritual, in another a form of government, and in another a method of doing its practical work. In Lutheranism neither a ritual, nor a form of government, nor a method of work is the thing of primary importance. Its bond of unity is a common faith which has been reached by a devout and painstaking study of the divine Word, accompanied by a free, untrammeled exercise of the right of private judgment. When a candidate for the ministry in our great Church accordingly is ordained, or a teacher is inducted into his office in a theological school, he voluntarily takes an obligation having all the sanctions of a vow made before God and the Church to preach or teach according to this faith. It is to be presumed that he has reached the Lutheran faith by a free and devout study of the Word; that it has not been imposed upon his conscience by unwilling constraints—that it is no matter of police authority, but that he gladly proclaims his purpose to preach or teach it, because he heartily believes it to be in accord with the sacred Scriptures. This is a proper requirement of the Church, and on any other conditions he would be rejected as a teacher of theology or a preacher in a distinctly Lutheran Church. This is a legitimate limitation, but such an one as does not renounce the man's right of private judgment. That is a right which no person should and no self-respecting person can renounce without sacrificing his Christian liberty. But the right of private judgment does not include the right to herald or teach doctrines inconsistent with the Lutheran faith in Lutheran pulpits or chairs of theology, or for a man to transcend the limits imposed by a solemn obligation voluntarily assumed. A Trinitarian might become a Unitarian, and no Evangelical Church would oppose the right to make the change; but that privilege to thus change would afford a man no right to teach Unitarianism in evangelical pulpits or schools. A Lutheran who in the exercise of his right of private judgment has ceased to hold the faith of his Church, should practice sound ethics and withdraw. To remain as a disturber, striving to substitute the conclusions of his private judgment instead of the faith which he has voluntarily promised to maintain, and which faith has stood the test of centuries, that course seems to be not only audacious, but likewise unethical. Heresy is not so great a sin as dishonesty. There may be honest heresy, but there can be no such thing as honest dishonesty. It is a significant fact, in the history of our Church, that it was rationalists, such men as Semler and Bahrdt, Wegscheider and Bretschneider, who first invented or acted upon the theory that a man could be a good Lutheran and at the same time assail the doctrines of the Church.

It comes within the scope of church authority also that it require at the hands of its teachers a particular kind of creed subscription. "Symbols are not to be subscribed until, as the result of their careful study and comparison with God's Word, they are recognized and cheerfully declared to be drawn from the pure fountains of Israel. This is a *quia* subscription [*vide*

"Book of Concord," Vol. II, p. 13, Jacobs]." On the other hand we call it a *quatenus* subscription when a confession is subscribed to in this way, "in so far as it is in accord with the Bible." The Church has the right to require a *quia* subscription—that is, "because the teachings of the Church agree with the Scriptures," and not the *quatenus*, because this latter is evasive. Men holding the most diverse views might all subscribe to the same confessions, in this way, which would allow all sorts of latitudinarianism and dissension. We Lutherans subscribe to the Augsburg Confession because we believe, as the Confession itself says, that these doctrines are taught in the Scriptures, and all that we as Lutherans ask is that if a man's private judgment of the Word of God does not make him believe the doctrines witnessed to in this great Confession, that he should not pretend to be a Lutheran and use the splendid name of a great Church as his shelter in undermining the faith of such as are committed to her spiritual care.

It cannot be known that we believe in accordance with the Bible until we declare or confess what we believe. No faith is intelligently formed until we are able to say what that faith is, and unless we do say we can never be known as partakers in the community of believers. Since all churches and sects appeal to the Bible and profess to accept its teachings, it becomes hypothetically necessary for each community of believers holding to a common apprehension of the faith to determine the sense in which it understands the Bible. Denominational honesty requires on the one hand that a church make a clear, unambiguous statement of its beliefs, and on the other an unequivocal and sincere assent upon the part of authorized teachers, without mental reservation and uncertainty.

What John Milton says of a good book, that it is "the life blood of a master-spirit," is much more true of a well-articulated creed which has been elaborated by master-spirits through study of the Scriptures, Christian experience, the conflicts of the faith, the battles for the truth and the sufferings of martyrs. Next to the Bible there is no book so full of theology, of church history and Christian life as Schaff's "Creeds of Christendom." The popular objections against the church requirement of an *ex-animo* subscription to its creed, are all founded either upon invincible ignorance as to the true design and use of a creed, or upon that presumptuous individualism that says, "I am wiser than the ancients," and which sets up its own private interpretation of Scripture, its unwritten creed, as the infallible standard of truth.

At no time in the history of the Church has it been more urgent for the Church to assert her authority in this important matter of creed subscription. Our generation is inflated and self-asserting. It has done a great deal, and it means that all the postcrities shall know it. Intellectually and religiously considered it has far more surface than depth of keel. It is many-sided, but in much of its religious life is disinclined to thoroughness. It will not bear much of what Master Ridley called "deep spading," nor further on what Master Latimer called "weeding" for the sake of a better crop. It is a time when the old words are often so skillfully used that the superficial hearer thinks that he is getting the Bible, and it is only the hungry soul that feels the want of living bread, and finds that some sophisticated Barabbas has been thrust upon it instead of the Lord from heaven.

We have to confront in the life of the Church in our time one of the most specious forms of religious thinking ever formulated. It claims to be more Protestant and Evangelical than the Reformers themselves, and more Christian than the Holy Catholic Church; it aims to increase personal piety, on the one hand, and the practical activities of the Church on the other; it has its church historian in Harnack; its theologians in Kaftan of Berlin and Hermann of Marburg; its critics in Schulz and Wendt, and it asserts with enthusiasm that it stands in possession of an entirely new method, whereby it can reach certainty of Christian truth, revolutionize the theology of the ages, and construct a new basis for Christian belief. It has been widely introduced into this country and has well-nigh overmastered in its New England home, the older theology of Emmons and Taylor.

At such a time the Church may be hospitable no less to all truth, but it is under special bonds to insist upon something explicit in its teachings, and by wise legislation authoritatively in the name of the Church, to set due metes and bounds for such as seek to become her teachers.

Surely no right-thinking religionist will advise us at such a time as this to give less attention to the past than to the present. We should be men of understanding, discerning the signs of the times and taking frequent soundings in the cross-currents of living thought; but the fact remains that what is sound and safe in religion has not only its roots, but in many things its matured growths in the past. The faith of the Church was once for all delivered unto the Church. As it came to us we are to hand it on. It can gain nothing in its substance, and it must lose nothing in our keeping. It enters the life of this age as it entered the life of the centuries behind us—as a finished force from without. By some of those centuries it has been rent in twain, by others sadly corrupted and obscured, by others restored to its early purity, but by none advanced beyond its primitive type. The matter is unchangeable. It is ours to see that its verities are maintained in their integrity.

THE SCOPE AND LIMITATION OF CHURCH AUTHORITY.

BY G. F. KROTEL, D.D., LL.D.

Although Luther, in the Smalcald Articles, says: "Thank God, to-day a child seven years old knows what the Church is, viz.: saints, believers and lambs, who hear the voice of their Shepherd. For the children repeat: 'I believe in one holy (Catholic or) Christian Church,'" he, and others in his day, and their successors down to our own days, have found it necessary to write many pages to show what the Church is, in order to dispel false conceptions of its nature and functions. It is with the doctrine concerning the Church, as it is with many other doctrines, although all we know about them is found in the Holy Scriptures: men have differed widely in their interpretation of the statements of Holy Writ. Many have undertaken to write the Life of Christ, and while all were absolutely dependent for their information upon the New Testament, the portraits they have printed have widely differed. All we know about the Church is in the New Testament, and yet men, taking its statements, have constructed theories of the Church differing as widely as those which the Articles of Smalcald opposed and those which they defended.

In the discussion of the theme: "The Scope and Limitation of Church Authority," we propose to confine ourselves altogether to the New Testament, as the only inspired, and therefore infallible source from which we can ascertain what the Church is, whether it has any authority, and how far that authority extends.

It is well known that the Gospel history, as recorded by the four Evangelists, contains but two passages in which the Lord Jesus Christ speaks of the Church, one being in Matth. 16: 18, 19. "And I say unto thee, that thou art Peter, and upon this rock I will build my Church, and the gates of hell shall not prevail against it. And I will give unto thee the keys of the kingdom of heaven; and whatsoever thou shalt bind on earth, shall be bound in heaven; and whatsoever thou shalt loose on earth shall be loosed in heaven." The other is in the eighteenth chapter, verses 17–20. "And if he shall neglect to hear them, tell it unto the Church: but if he neglect to hear the Church, let him be unto thee as a heathen man and a publican. Verily I say unto you, Whatsoever ye shall bind on earth, shall be bound in heaven; and whatsoever ye shall loose on earth, shall be loosed in heaven. Again I say unto you, that if two of you shall agree on earth as touching anything that they shall ask, it shall be done for them of My Father which is in heaven. For where two or three are gathered together in My name, there am I in the midst of them." Although these are the only passages in which the Lord speaks of the Church, they are full of meaning, are fundamental in their character, are in entire harmony with what we read in the rest of the New Testament, and are further illuminated by what the Apostles said and wrote upon the same subject. While we listen, with the profoundest reason, to the words which fell from the lips of the Lord Jesus Christ, we do not forget that he promised to His Apostles that *Comforter*, "which is the Holy Ghost, whom the Father will send in My name. He will teach you all things, and bring all things to your remembrance, whatsoever I have said unto you." Of this Comforter, or Advocate, or Paraclete, He furthermore said: "Howbeit, when He, the Spirit of truth is come, He will guide you into all truth: for He shall not speak of Himself; but whatsoever He shall hear, that shall He speak: and He will show you things to come. He shall glorify Me: for he shall receive of Mine, and shall show it unto you."

Whatever, therefore, the Acts and the Epistles of the Apostles, and the last book of the New Testament tell us about the Church, is to be received as additional teaching, coming from Him who is the Builder and the Head of the Church, and it will be found that in all that they have written they are in full accord with the fundamental conceptions set forth in the two passages in Matthew.

When He says, "I will build My Church," He undoubtedly refers to that of which St. Paul writes to the Ephesians, "And gave Him to be the head over all things to the Church, which is His body, the fullness of Him that filleth all in all;" and, using another figure, "And are built upon the foundation of the Apostles and Prophets, Jesus Christ Himself being the chief cornerstone, in whom all the building fitly framed together groweth unto a holy temple of the Lord: in whom ye also are builded together for a habitation of God through the Spirit." "There is one body and one Spirit," and the Church is the body of Christ. "One Lord, one faith, one baptism." "For the husband is the head of the wife, even as Christ is the Head of the Church," and therefore the "Church is subject unto Christ," who "loved the Church, and gave Himself for it." He nourisheth and cherisheth it, and the union between Him and his Church is spoken of as "a great mystery." He sanctifies and cleanses it, "with the washing of water by the word, that He might present it to Himself a glorious Church, not having spot, or wrinkle, or any such thing; but that it should be holy and without blemish." Such a body, with such a head, consists of living members and believers, that have the Spirit of Christ, for, as Paul writes to the Romans, "Now if any man have not the Spirit of Christ, he is none of His." When the great Master Builder says, "I will build My Church," we may be sure that He does not build this "spiritual house," except with "lively stones," living stones, believers, built upon the "chief corner-stone, elect, precious." There is but one such "spiritual house," one such body, one flock gathered around the good Shepherd.

As the great Head of the Church, and His inspired apostles speak of this one holy Christian Church, extending all over the world and throughout all ages, so He and they speak of those gatherings of believers, in His Name, for worship, for preaching and for hearing His word, and the administration of the sacraments instituted by Him, by the same name—"Church." "Tell it unto the Church," not unto that vast body of believers of which we have spoken, but to that smaller part of it which assembles in a particular place, and to which you and your offending brother belong. That small body is also called the Church, for it has the same Head, Christ, is animated by the same Spirit, has the same Gospel and sacraments, and where two or three are gathered in His Name, He has promised to be in the midst of them.

Again and again the Acts and the Epistles speak of such churches, churches in the provinces and cities, and "the Church that is in the house," as in the house of "Priscilla and Aquila," as well as in others. The Church assembled in such a house was a true Church of Jesus Christ. The Lord declared, "I will build my Church," and he has kept His word. He gathered the first stones, and laid the "foundation of the apostles and prophets," He himself being the chief corner-stone, so that no matter how we may interpret the words spoken to Peter, "and upon this rock I will build my Church," it must forever remain true that He himself is the only Rock,—"the chief corner-stone," "for other foundation can no man lay than that is laid, which is Jesus Christ," "the living stone, disallowed indeed of men, but chosen of God, and precious."

He called the first disciples, and by the word of which He himself said: "The words that I speak unto you, they are spirit, and they are life." But He also employed His disciples to be "workers together with Him," to call men to the great supper, and to the marriage, and to serve as builders. Paul says, "According to the grace of God which is given unto me, as a wise master-builder, I have laid the foundation, and another buildeth thereupon." At the close of the chapter that tells the story of the Day of Pentecost, we read, "And the Lord added to the Church daily such as should be saved." He himself had gathered the nucleus of the Church before that day, on which "about three thousand souls were added unto them," through the instrumentality of Peter, and to these others were added, by the same Lord, through human instrumentality.

Nevertheless, although the Lord builds the Church, and calls men through the Gospel, and there appeared among men a body called the Church, He distinctly foreshadowed the sad fact that there would be found in it those who were not true believers, nor His sheep, nor living stones. The seed is the Word of God, which He and all His co-workers sowed in that great field—the world. "The good seed are the children of the kingdom; but the tares are the children of the wicked one; the enemy that sowed them is the devil." Judas, though called by Him, allowed Satan to enter his heart; Ananias, Sapphira and other unworthy ones mentioned in the New Testament were members of the Church, but, for all that, were not members of His body. They belonged to the class of which He said in the Sermon on the Mount: "Not every one that saith unto me, Lord, Lord, shall enter into the kingdom of heaven; but he that doeth the will of my Father which is in heaven. Many will say to me in that day, Lord, Lord, have we not prophesied in Thy name? and in Thy name have cast out devils? and in Thy name done many wonderful works? And then will I profess unto them, I never knew you: depart from me, ye that work iniquity."

And yet, although such were found among those who professed to be followers of Christ, the apostles addressed their epistles to the bodies to which they belonged, as to churches of Christ.

Our theme takes it for granted that there is such a thing as Church *authority*. Authority means "the right to command, and to enforce obedience." If the Church is a body, it is subject to the laws upon which the existence and welfare of a body depends. There cannot be an organization without law and order. There cannot be a state without the observance of law, and some authority to enforce it. "The powers that be are ordained of

God," who is the Creator, Preserver and Supreme Ruler of the Universe. It could not continue to exist without submission to the authority of Him who is its author.

Paul says to wives, "The husband is the head of the wife, even as Christ is the head of the Church, therefore as the Church is subject unto Christ; so let the wives be to their own husbands in every thing."

He who built and builds the Church exercises supreme authority over it. His word is its law; His Spirit enlightens, guides, directs and restrains it. His Word spoken by Himself, and recorded by His chosen witnesses, the inspired evangelists and apostles, is her infallible rule of faith and practice. When visibly present with His followers, He said, "Ye call me Master and Lord: and ye say well; for so I am." And His word was their highest authority, from which there was no appeal.

The people who heard the Sermon on the Mount were astonished at His doctrine, "for He taught them as one having authority," and His chosen apostles and other disciples received the same impression, only more profoundly. He gave them authority, in certain directions, before His ascension, and when this was about to take place, and they were to receive their final commission, he said, "All power is given unto me in heaven and in earth. Go ye, therefore, and teach all nations, baptizing them in the name of the Father, and of the Son, and of the Holy Ghost: teaching them to observe all things whatsoever I have commanded you: and lo, I am with you always, even unto the end of the world. Amen."

More than once the chosen twelve disputed among themselves as to their rank in the kingdom of heaven, and on one occasion the sons of Zebedee, and their mother, made the request that one son might sit on the Lord's right hand, and the other on His left, in His kingdom. After His reply, the Lord said to the other apostles, who "were moved with indignation against the two brethren;" "Ye know that the princes of the Gentiles exercise dominion over them, and they that are great exercise authority upon them. But it shall not be so among you: but whosoever will be great among you, let him be your minister: and whosoever will be chief among you, let him be your servant: even as the Son of Man came not to be ministered unto, but to minister, and to give his life a ransom for many."

When John and James and their mother made the request, they evidently did not dream that their Master, when He said to Peter, "Thou art Peter, and upon this rock I will build my church; and the gates of hell shall not prevail against it. And I will give unto thee the keys of the kingdom of heaven: and whatsoever thou shalt bind on earth shall be bound in heaven; and whatsoever thou shalt loose on earth shall be loosed in heaven," thereby conferred upon him such a primacy and headship, as men subsequently were led to believe that he had. Peter himself could not have understood them as committing something to him which was not committed to his fellow-apostles, especially when he heard what the Lord said in Matt. 18:17–20; and saw how the risen Lord breathed on them as well as on him, and said unto them as well as to him: " Receive ye the Holy Ghost: whosesoever sins ye remit, they are remitted unto them; and whosesoever sins ye retain, they are retained."

Nothing is clearer from the Acts and Epistles than that Peter never arrogated to himself such a headship and authority, and that neither the other apostles nor the churches, in the East and in the West, recognized any such supreme authority. Although he seemed to be recognized as, in a measure, *primus inter pares*, he never claimed or exercised such authority as that which has been claimed for his boasted successors. In the meeting, composed of "about a hundred and twenty" disciples, after the Lord's ascension, it never entered into the mind of Peter to appoint an apostle to fill the vacant seat of Judas Iscariot. Neither he nor the other apostles had anything to do with the appointment of Paul to the apostleship. Peter did not preside at the council at Jerusalem; and at Antioch, Paul, who was not one of the original twelve, "withstood him to his face, because he was to be blamed," and Peter submitted to it.

If the New Testament teaches anything very clearly, it is, that the Great Head of the Church has not given supreme authority in His Church to any one man, and that the monarchical principle, as far as the Church is concerned, is altogether anti-Scriptural. The apostles and first Christians never forgot the words of the Saviour: "For one is your Master, even Christ; and all ye are brethren." Paul tells the Galatians, "Neither went I up to Jerusalem to them which were apostles before me: then after three years I went up to Jerusalem to see Peter, and abode with him fifteen days. But other of the apostles saw I none, save James the Lord's brother." And in the next chapter he speaks of "James, Cephas and John, who seemed to be pillars, as giving to him and Barnabas the right hands of fellowship," actually assigning to Peter's name the second place. No doubt the Lord gave the apostles certain authority in the Church, such as is clearly indicated in the words spoken to them, and already referred to. The Lord "gave some apostles, and some prophets, and some evangelists, and some pastors and teachers, for the perfecting of the saints, for the work of the ministry, for the edifying of the body of Christ." And the same Paul, writing to the Corinthians, tells them, "Now ye are the body of Christ, and members in particular," and then adds: "And God hath set some in the Church, first apostles, secondarily prophets, thirdly teachers"—and afterwards asks: "Are all apostles? are all prophets? are all teachers?" etc.

The Apostles were Christ's chosen witnesses and preachers of the Gospel. They were the founders, teachers, and spiritual guides and rulers of the Church, but they exercised their authority in the spirit of Peter's words, in his Second Epistle: "The elders which are among you I exhort, who am also an elder, and a witness of the sufferings of Christ, and also a partaker of the glory that shall be revealed, feed the flock of God which is among you, taking the oversight thereof, not by constraint, but willingly; not for filthy lucre, but of a ready mind; neither as being lords over God's heritage, but being ensamples to the flock." Paul writes to the Corinthians of "the power which the Lord hath given me to edification, and not to destruction," and in several other places refers to the "authority" which the Lord had given. He exercised this authority in preaching the Gospel, in the organization of churches, in the administration of discipline, and in the introduction of certain rules and observances in the churches, on the principle that "God is not the author of confusion, but of peace, as in all churches of the saints," wherefore he admonishes them, "Let all things be done decently and in order."

And yet an examination of the New Testament shows how far the apostles were from exercising their authority as if they were "lords over God's heritage," and how careful they were to recognize the rights of the congregations and individuals. Peter neither appointed a successor to Judas, nor did he urge the apostolic college to do so. He proposed his plan to the one hundred and twenty, and when two persons were designated or nominated, we have every reason to believe that the whole assembly took part in the proceedings. When it became necessary to silence the "murmuring of the Grecians against the Hebrews, because their widows were neglected in the daily distribution," "the twelve called the multitude of the disciples unto them," and said, "Brethren, look ye out among you seven men of honest report, full of the Holy Ghost and wisdom, whom we many appoint over this business." "And the saying pleased the whole multitude; and they chose" the seven men, generally called deacons, "whom they set before the apostles; and when they had prayed, they laid their hands on them." Peter did not appoint them, nor was it done by the twelve; but the congregation elected them, and then the apostles, by prayer and the laying on of hands, appointed them "over this business."

We do not know *when* the *elders* of the Church at Jerusalem, mentioned for the first time in Acts 10: 30, were appointed, but surely it is not unreasonable to suppose, that the manner of their appointment was similar to that of the seven (deacons) spoken of in Acts 6. When we read, in chapter 14 of the same book, that Paul and Barnabas "ordained them elders in every church," is it not natural to infer that they did so after the example set by the apostles in Jerusalem? And when Paul wrote to Titus: "For this cause left I thee in Crete, that thou shouldest set in order the things that are wanting, and ordained elders in every city, as I had appointed thee," we are at liberty to take it for granted that Titus pursued the same course.

When a question concerning fundamental doctrine and practice arose in Antioch, and Paul and Barnabas were not able to settle it, that congregation resolved "that Paul and Barnabas, and certain other of them, should go up to Jerusalem, unto the apostles *and elders* about this question," "and being brought on their way by the Church," and arriving in Jerusalem, "they were received of the Church, and of the apostles and elders, and they declared all things that God had done with them." We read further that "the apostles and elders came together for to consider of this matter," and a little later that "all the multitude kept silence, and gave audience to Barnabas and Paul." After James had made his address and presented his "sentence," the record goes on : "Then pleased it the apostles and elders, with the whole church, to send chosen men of their company to Antioch with Paul and Barnabas;" and in the letter which these messengers were to carry to Antioch, it was written : "The apostles and elders and brethren send greeting unto the brethren which are of the Gentiles in Antioch, and Syria and Cilicia."

A transaction like this gives us an admirable insight into the manner in which the apostles exercised their authority, in consultation with the elders and the congregation,—a manner as far removed from prelatical and priestly assumption and arrogance, as it is possible to conceive.

In that remarkable case, referred to in I Cor. 5, in which Paul gave the most striking manifestation of his apostolic authority, in an act of severe discipline, he acted in coöperation with the Church at Corinth, fully recognizing not only their duty, but their rights in the case.

Although the apostles were the divinely chosen teachers and guides of the churches, they never organized them into any ecclesiastical body, over which they ruled, or a representative body over which they, or one of their number, presided. There was no priestly or hierarchical rule, as far as they were concerned. They knew of "the Church" throughout the world, and of "the churches of Galatia," and other provinces, countries and cities, but they knew nothing of a church of a particular province or diocese. There was *the Church*, embracing all believers, and the *churches*, scattered over many lands. They strove to make them feel that all of them were churches of Jesus Christ, and told them what Paul wrote to the Ephesians: "There is one body, and one Spirit, even as ye are called in one hope of your calling; one Lord, one faith, one baptism, one God and Father of all, who is above all, and through all, and in you all." For this reason they were urged "to keep the unity of the Spirit in the bond of peace." Paul could appeal to the Corinthians that he and all the apostles preached the same doctrines, and administered the same sacraments. In order to keep up the feeling of unity and fellowship, he and the other apostles visited them as often as they could; sent to them their pupils, assistants and fellow-laborers; addressed to them epistles, full of instruction, encouragement, warning, reproof and consolation, and did what they could to introduce, and keep alive in every congregation certain usages peculiar to the first Christian churches. In this way, without any general organization and without the convocation of representatives of the churches in councils or synods, the churches and the Church flourished during the time covered by the New Testament record. We receive the impression that the churches governed themselves in accordance with the doctrines, principles, regulations and usages given to them by the apostles. If they needed instruction, the apostles were ready to give it, and if they departed in any particular from apostolic teaching and practice, the apostles would call them to order and correct the evil.

The germinal word of the Lord, "tell it unto the church," was fully understood and practiced, and each church was called upon to watch over its own household, to provide for pure preaching, the right administration of the Sacraments, an edifying common worship, exercise of discipline and the observance of apostolic usages.

To the Church and to the churches the Great Head of the Church, who is, and always will be, its invisible but ever-present Ruler, gave authority to provide for the preaching of the Gospel, and therefore the right to choose those who were to be the preachers and teachers, and to administer the Sacraments. To the Church and to the churches He gave the right of discipline, the power of the keys, the right to open and to close the door, to bind and to loose. He did not give it authority over the bodily life and over the earthly affairs of the individual and the community, for the Church has to do with the spiritual things. It is to watch over two things; first of all, over "the faith which was once delivered unto the saints," the pure faith of God's Word; and secondly, over the souls that belong to it. It is bound by its very constitution, to have no fellowship with those who teach "for doctrine the commandments of men;" and it is equally bound to have no fellowship, "if any man that is called a brother be a fornicator, or covetous, or an idolator, or a railer, or a drunkard, or an extortioner." If any man refuses to hear her in those matters in which she has the right to speak and to judge, the Saviour's word for ever stands fast, "let him be unto thee as a heathen man and a publican," until he brings forth fruits meet for repentance, when he is to be restored to the fellowship of the Church.

The constitution of the Church and of the churches is in the New Testament, and the scope and limitations of the authority therein given, if carefully observed, will prevent, on the one hand, priestly and hierarchical assumption, and on the other, the assertion of the self-will of the individual, and that want of discipline in matters of doctrine and practice that must lead to the destruction of the Church.

Although the New Testament does not say anything about the organization of a number of churches into a larger body, we do not believe it contrary to the spirit of the Gospel; if they do so for the purpose of strengthening and supporting one another in the maintenance and propagation of the Gospel, and in the promotion of such work for the glory of God and the welfare of men, as can be better accomplished by united effort. But in doing so the united body, no matter what its name may be, has no right to deprive the individual church of the authority given to it by Christ, even as the local congregation or church has no right to surrender what its Lord and Saviour has given to it as a priceless and inalienable possession.

REMARKS.

Rev. HAAS said:—A difficulty arises in the minds of plain people. Church authority implies discipline, but it is often asked why so little discipline is exercised. There are, *e. g.*, certain papers and publications with the Lutheran name attacking Lutheran doctrines and principles and they are doing it with impunity. What our people wish to know is, if we have authority why it is not exercised? Is our authority a rope of sand? This matter has important and vital bearings.

Dr. CHAS. S. ALBERT said:—It is a question whether we do not over-estimate the powers of a congregation made up of a few members when we recall what the Church meant in apostolic times. The Church at Jerusalem was the community of believers, not a number of small congregations, independent and distinct as with us. Such was the case too at Ephesus and Corinth. Authority was not vested in a handful. It may be seriously questioned whether we have not gone too far when we concede all authority to congregations made up of a few men and women, irrespective of the community of believers to whom they belong. It invites weakness of church government. Its intense individualism is provocative of anarchy and not of the communion of saints.

Rev. KUNZMANN said:—One of the difficulties of theology has been to define the Church and to differentiate between her and the Kingdom. "The Scope and Limitation of Church Authority" cannot be defined until we have correctly defined the term Church—her nature, sphere and purpose. *Εκκλησια* and *Βασιλεια*—Church and Kingdom—have been regarded as synonyms, and, in consequence, much confusion and many errors have resulted. Rome confounds them and in her definition of the Church assumes the powers of the Kingdom. Hence, she claims infallibility, miracles and temporal power. She claims in her imperfection to do and exercise functions, which God has alone promised to perfection. Concede her definition of the Church and her claims must be acknowledged. But here we come upon her fundamental error. Christ founded the Church, the association of believers, on the truth of Peter's confession, and to the Church is given the power of the keys. Here we see the relation of the Church to the Kingdom. Both are of heaven, and not of earth. But the Church is in order to the Kingdom, is to loose men by the power of the keys so that they may become members of the Kingdom. The little flock is first, and afterward, according to the good pleasure of the Father, will receive the Kingdom. The Church is composed of weak mortals, and in her experience answers to Christ's first coming in humility to suffer and die. The Kingdom is composed of resurrected saints and in its experience answers to the second coming in glory. The only power of the Church is the power of the keys, in the exercise of which she looses from sin and makes men heirs of the Kingdom. The same is shown in her commission. Whatever offices and functions as well as authority may be needed to perform this lowly and yet glorious work, belongs to her. The Church is cotemporaneous with the persecuting and ungodly world, out of which she calls the saints, heirs of the Kingdom. But the Kingdom supersedes and overthrows all the powers of earth. Our Confessors, in the 17th Article, clearly recognized that the Kingdom would and could not be established before Christ's second coming and the resurrection; and hence condemned the notions of the Anabaptists and Romanists, who thought to establish the Kingdom before the resurrection. The Church, like her Lord, ever ministers and is not to be ministered unto, but the Kingdom rules over all. God will not allow to the Church, imperfect on the human side, the functions and powers which will belong to her after Christ has presented her before the Father, having neither spot nor wrinkle. The Church first, the Kingdom afterward. Suffering with Him, then reigning with Him. This is the order. Miracles were wrought as signs of the age to come, but they are not a part of this age, and their pretense by Rome on the one hand and so-called Christian Science (which has been well said, is neither Christian nor science) are simply lying wonders. When men claim for the Church what alone belongs to the Kingdom, they must make pretensions of such lying wonders and lying sinless perfection. The scope of her authority is over the saints, and them alone; and her limitation is the power of the keys, the administration of the Word and the Sacraments; their guardianship and protection.

Dr. WOLF in reply to Rev. J. A. W. Haas said, a phrase of the last speaker offered a fitting answer: "the perfect order of things." This perfect state we have not reached. How can the Church proceed against the sinuous, slippery course of a writer or editor, who deals in insinuations and evasions, and contradicts in one paper the very position he maintained in another? We have now in this Commonwealth under indictment a man holding the highest office in the gift of the State, and serious and apparently well-founded as are the charges against him, there is a very general fear that he will escape conviction. The machinery of the Church for enforcing discipline upon those who injure her good name, is even more defective than that of the secular Courts.

Besides, the worst use that an errorist can be put to in these days is to let him pose as a martyr. His influence for harm is thus multiplied a thousandfold.

SACRAMENTAL IDEA IN LUTHERAN THEOLOGY AND WORSHIP.

BY PROF. A. SPAETH, D.D., LL.D.

In presenting as briefly as possible a few thoughts on the "Sacramental Idea in Lutheran Theology and Worship," I propose to confine myself to two points which seem to deserve special notice at the present time:

1. The *general* idea of the *Sacramentum*, over against the *Sacrificium*, Sacramental over against Sacrificial, in the relation between God and man and their dealings with each other.

2. The *specific* meaning of the term "Sacramental," as describing the *union* between visible earthly elements and invisible heavenly things, and the manner of reception or *fruition* in those New Testament ordinances, Baptism and the Lord's Supper, particularly the latter.

I.

The general idea of the Sacramentum as over against the Sacrificium, in the relation between God and man, and their dealings with each other, is presented in the Apology, Article XXIV., De Missa, where Melanchthon answers the question: Quid sit sacrificium et quæ sint sacrificii species? Quid patres de sacrificio senserint? De usu sacramenti et de sacrificio. The importance of the distinction between sacrificium and sacramentum is emphasized. Both may be comprehended under the generic name of ceremonia, holy rites (Opus sacrum). Sacramentum est cermonia vel opus, in quo Deus nobis exhibet hoc quod offert annexa ceremoniæ promissio, ut Baptismus est opus, non quod nos Deo offerimus (geben oder anbieten), sed in quo nos baptizat, vid. minister vice Dei, et hic offert et exhibet Deus remissionem peccatorum, juxt promissionem (Mark 16: 16.) Econtra sacrificium est cermonia vel opus quod nos Deo reddimus et Eum honore afficiamus. The sacrament accordingly is a divine act exhibiting, offering and conveying divine grace. On the other hand the sacrificium is a human act rendered to God by man to give Him His due honor.

Eleven years before the Apology was written Luther in his Sermon "Vom Neuen Testament, d. i. von der Messe" (Erlangen Edit., Vol. 27), had treated the same subject even more fully. He says, "In all the dealings of man with God the proper way and order must be this: Not that man should begin and lay the foundation stone, but that God alone, without any endeavor or effort on the part of man, must come first (zuvorkommen), and give His word of promise. This word of God is the first thing, the foundation and rock on which afterwards all words and thoughts of man are built. This word must be thankfully received by man, confidently believing the divine promise, not doubting that it is and will be done even as He promises. Such faith is the beginning, middle and end of every work and righteousness of man. For inasmuch as man giveth the honor to God, taking Him and confessing Him to be true, he thereby finds a gracious God who, in turn, will honor him and confess him. It is therefore impossible that man by his own reason and strength should ascend into heaven with works of his own, and prevent (zuvorkommen) God and move Him to be gracious—but God must come before all works and thoughts of man, and must give a clearly expressed promise of His word which man is to grasp and to hold in firm faith. Thus follows the Holy Ghost that is given to man through the same faith.".... After a brief survey of the divine promises of grace and salvation in the Old Testament, Luther comes to the "Testament" of the new covenant, the sacrament of the altar, in which he sees "a brief summary of all the miracles and graces of God, as fulfilled in Christ.... A testament is a Beneficium datum. It bestows a benefit upon us, it does not receive a benefit. Who has ever heard that a man who receives a testament is doing a good work? He simply takes a benefit to himself,—appropriates it. Thus in the Mass (Lord's Supper), we do not give anything to Christ, we only take from Him. Likewise in baptism, which is also a divine testament and sacrament, no one gives anything to God, but receives from Him; so also in the preaching of the Word. There is no work of man in all this, but simply the exercise of faith on the part of man. There is no Officium, but Beneficium, no work or service, but only fruition and benefit."

In this wider sense then the "Sacramental Idea in Lutheran Theology and Worship" represents the very heart and centre of the great Reformation of the sixteenth century. It is the restoration of the Gospel of God's free and sovereign grace. It sets forth and emphasizes the divine initiative in the whole plan and work of our salvation. It ascribes all power and honor exclusively to God's grace over against any work of man. God comes, God works, God gives; His are also the means and methods by which He has chosen to work out our salvation, the means of grace and ordinances which are objective divine realities to offer and convey God's saving grace to the individual. God first loves, He makes known his love to the individual, and being assured that we are "beloved" we believe,—our faith itself being altogether God's own work, God's gift.

Now this position is of necessity a protest against the principles developed by the Mediæval Church which is characterized by a general tendency to substitute the sacrificium to the sacramentum, the human act and performance to the divine gift and work, or at least to exalt the sacrificium over against the sacramentum in such a manner that God is robbed of His honor, the exclusive and absolute power of His grace is denied, and man's work is considered as either directly or indirectly meritorious and efficacious toward his salvation. A few references to the practice and teaching of the Mediæval Church will clearly illustrate this statement. The whole service of the Church and the participation of the Christian in that service is looked upon as in itself a good work that tends to merit the good pleasure of God. In the Roman practice of Confession and Absolution the sacrificial side, the human confession of sin, is made the principal feature. For this confession completeness and perfection is demanded and claimed, and the extent, power and application of divine forgiveness is limited by, and made subject to, the exact enumeration of all sins. On the other hand, for the Church of the Reformation, in this rite of Confession and Absolution, the sacramental side, the divine word and act of grace, in the forgiveness of sin, is the principal feature; confession itself, as a human sacrificial act, is admitted to be of necessity imperfect, fragmentary at the very best; but the sacramental side, the divine act and declaration of forgiveness, is considered as perfect and complete, and so to be taken and honored by the believer. Again, take the Sacrament of the Altar itself as the strongest illustration of the point in question. To the Church of the Reformation the Lord's Supper is the culmination and concentration of all that God has done and is doing for the salvation of man, the greatest of all His gifts, and the most direct personal application of this gift. To the Mediæval Church it is the culmination of all human offerings and sacrificial acts, the unbloody sacrifice, with propitiatory power for the living and the dead, the greatest of all human acts and performances in the sphere of religion.

It is, however, not only in the Church of Rome that such erroneous views and practices are found concerning the relation between what is sacrificial and sacramental. There are features also in the Protestant denominations around us which indicate that with them also the proper balance between the sacrificial and the sacramental is frequently disturbed, and that the former is being exalted at the expense of the latter. The sacraments themselves are almost entirely stripped of their proper sacramental character, and turned again into sacrificial acts of man. They are chiefly considered as human acts of profession. God is no longer seen in them as the principal actor and giver. Man is acting, presenting himself, making a profession of faith. From this position results the common widespread indifference toward Infant Baptism, even among those Protestant bodies which are still pedobaptists in their theological standards. Consistently carried out this view leads to the final rejection of Infant Baptism. I may also point, in this connection, to the modern prayer meeting in which prayer is treated as a means of grace, a kind of sacramental power is ascribed to it, while in its very nature it can never be anything but sacrificial.

In the service of the Lutheran Church our sound and Scriptural position in this respect must naturally express itself. We look upon our service as the means to establish, to preserve, to cultivate and to demonstrate our communion with God. God's side, the sacramental, representing divine action, must be to us the prominent, the domineering feature. His work in the means of grace, the Word and the Sacraments, secure to us all the benefits to be expected from our communion with Him. Naturally, then, our service culminates in the celebration of the Sacrament of the Altar, whereby the New Testament grace of forgiveness, life and salvation is sealed to us individually by the reception of the Body and the Blood of Christ under the elements of bread and wine. But the sacrificial side is by no means overlooked in our service. We bring to God the sacrifices of our prayers, praise and confession, of our gifts and our persons. We want a congregation of spiritual priests, worshipping God in spirit and in truth; but all their sacrifices without propitiatory power, only eucharistic, rendering thanks to God for the grace received. A significant and appropriate expression of these two sides in the service, the sacramental and the sacrificial, is the change of position on the part of the officiating minister at the altar, as prescribed in many of our old Agenda. In all the sacramental parts of the service, whenever the minister has a divine message to deliver to the congregation, he faces the congregation. In all the sacrificial parts, when he speaks with and in behalf of the congregation, he stands, as the other members of the congregation, facing the altar.

II.

But there is yet another specific meaning of the term "sacramental," of which we propose to say a few words. It is that sense of the word by which we describe the mysterious union between visible and invisible things, the earthly elements and the heavenly gifts, and the peculiar manner of fruition, which we call sacramental, in those New Testament ordinances, Baptism and the Lord's Supper, particularly the latter.

To our Lutheran Church it is an essential feature of those divine ordinances which alone she calls sacraments, that there should be not only a direct appointment by Christ Himself, not only an offer and promise of New Testament grace, but also the choosing and appointing of certain earthly elements, to be connected with the word of grace, so as to become the visible organs by which heavenly gifts are conveyed to the recipient, and the New Testament grace is sealed to him individually. Sacramentum visibilis forma invisibilis gratiæ. (Luther.) Things which in themselves belong to the kingdom of nature, like water, bread and wine, are by Christ's own appointment transferred into the kingdom of grace, and thus become actual and real means of grace through their connection with the Word. Accedit verbum ad elementum et fit sacramentum. For this very reason we draw the line between those two ordinances, Baptism and the Lord's Supper, and other sacred rites and institutions, like ordination, confirmation, absolution, etc., which we refuse to call sacraments because they are without that sacramental union between earthly elements and heavenly gifts.

Now this sacramental union, however mysterious, is to us altogether real. Independent on human belief or unbelief, its reality is based on and assured by the divine word of institution. The water and the Spirit, in Baptism, the bread and wine and the Body and Blood of Christ, in the Sacrament of the Altar, are united, not by the faith of the recipient, but by the powerful, true and abiding word of Christ which appointed such sacramental union, not for the union as such, but for the communion of the recipients and the strengthening of their faith. The reality and objectivity of this sacramental union carries with it the reality of the sacramental fruition on the part of all recipients. There is in the Lord's Supper, not the reception of the elements alone for those who do not believe, and the reception of the Body and Blood of Christ for those who believe; but the sacramental fruition of both, the elements and the Body and Blood of Christ, in their sacramental union. This is the clear teaching of our Augsburg Confession, that the true Body and Blood of Christ, truly present and truly communicated under the species of bread and wine, are received by all communicants. All who come to the Supper receive sacramentally the Body and Blood of Christ, while those only who receive in faith receive savingly the Body and Blood of Christ as the seal of their forgiveness, life and salvation.

This truly scriptural realism which our Church maintains is most beautifully adapted to the needs of our human personality in body and soul, conveying the most direct assurance of personal salvation. It is deeply rooted in the very centre of God's revelation, the mystery of the incarnation. And it represents a guarantee and a type of that future consummation when our heavenly citizenship shall be fully realized, when our Saviour Jesus Christ shall fashion anew the body of our humiliation that it may be conformed to the body of His glory, when we will understand the deep truth contained in the saying of the Suabian theologian, Oetinger, "Das Ende aller Wege Gottes ist Leiblichkeit."

THE SACRAMENTAL IDEA IN LUTHERAN THEOLOGY AND WORSHIP.

BY J. C. KOLLER, D.D.

It is intensely interesting and highly gratifying to a Lutheran to know that his church believes and maintains the conception of the Holy Sacraments as set forth in her confessions. An attempt to translate the magnificent doctrine into practical uses is a task for the master. Some of you have, doubtless, heard the story of Handel, how when asked to play the concluding voluntary at a Sunday morning service in a country church, he kept the people spell-bound within their seats, until, at the first impatient touch of the regular performer, the congregation walked out as usual. That much depends upon the interpretation. Perhaps I have not even apprehended the purpose of my appointment, to say nothing of throwing additional light upon the fundamental teaching.

However the formulation of the subject presupposes a sacramental idea in theology and worship other than Lutheran—an idea founded chiefly either in metaphysics or sentimentalism, Roman Catholic or Zwinglian, whilst the Lutheran has its authority from God and the pure enlightenment of his Word. It is therefore not encumbered by mataphysical distinctions. Whilst in Romanism we are limited to an *opus operatum* and in Zwinglianism to a vivid imagination, Lutheranism confines us to a spiritual perception. In the one system of theology and worship the idea is only an ecclesiastical dogma; in the other an intellectual proposition; and in the Lutheran it is a supernatural fact and distinctively the content of a living faith—yet not as if its efficacy depended upon the communicant's heart any more than the theologian's mind or the priest's manipulation. The real and the practical have therefore an immense advantage over the theoretical and experimental. We believe, therefore we receive the regeneration in baptism and the sustentation in the Lord's Supper.

It has been said that the Reformation was born in Luther's inner consciousness: it is no less true of the Sacraments as he understood them; they had become a mighty reality in his experience; to him they were living entities, rather than the products of logical deductions. To the great comfort of his adherents his views reached a very conservative standpoint as he advanced toward the completion of his masterly work. Even Canon Luckcock notes, with great satisfaction, that the Holy Communion found so fair and lucid a definition in the Protestant Confession at Augsburg.

But so intimately associated with the Lord's Supper is Holy Baptism that according to Martensen the latter is the sacrament of the children, as the former is the sacrament of such as are of riper years. Baptism is the setting up of the new covenant; not the introduction of a germ, but the implantation of a life; the Lord's Supper is its renewal and nourishment. By Baptism a man is incorporated into the new kingdom and receives a new personality. By means of the Lord's Supper this new personality is brought to perfection. The differences of interpretation are accounted for not by the nature of the sacraments, but by individualistic opinion.

Hence the two sacraments contain the pivotal doctrines upon which the facts of Lutheran theology and worship revolve; the sacramental idea is the incorporating and energizing element in the life of the Church. Here the Divine mysteries reveal themselves to the humble investigation of the true believers.

Thus the Confessors say: "Concerning the use of the sacraments our Churches teach, that they were instituted not only as marks of a Christian profession amongst men, but rather as signs and evidences of the will of God toward us, for the purpose of exciting and confirming the faith of those who use them. Hence the sacraments ought to be received with faith in the promises which are exhibited and set forth by them.

They therefore condemn those who teach that the sacraments justify by the mere performance of the act and do not teach that faith which believes our sins to be forgiven is required in the use of the sacraments."

Harnack of Dorpat maintains that the administration of the Lord's Supper is the culmination of the Divine worship—the nerve and sinew of the public worship of Christians, as Gerhard teaches, for with it we reach the most solemn of all worship, namely, the thanksgiving Collect and Benediction. That is soundly scriptural. Thanksgiving and Benediction—surely it is only Christ in our praises and prayers that makes them worship. True, some one forcibly remarks that "to an æsthetic or literary or (most odious of all) to a stagey piety this truth may seem both narrow and inhumane"—slow and formal. But this sacramental idea is not responsible for the æsthetic or literary, or stagey construction placed upon the sacred mysteries.

A few things are definitely settled in the Lutheran Church, and believed on, notwithstanding our many "isms." First, that the sacraments are *acts*, natural and supernatural, realistic and substantial actualities, not formalistic practices. The strongest emphasis is laid upon this principle by the leading theologians of our Church from the beginning, which, to say the least, is a most encouraging thought to the communicant. Luther says the sacraments are actions; not permanent creations (*stantes factiones*). To which Melanchthon replies, "that there is no sacrament outside of the sacramental action;" from which it follows, says Köstlin, that the host is not to be enclosed in a casket, and carried about. Neither, we may add, is it to be transformed into a photograph, as of some beloved one, and held up for sorrowful contemplation.

Lutheran expositors could be multiplied indefinitely, who laid very emphatic importance upon the act of the communion to preserve it from the subjective on the one hand and the mechanical on the other. But just as in the Church of England the ninety-eighth Psalm was substituted for the Magnificat to pacify the extreme Protestants who were afraid to use the triumph song of the Virgin Mary, so some Lutheran writers have fallen back upon memorialism in order to escape materialism, and thus have missed the better way we have come to magnify.

Dr. Forsyth of Cambridge, England, has manifestly caught the genuine signification: The Communion is an *act*. It is not simply a feeling nor a contemplation. So far it may be described as an *opus operatum*. "Do this" is the word, not "consider this." *Am Anfang war die That*. "The Saviour in that hour did not think of Himself æsthetically as an object of contemplation." He was really present breaking the bread and pouring out the wine. The disciples were actually there eating and drinking, not exercising their memory, but believing on Him. The emphasis is not on "remembrance," but on "Me." Everything turns on the personality of the speaker as he defines, illustrates and seals the atoning work. *Accedit verbum ad elementum et fit sacramentum.* The audible Word, the visible Word, the personal Word. In the beginning was the Word, and the Word was with God, and the Word was God. The sacramental *act* is unthinkable, aside from the real presence of Christ in the communion.

The Lutheran idea of the sacraments gets its argument from the Divine revelation. The sacraments are not an invention of the Reformers. They are not one of Luther's original discoveries. The continuity of the Divine thought takes us back at least to the Circumcision and the Passover, and comes to evangelical operation in the Gospel economy, where the efficient agency of the Holy Spirit, who leads to the Son and is the dispenser of the life which proceeds from the Son, is bound to the use of ways and means. These so-called means of grace are distinguished as the Word of God and the sacraments; through them the word and the act—the grace of God—reaches us, as Von Berger explains, and becomes a factor of our consciousness. They are, so to speak, the channels through which the fountains of life, as they proceed from the Holy Spirit and the Son of God, supply to our faith, power and fruitfulness. The differentiating peculiarity of the sacraments with the word of God are visible signs with which the word is intimately connected, together with the accompanying consecration and administration. Consequently it is demanded by Chemnitz that the words of the institution be not read in the style of an historical narrative, but in such a manner and expression that Christ Himself, according to His command and promise, and through His word, be set before the congregation as really present in the service of the Holy Supper, and by virtue of His word His body and blood are imparted to the communicant, for it is He who administers Himself, and says, "This is my body."

This Lutheran doctrine leaves nothing unexplained, as far as the divine mystery admits of explanation. There either takes place a full identification of the mystical and the visible element, without, however, effacing the outward sign; or there is presented the promised blessing of the glorified body and blood of Christ, as conveyed in, with and under the visible signs. Therefore the material signs are the bearer or vehicle of the invisible grace. The natural is indeed the image and sign of the supernatural, yet the supernatural is inseparably joined with the natural, so that each communicant who receives the natural sign during the communion also becomes a partaker of the supernatural blessing, either to salvation or condemnation, for St. Paul will have it that worthiness or unworthiness depends upon the discernment of the Lord's body. The genuineness and integrity of the sacrament are consequently not conditioned on our faith; but the *saving power alone*. Only to him who receives and appropriates them do they become the life of the soul.

Here and there we may incur the charge of superstition by emphasizing this real presence—for not all Lutherans hold the Lutheran idea; but the truth is not bound to apologize to such as renounce one distinctive feature after the other until the margin becomes perilously limited. At any rate there is no fear so long as we urge that the real presence is a reality of *present act and will*, and not of mere substance.

Second. It follows as a natural consequence that the sacramental idea in Lutheran theology and worship is *inseparable from the Church*. The sacraments are not only acts, but acts of the collective body of Christians. Individualism is no authority on the central doctrine; neither is the communion the privilege of individualism. We are not to be robbed of the high standard of doctrinal statement by a few latitudinarians who parade their views in the name of Lutheran liberty and independence. One of the most pronounced friends of religious liberty in the present day reminds us of the fact that it was not a group of individuals to whom that command was given, but to a body already organized into a unity by the life and purpose standing in their midst. "They were not united to each other except in so far as each was personally united to Him. The Church is the body of Christ. What was done at the institution, was not the act of so many units in combination. It was the act first of Christ, and then of a living community capable, by a common soul, of a unitary act. These disciples, forming the first church, were not a fagot, but a tree; not a basket of summer fruit, but a cluster on the true vine." We readily subscribe to this language even when the question of clinical communion is raised, where Chemnitz makes indispensable the consecration of the elements in the presence of the sick, for Jesus uttered His words at the time and place of the institution and directed His words not to the elements, but to people to whom he was about to communicate His body and blood. If the priest can transubstantiate the bread and the wine, then the presence of the congregation is not necessary. But that is not a communion.

A faithful Christian invariably declined to commune with her afflicted sister because she believed that the communion was for the congregation, not for the private home; though, like Luther, she would not debar the sick from receiving the communion in their own home, in accordance with the recognized order of the Church; but she only reprobated the custom of "peddling" the elements used at the public service and giving delusive comfort to the indolent. Neither would she detract in the least from the necessity and privilege of making her act an intensely personal and individual communion.

Third. It is to be added, also, that according to Lutheran theology and worship the sacraments involve *responsiveness*. The sacramental act is not an external imposition. "Its nature is not met by sitting around a table or kneeling at an altar," partaking the elements and calling the history before our moved minds, much less is it mechanically bowing before a transubstantiated substance. Kleifoth reports the experience of St. Augustine: "On account of the consciousness of sin he knew that man cannot serve God, in his natural state, but on the sole ground of the sacrifice once made for sin, born again in baptism, called and enlightened by the word, nourished through the flesh and blood of our Lord. So rigidly is this principle defended that, according to Martensen, the communion of children must be taken exception to and only confirmed Christians must be admitted to it. And so fervently does the Lutheran adhere to his liberty and personality, which the sacrament supplies, that it should never be given to those who have lost consciousness, to the insane, or to the sick and dying who are in an unconscious state, and above all is it obligatory that the most sacred ordinance of Christian worship be withheld from the unworthy. *Sancta Sanctis* was a symbol of the early Church."

Nothing is truer than that the Holy Son of God stands ready to respond in this precious ordinance of His own appointment to the penitent and believing child of God; neither is a more solemn admonition addressed anywhere else to the unresponsive, impenitent, formalistic, unbelieving. "As often as you eat this bread and drink this cup, ye proclaim the Lord's death till He come." Where there is no believing proclamation of the Redeemer there is no joy and peace. Consequently there is the marvelous beauty and helpfulness of the Lutheran typical form of worship in which the minister and people are alike not only the recipients of the Divine blessing, but mutually the active participants in the Holy service. Here is no celebration of the Mass; nor any Romish weakness or Romeward folly. It is the testimony to the power of God unto salvation.

On the other hand, the sacramental idea is as distinctively scriptural, practical and beneficent in Lutheran worship as it is in theology.

For instance, it is the *remedy for ritualism* because it exalts the spiritual act above the material performance. There is no worship of the bread and wine in the one and water in the other, as symbols deified by priestly manipulations. *Hoc est corpus* is not a hocus pocus, as some one forcibly expressed it. Among us the symbolism is in the Church's act—in the breaking and pouring out of the elements and the receiving and partaking of them. The material objects are not the symbols; they are only symbolic of the acts in the worshipping congregation—the "Handlungen" in thought, word and deed. This removes the sacramental thought to an infinite distance from a mechanical performance, whether that be the elevation of the host or the mere exaltation of the rite; the worship is not a matter of the emotions any more than of superstition, but rather spiritualized activity.

Said the old priest to the novitiate: "What wouldst thou do with the consecrated host in crossing a stream should the broken bridge go down in your passage?" The answer came after a moment's reflection: "The bridge would not go down when I am carrying the host across." Such idolatry is an impossibility in purely Lutheran worship; no matter how much it catches the admiration of symbolists, or repels the devotion of ceremonialists. Worship in the Lutheran Church is free from fatalism, because the sacramental idea pervades every phase of the service—preaching, singing, praying. True we must admit that there is a deep distinction between the communing and ordinary acts of worship. In these we chiefly go to God, but in communion God chiefly comes to us, and speaks to us, and through us.

The teaching is very explicit. The Lord's Supper is a eucharistic festival according to which the body and blood of Christ are administered and imparted, *in with and under* the consecrated elements, to all the participants in order that they may praise and thank God for such a rich, comforting and blessed testament. This is not ritualism, it is Lutheranism. It commends itself to every devout and thoughtful Christian. A little boy standing beside his parents during the baptism of his infant brother made reply to the questions and joined in the repetition of creed and prayer. To him the sacrament was a worship. The impression upon the father has been most salutary, and his attendance at the services in the sanctuary, accompanied by the child, is a new revelation of the sacramental teaching of our Church. "Things which are hidden from the wise and prudent are revealed unto babes."

Again it follows without dispute that the sacramental idea of the Lutheran Church marks the downfall of priestism as a factor in theology and worship. The sacrament is not something to juggle with. Give to it the interpretation of extremists either of the spectacular order or barren sensationalism, and the jugglery of popery is always possible; but apply the Reformation ideals and the power is taken out of the hands of the manipulator and placed in the range of divinely appointed ordinances—the true symbolism of a living actuality. One who is not a Lutheran pronounces sacramentalism the remedy for sacerdotalism. It is its death-blow; it abrogates the worship of the elements. And yet the safeguard against priestism is not an attenuation of the sacraments but their true interpretation.

Transubstantiation allows no part to the believer because its metaphysics smothers faith, which must be allowed the play of activity and witnesses to Luther's positive declaration that "nothing can be substituted for the divinely imparted gift in the sacrament, which the communicant is to receive in simple faith. Not any human work—whether it be the sacrificial act of the officiating priest, or the meritorious deeds of the communicants, or their devout religious ardor and self-mortification;" for the sacrament is not a sacrifice; it is the gift of God which we receive with thanksgiving.

We may conclude by stating that the sacramental idea in Lutheran worship is far in advance of a mere commemoration of something which transpired long ago. We can easily agree with a modern definition that a simple commemorative sacrament is but the relic of a dead Christ and the badge of a dying church. A memorial of the crucified rather than a realization of the risen Christ is an inadequate sacrament. It is not possible for a congregation assembled in the name of Christ and engaged in the worship of Him crucified to continue looking upon the sacrament as a mere souvenir. No wonder the priest steps in and attempts to supply a stirring need of the soul. Not even the most constructive imagination can be permanently substituted for a living faith. The advocates of barren commemoration misuse the word symbol; they insist that it only reminds of a reality signified; without stating the reality; but the advocates of the real presence declare that the symbol passes us on to the reality *in with and under* the material elements. That which has turned these terms into a battle ground for controversies full of misunderstanding, misapprehension, misrepresentation, is emphatically a subtle and dangerous rationalism. But we can not part company with the spiritual intimacy and profundity—the mysticism, if you prefer,—simply because the good man on the street cannot realize it.

The following are strong words by a non-Lutheran: The soul-sterilizing and church-destroying memorialism starves and palters with the rite without the courage either of taking it in earnest or letting it go. Such paltering is no better than ritualism. It clings to a rite which is little better than a rite, and is slowly ceasing to be either a pledge, a seal, or a power.

It remains to say that the Christian will find no difficulty in apprehending the sacramental idea in Lutheran theology and worship who accepts *ex animo* and *ex fide* the two principles of the great Danish theologian: First, That worship as a holy act finds the highest expression in the sacraments, for in action there is a living union of the internal and the external, the invisible and the visible, the spiritual and the corporeal. Second, That all the intuitions of Christendom are reflected in the sacraments, for in them Christ communicates Himself not only spiritually, but in His glorified corporeity. The final goal of God's kingdom is not only that history, but that nature also shall be redeemed and glorified.

REMARKS.

Dr. JACOBS: The sacramental conception is of wider extent than the sacraments themselves. In the wide sense of the term, any act whereby God comes to man and communicates His grace, is a sacrament. The Reading of the Word and the Preaching of the Gospel are thus sacramental. Before the sacrificial element can be found in worship, the sacramental must be there. This means, in plain language, that God comes to man before man ever thinks of coming to God. This illustrates a principle we were discussing yesterday, when the subject of Prayer was under consideration. It was said, with entire correctness, that where God's Word is not, there is no prayer. Prayer is not just any address made to God; nor is it even every sincere desire of the heart. But it is an utterance of the heart called forth by some particular word and promise of God. Prayer is the voice of faith; but faith is the response of the heart to some word of God. God gives some promise. Faith takes this promise, and carries it to God. Faith reminds God of His promise, and asks that it be fulfilled. The promise is the sacrament; the eucharistic sacrifice is faith.

If the question, then, be asked, as to what is the distinctive characteristics of the sacraments in the narrower sense of the term, viz., Baptism and the Lord's Supper, as contrasted with the sacramental element in the reading and preaching of the Word, the answer is that in these two holy ordinances the promise of the Gospel is specialized or individualized. In the general preaching of the Word, whether in the Church, or as we read it in our homes, we hear that, wide as is man's sin and ruin are the provisions of the Gospel for his recovery. Christ has died for all, and the blessings of God's grace are intended for all. The invitation is addressed to all who labor and are heavy laden; and the encouragement is that whosoever will may come. But, in the sacraments, it is no longer a general or indefinite matter. The offers are no longer universal or to classes. The great congregation passes out of view, and a particular individual is singled out. The pledge is given this individual that forgiveness of sins, and sonship with God, belong to him as truly and completely as though, beside himself, there had never been a person on earth that needed the assurance of God's pardon and presence. The sacraments are intended to emphasize the little words: "FOR THEE."

For years I had been trying to teach theology before I learned to know the meaning of a well-known passage in Luther's Catechism. It is where the Catechism teaches that the chief thing in the Holy Supper is not the bodily eating and drinking, but the words: "For you." This I once thought referred to the bodily eating of the bread and wine, but learned that it was the Body and Blood of Christ that are here meant. Precious as is the assurance of the presence of the Body and Blood of Christ and their reception by the communicant, all this is subordinate to the word of grace which accompanies this eating. The chief thing in the sacrament is not the Body and Blood of Christ, but what is still greater, the promise. It is as though, for a moment, all others were excluded from Christ's thought, and he said: "Thou art a redeemed and forgiven one. That, in thy weakness, thou mayest be sure of this, I give thee the very Body and Blood, that have purchased thy salvation." Without the word the presence even of the Body and Blood of Christ do not profit. Faith is strengthened, not by our reception of Christ through the bodily mouth—although this occurs—but by the word of the promise which it takes to heart.

Just as important as the definition of an Article of Faith itself is the place which is given it in the system of doctrine. It is possible to hold correctly concerning the nature of the Real Presence; to avoid the extremes of transubstantiation on the one hand, and a mere commemorative ordinance, or a presence only to faith on the other; and, nevertheless, entirely misapply the doctrine. This we believe to have been done in many cases by the ritualists in the Church of England and elsewhere. The mere definition of the mode of the presence sometimes seems correct. But where this is used to uphold the theory of a sacrifice in the Mass, the entire sacramental conception vanishes; and transubstantiation itself would not make the perversion much more pernicious. Or where the Real Presence is regarded as the basis for a channel for the impartation of spiritual life in some other way than through the words: "Given and shed for you for the remission of sins," received by faith, the doctrine is certainly not that of our Lutheran Confessions.

Dr. Wolf. What, then, do you think of the administration of the communion without the words of distribution?

Dr. Jacobs. It is no communion; since one of the essentials, and that the most important, the word of promise, is lacking.

Rev. Groff expressed mortification at the thought that in the Lutheran Church, where the Lord's Supper receives so high a place of honor, there should be less frequent celebration of communion than in others where it finds a much lower place.

Dr. Spaeth gave the Lutheran view as over against other views by a quotation from Luther: "The Pope makes visible what God has made spiritual, and Carlstadt makes spiritual what God has made visible; but we go between and leave corporeal what God has made corporeal and spiritual what God has made spiritual."

PROBLEMS IN FOREIGN MISSION WORK.

BY GEORGE SCHOLL, D.D.

The cause of Foreign Missions is, in itself, not a problem. The obligation of the Church to preach the Gospel to every creature is no longer questioned by Christian men. The command to disciple all nations is plain and direct. The authority of the Commander is undisputed. The object of a divine revelation is to establish the Kingdom of God not in this land or on that continent, but in the earth. The Bible is not only a Missionary Book, but it is the Missionary Book. The Scriptures and Christian Missions stand or fall together. While with bated breath and expectant spirit, flooded all about with the "glory of the Lord," we listen to the announcement of the angel on Bethlehem's plains, "Behold, I bring you good tidings of great joy, which shall be to all the people," there must of necessity flash into our inmost being the conviction that now it is our heaven-appointed mission to publish these good tidings of great joy to all the people.

This certainly was the impression produced on the minds of the shepherds, for they at once said one to another, "Let us now go even unto Bethlehem, and see this thing which has come to pass, which the Lord hath made known to us. . . . And when they saw it, they made known concerning the same, which was spoken to them about this Child."

Here, as it seems to me, we have in the very opening hours of the blessed Advent, flashed out of the Heavens and set to the music of the angel choir, the pictured story of the world's evangelization: Heaven publishing good tidings of great joy, those who hear verifying the truth of it in their own personal experiences, and then hastening to tell it to others.

And when this wondrous Babe of Bethlehem, whose advent into the world was already made the occasion for heaven's intimation of the method of the world's evangelization, had reached the full estate of divine manhood, there does not seem to have been the shadow of a doubt in his own mind as to why he had come from heaven or what might be his mission on earth. He said to those about Him, "Follow Me, and I will make you fishers of men." Whether in the way of command or invitation, He was continually saying, "Follow Me, follow Me." And then, after a suitable preparation for the work, the disciples having, in some faint measure at least, caught His Divine Spirit, He said to them, "Go ye into all the world, and preach the Gospel to the whole creation," while in what might be called his prayer of consecration He said, "As Thou didst send Me into the world, even so send I them into the world."

No, the cause of Foreign Missions, by which is meant the preaching of the Gospel to heathen nations, is not a problem in the sense of being involved in doubt or uncertainty. The Master's command is, "Go." It is not an open question. With the Christian it is not debatable. For or against Missions is for or against the Master. So far as the Church is concerned there remains absolutely nothing to be done except to carry out the command of the Great Head of the Church. But now this brings us to the point where the problems begin to present themselves. They come thick and fast and are by no means easy of solution.

After almost twenty-two years of close connection with and active participation in this department of the work of our Church, and after a more or less careful study of the plans and methods of other societies, I trust it will not be regarded presumptuous on my part to state what I consider to be the most vital and immediately practical problems in Foreign Mission work. In the time allotted I cannot, of course, undertake to refer to all the important phases of this subject, but shall confine myself to a few of the leading problems, believing, however, that these will be recognized as fairly covering the whole field of inquiry.

1. *Who shall engage in this work?* The effectual call to labor in the foreign field comes to comparatively few men and women. In one of the most active communions in this country about one in a thousand of its communicant membership is enrolled as a foreign missionary. There are other communions which send only one out of five thousand, or one out of ten thousand of their communicants to the regions beyond. This fact in itself furnishes sufficient ground for the claim that great care and discrimination

should be exercised in the selection of men for the foreign field. If the Church can send only one in a thousand, or possibly only one in five or ten thousand, surely only the best ought to be sent.

But there are other and more cogent reasons for this claim. In a country like this, where Christian work is more or less thoroughly organized, the principle of the division of labor is generally recognized and practiced. In the Church, as in the learned professions and in business and industrial pursuits, we have specialists. The individual devotes himself to one particular department of work in the upbuilding of the Kingdom, and by concentrating all his powers and energies on that one thing he may, and often does, become an expert in that department. In the work of establishing the Church of Christ in Pagan lands, however, it is quite different. In the beginning of the work—and up to the present time it can hardly be said to have advanced beyond that stage—the individual missionary, if we may reasonably expect his labors to be fairly successful, must embrace in his personal make-up a combination of qualities and qualifications that, to say the least, are somewhat rare. In the home Church we have preachers and pastors, superintendents and teachers, presidents and professors, secretaries and treasurers, elders and deacons and deaconesses, and what not. The man who becomes the pastor of a fairly well-established congregation will find the majority, if not all, of these functionaries already installed and at work in his parish and in his church of which his parish is a part, while the man who is called to labor in the field will not only have to exercise all these functions himself, but is compelled to do so among a people who have not yet learned the simple rudiments of Christian faith and practice. He may be so fortunate to have associated with him, for advice and counsel, fellow-missionaries of larger and riper experience; but in many instances, because of his isolation, he is compelled to stand alone. As a pioneer in the work of establishing the Church he must be an organizer, laying the foundation wisely and well and shaping the superstructure, if the edifice is to endure, with the skill of the master builder. In his contact with the government of the country in which his field is located, or possibly in the effort to organize some form of government for the rude people among whom his lot is cast, he may discover that even some of the instincts and aptitudes of the diplomat and statesman do not come amiss.

He must also be physically sound. If after a thoroughly rigid examination it appears that he is not normal with respect to all his vital organs, his application, whatever his other qualifications may be, cannot be entertained. The vital current must run deep and strong and steady in the man who hopes to endure and be of service in the tropics. Foreign missionaries ought to be selected with as great care and intelligent discrimination as that exercised by a Kane or a Greeley or a Nansen in picking their men for an Arctic expedition.

It is not every man that is endowed by nature with an aptitude for the acquisition of a new language, and as his usefulness as a missionary depends very largely on his ability to communicate with the people among whom he labors it is a matter of prime importance that he be a man of linguistic talent.

A high grade of scholarship is also called for. There seems to be a popular impression that a man of mediocre scholarship, if he is only thoroughly pious and consecrated, will do to send to the heathen; and one not unfrequently hears the remark that such and such a man is too good to be sent to the foreign field. The fact is that in oriental countries he will come in contact with the keenest and most subtle intellects of the world, while by the rude pagans of Africa he will be read and judged as by the penetrating light of the Roentgen rays. The claim has been made that there are no better judges of human nature and none quicker to detect intellectual pretension or moral fraud.

An all-embracing love for souls, a firm and clear-cut faith and a consecrated piety are of course absolutely essential to success, but of these I will not speak at length. They are to be taken for granted. No ordinarily intelligent or fairly honest person would so much as take a single step in the direction of the foreign field without them.

But there is at least one more important qualification that should be mentioned, for without it any or even all the rest, if they could be secured in any single individual, would prove unproductive of good results. I refer to that well-balanced combination of faculties and powers, that harmonious blending of reason, will and conscience, that sound practical judgment, which we call common sense. It is absolutely necessary in the missionary as the crown of all the other qualities. "To understand one's self and others, to control one's self and others," to seize the opportunity and make the best of it, to adapt one's self to new circumstances, conditions and surroundings,—this is a faculty that is called for in the missionary as perhaps in no other calling in the whole sphere of Christian activity. To find men for the service who possess these qualifications in a fair degree is the first problem that confronts us in this work.

2. *Where shall the Missionary do his work?* This is another question that, in some quarters at least, is still calling for an intelligent and satisfactory answer. Since the Church does not seem to be able as yet to send more than one out of five or ten thousand of her members into the foreign field, it would seem to be the part of wisdom to place them where they are most needed. If the aim of foreign missions is to give the Gospel to those who have it not, then surely the missionary should go, primarily, to those lands where there are still millions of people who have never so much as heard the message, rather than to countries where the social, intellectual and national life of the people is not only largely dominated by the teaching of the Gospel, but which themselves have been centres of Christian activity for the propagation of the Gospel in heathen lands for a hundred years or more. Neither the Papal nor the Protestant Church have yet attained that degree of spiritual excellence which answers to the Apostle's description of "Not having spot or wrinkle or any such thing," but that does not justify the Propaganda at Rome in viewing the United States as distinctively mission ground nor some branches of the Protestant Church in this country in sending its missionaries to Germany and Scandinavia, or even to Italy, as long as there are millions of people, sunk in the lowest depth of heathenism, who are still waiting to hear the good news of salvation for the first time. And not only is the missionary to be sent to heathen rather than to even nominally Christian people, but preference is

to be given to such parts of heathen countries as have not yet been reached by others. But such a spirit of comity is not always observed. Dr. Lawrence, in his mission tour around the world, found fourteen or more societies in Tokio, eleven in Shanghai, and about as many in the cities of Madras, Calcutta and Bombay. Had he gone out from these large centres into certain sections of the country he would have found scores of little villages where rival congregations were struggling to maintain an existence each to the hurt and serious disadvantage of others, while in an adjacent district there were still one hundred thousand souls to whom no missionary had ever come. A true mission comity would render such a thing an impossibility. To plant in a heathen village two churches that are not only weak, but also contending about some minor distinctions that are utterly foreign to the thought and history of the people presents a spectacle that is anything but helpful in the work of winning the people to the new faith. As long as the inculcation of some minor peculiarity in doctrine or church polity, such as immersion or apostolic succession, is thought to be equally as important as the winning of souls to Christ, the Church will be sadly crippled and one of the most serious problems connected with the whole work will be awaiting its solution.

Encouraging progress has been made in late years in the direction of mission comity both between the various societies in this country and between their representatives in the foreign fields. More and more the sentiment is coming to prevail that if the agents of one Society are occupying a given territory, and are cultivating it with fair success, the field should be left to their exclusive care. On this point, as long as there is so much unoccupied territory, there ought never to have been a difference of opinion among the various branches of the Christian Church.

As evidence of a better condition of things prevailing we note the organization of the Conference of Foreign Mission Boards in the United States and Canada, which holds its seventh annual meeting in New York City, January 10-12, 1899. This Conference is composed of representatives of well nigh all the Boards and Societies in this country and Canada. Questions of vital interest to the cause are considered with reference to the administration of the work, views are exchanged, plans of work are discussed, a broad survey of the field taken and thus the representatives of the different Boards are more and more coming to see eye to eye on all the great questions that are essential to the success of the work. The General Conference held in London in 1888, the Decennial Conference of all Protestant missionaries in India and various other conferences of a similar character, are doing much toward bringing about a practicably operative spirit of comity in the work. Such united effort of Christendom in the prosecution of mission work is needed as an evidencing power. The task of the world's evangelization is such a stupendous one that it calls for the most careful distribution of territory, division of labor and economy of expenditure and effort. Any selection of a missionary field, or distribution of missionary force, or expenditure of missionary funds that aims at anything else than the giving of the gospel to the largest number of those who have it not and who, except as the foreign missionary brings it to them, have no possible chance of hearing it, does not seem to be under the guidance and control of sanctified common sense.

3. *The Problem of Education* is perhaps second in importance to none in the work of foreign missions. Wherever the missionary has gone educational work has been established primarily with the object of preparing the converts to do evangelistic work. In some instances the school work seems to have outgrown other forms of mission, though not without protest from some of the workers in the field. These argue that the divine command and commission is to preach the gospel and not to teach school. In well nigh every important station the claims of these two departments of work have been urged by their respective advocates with great earnestness.

It must be evident, however, to every thoughtful person that if the gospel is ever to be preached to the millions who are still in heathenism it must be done chiefly through a native ministry. Such a ministry, if the native Church is to become self-propagating and self-directing, must be more or less thoroughly educated. And not the ministry only, but the membership as well. Indeed, in many of the fields some degree of education is an absolute prerequisite to the introduction of the Gospel. Very little can be expected in the way of Christian life and character, and still less of activity and growth, from people who cannot even read the word of God; and in general, other things being equal, the progress and stability of the Church will be in proportion to the intelligence of her ministry and laity.

The great bulwark of heathenism is ignorance and superstition, and of these education seems to be the universal solvent. A purely scientific education has brought many a student to the point of utter dissatisfaction with his system of religious faith, and has thus cleared the way for something better, while many, in a caste-ridden country like India, can be reached only through the schools. So important is this form of missionary effort regarded that one of large experience, who has been eminently successful in district or evangelistic work, declares that in beginning a new work he would rather have in a village a school without a church than a church without a school. The command is indeed to preach the gospel, but the missionary who, in his school, trains up an efficient corps of native evangelists is filling the spirit of this command, and that, possibly, in a much larger measure than the one who engages in the direct work of preaching. In a country where millions of dollars are spent on educational enterprises, and where the aim is to give every person the opportunity of securing an education, it is hardly necessary to defend the school, and yet there have been and still are some very excellent missionaries who would place the emphasis entirely on evangelistic effort through the preaching of the Gospel and who have little or no sympathy with educational work in general.

4. *The Native Church* presents another problem for our consideration. It has perhaps more difficulties connected with it than any other. On what general plan should it be organized? What connection with the home church should be maintained? To what extent, if any, should it be controlled and governed by the home church?

What should be the relation of the different mission churches in a given field to each other? What shall be the condition of entrance, and what standard shall be maintained? These and other questions will continue to come up for solution as long as beginnings are being made in the organization and building up of the church among those gathered out of heathenism.

We will have made some progress toward the solution of this problem by getting a clear idea of the aim and object of Christian missions. Is it the salvation of sinners, the conversion of the world? That is the aim of all religious effort and cannot, therefore, be said to be the distinctive aim of missions. Not only are souls to be brought to Christ, but they are also to be organized into churches, and then built up in all the graces of the Christian life and so trained in Christian activity as to make those churches an agency for the further propagation of the Gospel, along all lines of Christian effort.

The Church is God's agency for the salvation of the world, and missions not only have their origin, but their end in the Church. In other words, the aim of missions must be to establish the Church of Jesus Christ in the earth. As Dr. Lawrence puts it, "The primary aim of missions is to preach the Gospel in all lands; the ultimate aim is to plant the Church in all lands. When they have done that their work is accomplished. Then the Church of each land thus planted must win its own people to Christ. The converts must convert. The new Church must evangelize and Christianize. India, China, Japan are each to be turned to Christ, not by missions, but by the Indian, the Chinese, the Japanese churches, when these churches shall have been securely planted by missions."

The Rev. Henry Venn, former Secretary of the Church Missionary Society, has expressed it in yet more condensed and classic form. He says, "The object of missions is the development of native churches with a view to their ultimate settlement upon a self-supporting, self-governing and self-extending system." By steadily keeping this end in view, we will be materially assisted in determining what course to pursue in the organization and management of the native Church. It is evident that from the beginning its connection is very close with and dependent on the home Church. But soon it will be seen that the conditions in India or China or Africa are so much unlike those in Christian Europe or America that the one cannot be modelled after the other except in its more general features. The great underlying principles of the Gospel will apply equally well to Oriental forms and customs as to the Occidental, and even better, since the Scriptures have come to us in an Oriental setting. Christianity is not intended to denationalize any people. It is for the Icelander or Esquimo in his igloo as well as for the African in his kraal, but both cannot be cast together in the same mold as far as the organized body of believers is concerned. As regards admittance into the Church, comparatively few come into it from disinterested and lofty motives, but coming as they may they are not to be sent back into heathenism, but taken into the school of Christ and instructed in Him. Possibly, for years the standard cannot be made as high, as with those of us who are the product of a thousand years of Christian evolution. As rapidly as possible the native Church should be brought to a condition of self-support, and this not particularly to relieve the home-land. It is a distinct and positive wrong to a Church to continue its support longer than may be absolutely necessary to give it an adequate start in its corporate life, for, like its Great Head, it exists, "not to be ministered unto, but to minister."

With self-support must also come self-government and self-propagation. In this country we have taken high and decided grounds against anything like foreign control in Church and State. The time was when we welcomed missionaries from Europe, and there was need of them, but now we stand alone without any organic connection with the mother country or mother Church. The sooner that is the case with India and Africa, with China and Japan, the better will it be for the good of the Church in those countries.

It is also a grave question as to the extent to which it will be wise to teach those denominational peculiarities that, throughout Christendom, are recognized as non-essential to human salvation. Shall only the essential and fundamental truths of Christianity be given to the converts and they be allowed, by natural process of ecclesiastical development, to organize themselves into a native

Church with such peculiarities of government and usages as may best comport with the circumstances of the situation, or shall the future Church in India or China or Japan present the almost endless divisions that characterize the Church in this country? In India thirteen different Presbyterian bodies are at work. Is it necessary or wise to impose upon the Hindoos the necessity of supporting thirteen different ecclesiastical establishments, and thus perpetuate in that country differences which here at home are more honored in the breach than in the observance? Shall the Leipsic, the Berlin, the Gossner, the Basel, the Hermansburg, the General Council, the General Synod and other Lutheran missions in India form, in the not far distant future, one grand united Lutheran Church in that country, or shall we largely waste our strength and minimize our influence by standing apart and emphasizing the minor points that separate us? The missionaries of these respective branches of our Church have sat together in conference in India, even as we do to-day, and they were able to see eye to eye, on all questions referring to the Christlike work that took them to that country. May we not hope that the ranks of our workers in India may never be invaded by the ecclesiastical microscopist who can point out differences where none appear to the unaided eye; but that, on the other hand, the delightful spirit of harmony and singleness of aim and purpose that characterized the conference of our representatives in India may somehow be communicated to the home Church in yet larger and ever-increasing measure?

THE COMMON BOOK.

BY L. A. FOX, D.D.

By the Common Book, as announced in the programme, is meant one book of worship for all Lutherans using the same language. We are to consider an eminently practical subject, and we ought to look at it in an earnest, practical way.

1. *The Need of a Common Book.* We need it for several reasons.

a. We need it as a bond of union. Difficult as it is for strangers to understand it, our Church is not made up of a number of different denominations or branches, but is one communion. There are not different names, but one common name: Lutheran. We are not Old School and New School, not American and German, not High Church and Low Church, not Northern and Southern, not General Synod and General Council, Ohio and Missouri Lutherans, but all are simply Lutherans. We have one common history, of which we are all alike proud. We have one common confessional basis: The Augsburg Confession. Some of us, it is true, have subscribed to the other confessions, but only so far as they are fuller statements of the Augustana. We have a common book for the instruction of the young: Luther's Catechism. We have one common spirit and life. The evident extremes among us have more in common than either extreme has with the Church with which it seems to have most affinity. Once imbued with the Lutheran spirit, one can never feel at home in any other Church. We have different organizations—different general bodies, different theological seminaries, different publishing houses, different quarterlies, different hymn books, different Sunday-school lessons, etc., but not one of us will allow that there are different churches. We have only one clerical register. Our ministers are all Lutheran ministers, our Synods are all Lutheran Synods. We all are members of the same great Church.

But this unity is not fully realized. We have a great many divisions. We have the General Synod, the General Council, the Synodical Conference, the United Synod of the South, the Joint Synod of Ohio and the Iowa Synod, besides thirteen or fourteen independent Synods. There are various reasons for these separate organizations. Some of them are formed chiefly on geographical lines. This is true of the United Synod of the South and the Texas Synod. Some of them grew out of a difference in language. This is true of the Swedish and Norwegian Synods. But others are based upon different conceptions of the common Confession and of methods of work. It must be added that personal feelings enter as an appreciable element, at least into the preservation of some of them. Two of our general bodies occupy precisely the same territory. Not infrequently congregations of two or three different synods are found in the same town. Many of these synods have no association with each other. When their work is contiguous, there is an unseemly rivalry, and often bitterness of feeling. Our Church is broken up into different parties. There is something among us very much like what Paul called schism in the Corinthian Church.

This division into unsympathetic parties is unnatural. The members of one household are divided against each other. Brethren are out of harmony and have sometimes fallen into discussions so heated as often to appear like quarrels. Our points of agreement far outnumber and outweigh our points of difference, but in our zeal to emphasize the difference we lose sight of the agreement. Different shades of conceptions completely conceal the substance of the common faith. Other churches with far more widely divergent tendencies and with much greater and more serious extremes remain in organic union; but we wrangle and split into hostile parties over matters of relatively little importance.

This division is injurious. We lose the moral force of a great concentrated body. We divide our efforts and weaken ourselves. We squander money in supporting rival institutions. We set up rival congregations and build separate churches and support separate pastors, when there ought to be but one strong church. A party spirit is engendered and fostered by repeated conflicts, and we are often moved more by that spirit than we are by a love for the Church. Sometimes a feeling of bitterness is manifested, and we let our members go into another denomination rather than encourage them to go into the congregation of an opposite party. It is a suicidal policy, and we have lost thousands of members because of it. Our growth has been marvelous, but we must not mistake the cause. It is due to immigration more than to wise and aggressive work. If Lutherans had ceased to come to America a half a century ago we would be still one of the small and insignificant denominations of our country.

We inherit weakness in organization from our Reformation fathers. Among Luther's wonderful and diversified gifts, the organizing faculty was wanting. He was strangely lacking in even an appreciation of its importance. In this he was very much unlike Calvin. He might have seen its power in the Roman Church and in the Reformed Churches; but either he did not, or he was afraid of it. He relied so implicitly upon the power of the truth that he overlooked or rejected subsidiary agencies. Not until the work had gone on for several years and there were some sad disturbances through the Anabaptist influence did he undertake anything like a system of congregational visitation. Even that was merely temporary. He turned over to the rulers of the State what properly belonged to the Church, and left each sovereign to govern the congregations according to his own plan. Each State had its own ecclesiastical government, and when a ruler changed his faith he carried with him his country. The Jesuits availed themselves of this policy, and insinuated themselves into royal families to become teachers of the heirs apparent, and made perverts to Rome. But still there was no radical change of policy. Luther's greatness was so overshadowing that if there were men who had a gift for organizing, it never became operative. His spirit was so masterful that it has indelibly stamped itself upon the Church, and in this respect we have never been able to rise above his defect. He was right in holding that the supreme power is in the word of God; but he was wrong in supposing that there was no need of accessory instrumentalities. Superior as we believe we are in many respects to the Reformed Church, we must acknowledge ourselves its inferior in thoroughness of organization. We have surely felt the effects of this inferiority.

We are by no means ready yet to break up our Synodical organizations and reorganize upon strictly geographical and linguistic lines. We may not be able to do it for several generations to come. It takes a long time for feelings created by conflicts to die and old contests to be forgotten. Long standing wounds frequently fretted by friction are not soon healed. Cherished crotchets are not readily abandoned. But if organic unity is impossible, a fuller consciousness of the unity of faith and spirit is not. We are already beginning to realize something of the unnaturalness of our divisions, and there are movements already commenced towards closer relations. We look with great pleasure upon this part of the work of the Luther League. Our young people fraternize and co-operate. There are other but less conspicuous associations in which men of different parties meet in informal and fraternal conference. The sense of unity lying behind these external divisions is growing, and we are getting ready for a common book of worship, which will bind us still more closely together.

Our different books have done a great deal towards weakening the sense of Lutheran unity and keeping alive our unnatural and hurtful divisions. With a separate book for every party, so much like different denominations, our own people as well as strangers find it diffcult to believe that we are not so many different Lutheran denominations. But with one common book, a Lutheran attending the service of any party or Synod, and finding the same forms and the same hymns, will feel that he is at home in the same great family. When we have grown warm over our discussions we will take up the same book and realize that after all we are brethren. We can appeal to facts in proof of the unifying influence of such a book. It may be seen in the Prayer Book of the Episcopal Church. In England narrow Tractarianism and broad Liberalism, Pusey and Maurice, gather themselves under its fold. In America we have tendencies closely approximating Romanism on the one hand and Unitarianism on the other, kept in the same communion. The bond of union is not so much the Episcopacy as the Prayer Book. Without the Prayer Book the Episcopal college would dissolve. We may see the effects of a common book in the United Synod of the South. Our ministers were educated at different seminaries, some at Philadelphia, some at Gettysburg, some at Chicago, some at Newberry and some at other places. We have some who sympathize more with the General Council, some more with the General Synod and some more with the Synodical Conference. We have some who hold in almost extreme reverence the Book of Concord, and some who cherish the memory of the Definite Platform. But we all work together in harmony, and there is no bond except our Book of Worship and our mission in Japan. The Tennessee Synod, which withholds full co-operation, has a different book. Can we not see the same influence already in the effects of the Common Service? We do not propose to substitute a book for the Lutheran faith as the fundamental tie. We do not want a book like the Prayer Book with its cast-iron rubrics. But we do need a common book as an expression of unity and as an accessory bond.

b. We need a Common Book for the highest development of the religious life of our people. Worship is the expression of the religious character. It is the divine life in us reaching out towards God. In somewhat Hegelian language, but not in the Hegelian sense, it is the divine nature of which we have been made partakers seeking to return to God. This life is given and increased only through the Word and Sacraments. But worship reacts upon that life, and like physical exercise in the physical life, or like the effort to impart instruction in the intellectual life, worship develops it. Every Christian has felt this in both his public and private devotions. In his closet when he begins to speak to God about his feelings of reverence, of gratitude, and of sinfulness and wants, these feelings become deeper. In the sanctuary his worship is joined with others and he is lifted out of his own little sphere into a fuller life. His heart is expanded into broader sympathies, wider interests and deeper affections. His piety has a larger field. But the form of the service has much to do with this reflex influence. The better the expression, the more he is helped. To accomplish most in this direction our book of worship should be the voice of the great Church.

No one of our Lutheran parties represents the whole of the Lutheran life. There is narrowness and littleness about each one of them. The horizon of each is contracted. One may be better than the others, may be nearer the true Lutheran spirit, but not one of them fully represents it. Each one in some respect is a better exponent of one of the various phases of the Lutheran life than any other. We can have the best service only when we all unite to form it. When Edward I established Parliament he gave this common-sense reason for it: "What concerns all should be approved by all." The Constitution of our National Government was framed by compromises. It was formed by the representatives of the different sections of this country, who gave up sectional preferences and interests. No one was perfectly satisfied with it, because it did not embody his individual notions of what the government should be. It is not perfect, but it is a wonderful instrument. Without amendment, save only in the manner of electing the President, it directed the administration of our national affairs until after the Civil War. Even then there was need of nothing except some added articles to meet the new conditions. It may, perhaps, be expanded to meet even the radical new conditions into which the last war has involved us. It was far better than any one of the great statesmen of that day could have framed. Washington, great and broad, honest and patriotic as he was, could not have done it. The Constitution was the product of the great body of the people, the will of the nation. So the best Common Book must be the product, not of an individual, not of a party, but of the whole Church.

If it be true that the Common Book is so important to the development of the life of the Church, we owe it to the Church to secure it. We are responsible for all the possibilities in us. But there is even a higher view. The Lutheran Church is not an end, but a means. It has no reason for its existence, and no claim upon our affections and service, except so far as it makes men Christians. We love it and work for it, because it promotes the Kingdom of God among men. Will this book make us better and holier? If the answer be affirmative, the duty is unquestionable.

c. We need a Common Book to awaken a deeper Church love. This follows necessarily from the preceding facts. Whatever will give them a new sense of the greatness and unity of the Church, and especially whatever will create in them a higher spiritual life, will have their profoundest affection. But there are also other things which emphasize this point. We believe that the Lutheran Church is the purest part of the Church on earth, and therefore we want to make the largest possible number of Lutherans, and to lead them to a true appreciation of the Lutheran Church. We may have our people very decided and positive Lutherans without being bigots; love it as the *best* Church, without believing that it is the *only* Church. We must not forget that the great glory of our Church is her pure faith. Her creed constitutes her essence. We can make true and staunch Lutherans only by thorough indoctrination. We must rely primarily upon thorough catechization. Our people love our Church as they understand her doctrines. But our faith is not our *sole* glory. We have also a pure worship. Our liturgy and our hymns have been little less admired by candid non-Lutheran scholars than by ourselves. A Common Book can be made the pride of our people. Not every one can be brought to the clear understanding of our distinctive doctrines, but all can be taught to love a Common Book. We do not have many of the secondary means of a Church love. We have no college of bishops to rally us. We have no great institutions. We are strangely destitute of many of those attractions which our neighbors have. There is not much probability that we could have them very soon even if we desired. But we can have a Common Book that will awaken a devotion to the Church deeper than any episcopate or great institution can.

2. *The Contents of the Common Book.* It would be very presumptuous in any one of us to attempt to say just what that work should be, but one may be pardoned for suggesting a general outline of what it should contain. Indeed we have approved plans.

While Rev. Dr. D. M. Gilbert was the youthful pastor in Staunton, Va., he proposed through the *Southern Lutheran* a Book of Worship for the Southern Lutheran Church. He suggested that it contain a Liturgical Service, Œcumenical Creeds, the Augsburg Confession, Luther's Small Catechism, some Psalms for responsive reading, Ministerial Acts, and a collection of Hymns. The suggestion was adopted by the Southern General Synod, and the Book of Worship was formed. That book passed over from the General Synod to the United Synod of the South. We have adopted the Common Service and incorporated it, but in other respects, the book remains what it was when adopted thirty-five years ago. We of the Southern section do not offer our book, but our plan.

We think that the Common Book ought to have the Common Service. It has been already adopted and offers itself as the first step toward a Common Book. It may not be just what some of us prefer, but now that it has been officially adopted by our general bodies, it ought to be accepted by all of our pastors. No one has said that it contains any doctrinal errors, or that it is really un-Lutheran, and therefore no great tax is laid upon any man's conscience. It allows us to omit certain points, provided we follow the general order. It takes away, therefore, very little of any man's liberty. The discussion has been chiefly whether certain quite subordinate points should be retained or not. To some it seems to be an effort to determine the difference between tweedle dee and tweedle dum. If we persist in contending for the unimportant, we doom ourselves to our present divided condition. We sacrifice the whole Church on the altar of a party. If Patrick Henry and George Clinton could have had their way about States' rights, and Rhode Island have remained out of the Union because it wanted to regulate its own commerce, there had never been this great nation of the United States. Ruin awaited all. If men then made compromises for the sake of the public good, can not we for the sake of the eternal welfare of souls? They did it to secure the well-being of the State, and shall not we for the benefit of the Church? They surrendered their individual narrowness, and rose into a broad patriotism, and cannot we, that we may rise up to a wider Lutheran life? The Common Service is not perfect, but time and grace will perfect it.

The Common Book ought to contain the Œcumenical Creeds, the Augsburg Confession and Luther's Catechism. The reasons for this are so manifest that they do not need enumeration.

The Common Book ought to have orders for ministerial acts, both for convenience and instruction. This is the first difficulty. We seem to be quite far from agreement upon these forms. The general bodies have found difficulty in agreeing upon them for themselves, and it seems much more difficult for all to do it. But the difficulty is not insuperable. These forms are not of vital importance. We could agree upon certain tentative ones, and allow large liberty to pastors in using them; or we might allow the general bodies to have special editions of the Common Book containing their own forms. In the Southern Church we have no trouble in this matter. Some have other forms, but most of us use those recommended for the time by the United Synod. Few of us think that they are the best possible, but until we have something better, they will do. We have grown so accustomed to this state of things that we do not quite appreciate the difficulties of some of our brethren.

The Common Book must have a common hymnal. This is the second, and perhaps the greatest, difficulty. Some of the Synods are so pleased with their present collections that they think they could accept no other. Some others are changing theirs, and would not object very much to an entirely new one. We of the Southern Church, while offering our plan, do not offer our hymns. They were collected by a man regarded as the best hymnologist among us, but some of us regard this collection as the very poorest in use in any part of the Church. We are exceedingly anxious for something better, and this is one of the reasons why the idea of a Common Book originated among us.

There is place for the suggestion of only a few, very few, of the principles upon which this common hymnal should be formed.

It is a book for use. It should have only such hymns as a majority of our congregations can sing. There are translations of German hymns loved by our fathers, and we may like to have them for their historic interest, but the reason is not sufficient for retaining them. Our children love only what they sing, and can be made to take interest in no others.

The hymns should be orthodox. They should be really hymns, and not merely good religious poetry. How far admonishing one another in psalms and hymns and spiritual songs can go is a difficult question.

Our hymnal must meet the wants of our Churches. It cannot embrace all the good hymns, and in any collection that could possibly be made, all of us will miss some that we love. But we can have a book that will meet all reasonable demands. It is a little remarkable how small a number most pastors use. We have heard of a few ministers who tried to have all the hymns sung during a certain period. Young ministers usually want a large number from which to make selections, and to every sermon they want hymns specially adapted. But as we get older, we narrow the range until most men of experience do not use more than forty or fifty. This suggests a plan. Let the committee on the hymnal address every pastor, asking him to give the fifty hymns he most frequently uses; and from these answers make up the collection. We would get in this way the voice of the Church and be able to form the best possible book.

The Common Book is not then an ideal something, a dream, a matter to be talked about, but unattainable. It can be had, and that in the near future. No, it will be realized as soon as the love of the Church overrides love of party.

REMARKS.

DR. JACOBS: Without entering into a discussion of a number of the questions suggested by the interesting paper of Dr. Fox, I may say that whatever may be the difference concerning the details of his argument, there is substantial unanimity as to the end proposed—the Common Book. So far as legislation can effect anything, that is already accomplished. Our General Bodies have already acted, and instructed their representatives on the Joint Committee, and that Committee has appointed a sub-committee to report a plan for the work. The Committee, while fully aware that the project will encounter peculiar difficulties, and that years must intervene before the wishes expressed can be gratified, can only follow instructions. Books that may have recently appeared, or may soon appear, need be no hindrance to the ultimate attainment of the end. As Providence opens the way, we must advance. The difficulties, great as they are, are no greater than those which seemed to some of us to obstruct the way, when the Common Service was proposed.

DR. SEISS cited Lutheran authorities in favor of uniformity in the services and ceremonies in the Church, and urging the advantages and necessity of a common Book to be used as far as possible by all. These quotations were collected by Dr. Seiss, and meant to be read in the Conference when the subject of One Book was under discussion. The worth of these expressions entitle them to a place in this connection.

Klieforth describes the feeling and opinion of the Lutheran Church from its beginning in the words following:

"While the Lutheran Church in theory considered and treated the forming and changing of the Liturgy as a right of the Church, she held congregations and individual ministers bound by the decisions of the Church general, insisted on uniformity of ceremonies, forbade all arbitrary alterations, and fully acknowledged the great practical evil of inconsiderateness and disposition to change. History teaches most clearly with what steadfastness she met the insubordination of individuals, from Carlstadt down."

The correctness of this statement appears from various official and authoritative utterances, among which are the following:

Luther himself, in his *German Mass*, says: "It is true we have freedom; but freedom should be used for the benefit of one another. For love's sake, therefore, we should try to agree, and, as far as possible, have a uniform manner and uniform ceremonies, just as all Christians have one Baptism and one Eucharist . . . . There have always been different rites; but it would be good if, throughout each realm, the same order were observed."

So in the *Apology*, while the Augsburg Confession declares that it is not necessary to the Unity of the Church for "human traditions, rites, or ceremonies instituted by men, be everywhere alike," there is this further statement: "It is pleasing to us that, for the sake of unity and good order, common rites be universally observed; just as we willingly and gratefully observe and embrace the profitable and ancient ordinances, especially as they instruct and educate the people."

The Churländ *Kirchenordnung* says, "It is greatly to be desired that uniformity of ceremonies should obtain throughout the whole land. It would make a favorable impression on the people, and secure no small advantage to the growth of the Church. For if the people see a different Order of Services and ceremonies in one place from those practiced in another, they are disturbed and perplexed about the whole matter of religion, and the want of conformity becomes a stumbling-block and offence to them. Therefore it shall ever be our earnest endeavor to secure decent and Christian order in the churches of this Principality, and we will in no degree give way to the fanaticism of the Calvinists, who, in their blind perverseness, will not understand that God is not a God of confusion and disorder."

The Pomeranian *Agenda* says, "Inasmuch as God is not a God of confusion, but of peace, and wills that in congregations all things should be done decently and in order, there is no doubt that it is a service peculiarly acceptable to the Divine Majesty when a uniform, spiritual, and edifying form of worship is adopted and maintained.

In addition to manifold other blessings which it brings with it, it tends to secure unity in the doctrines of God's Word, and to remove many causes of stumbling to the common people, who judge of doctrines, sacraments, and the whole work of the ministry from outward forms and ceremonies. On this account the appointed Order of Hymns, Lessons, forms and ceremonies is to be observed in our churches. And where this has not hitherto been the case, Pastors should comply with this Order, and not depart from it without special and important reasons, but cheerfully conform to it out of willing Christian love, in order that divisions or dissensions among the people may be avoided; for they are not to be allowed arbitrarily to reject or alter the appointed Order according to their own pleasure."

In full accord with all this, Henry Melchior Muhlenberg, near the end of his life, wrote: "It would be a most desirable and advantageous thing if all the Evangelical Lutheran congregations in the North American States were united with one another, and all used the same Order of Worship, the same Hymn-book, and, in good and evil days, would show an active sympathy and fraternally correspond with one another."

COMMON SUNDAY-SCHOOL LITERATURE.

BY REV. L. L. SMITH, A.M.

No subject is of more importance than the type of literature used in the Sunday-schools in connection with our Lutheran congregations. The children of to-day in the Sunday-school will make up the active, intelligent, and dominating membership of to-morrow in most of the congregations. So it can be positively prophesied that according to the teaching, worship and spirit in which the Sunday-school is conducted to-day, will largely mould and develop the Church life and attitude of the next generation. And it is well for our Church to realize the problem of the great power of the modern Sunday-school system in guiding and directing the Church life and spirit, not only of our denomination, but of all the churches of this great nation. When we recall the fact that about 1,200,000 laymen engage in teaching ten millions of children every Sunday, in the cities, towns and country, the possibilities of this institution are beyond estimation. The teaching and no teaching accomplished by this vast aggregation tell us plainly that it will have a mighty harvest of good and evil in the religious life of this land. And in the midst of this vast aggregation of all kinds of teachers, and every type of literature, and the multitudinous sensational and unscriptural devices and methods, the Lutheran Church is placed by divine Providence, to bear the light and blessings of her own pure truth and worship and practices. It is true of the Church as it is of the individual, she liveth not to herself; and surrounded on all sides by the vagaries and departures from truth by scores of sects and religious parties, it behooves her to earnestly lay hold of this institution, to feed and nourish the lambs of the flock in her own doctrine, worship and church life. If our Church has a reason, and a scriptural reason above all, for her own distinctive life and existence, and of this there can be no doubt, then it follows to be true to God and true to herself the teaching and training of her children is the supreme question.

This brings us to the question, what is the Sunday-school? To this inquiry the answer is variously given both in theory and in practice. The answer is colored by the peculiar views held by the different religious forces. Largely the view of the Church dictates the view of the Sunday-school. According to Luther, the Family, the Church and the State are the three divine institutions. The family is the foundation of the whole Christian fabric, and for that reason, Luther prescribed as the opening direction to the five parts of his catechism: "in the plain form in which the head of the family should teach it to his household." This places the responsibility for the children where the Lord places it, primarily, with the parents. No agency of the Church can possibly set at nought that obligation. But, though that be true, has not the Church a binding obligation to teach, to instruct her children? That a leading duty of the Church was to teach all nations was made plain in the great commission of our Lord to His disciples. That little children are included in the scope of that commission was evident from the Saviour's own commands, "Suffer little children to come unto Me and forbid them not," as well as from His impressive charge to Peter: "Feed my lambs." This duty has been solemnly performed by the

Church in every age from Abraham down to the present, whenever she has been faithful to her great Head. The patriarchs like Abraham, Job, Jacob, Moses and others taught the children, and it is well to remember how Ezra gathered the people with the children together, and required the priests to explain the meaning of the law of God. Afterwards the schools attached to the synagogues in the New Testament period, followed by the catechetical schools of the early Christian Church, then Luther at the time of the Reformation, as he so plainly states in the preface to the catechism, give an unbroken historical chain of testimony to the fact that the Church has always had, more or less, a conscious realization of this duty and privilege. Therefore the modern Sunday-school is simply the Church performing one of its divinely given functions, teaching. And this, primarily, to the infant or child membership of each congregation, but no less a blessing to all who may attend upon its services. The Sunday-school, therefore, is not a new institution. It is not a separate agency, distinct from the Church, with the officers, and teachers, and scholars only to follow their whims and notions,—a little Church, sadly in some cases an opposition,—but the Church performing her great and holy function of teaching. Thus the Sunday-school is the Church organized for this specific work of instruction after the catechetical method, the pastor *ex officio* its superintendent, the congregation's officers its governing board, and the congregation fulfilling its obligation of instruction and training.

With the Church thus ready to teach and to train, to whom shall instruction and training be given? First and chiefest, children, baptized children, children in the Church. The Scriptures teach that all are conceived and born in sin; that children inherit from their parents, and they from Adam, a sinful nature; that our Lord took upon Himself our nature, that He became the second head and parent of our race, that we might receive a new nature; that children only become partakers of this new nature by being grafted into Him; that children are thus grafted into Him and become members of Christ, the second Adam, children of God and heirs of the kingdom of heaven, in holy baptism. As there is a natural life, so is there as well a Christian life; as there is a natural birth, so is there a spiritual new birth. Therefore, holy baptism begins Christian training. Without it, whatever other training may be given, Christian training is an impossibility. Christian training differs from all other training in this one respect, that it believes in an implanted supernatural life, which can be and must be developed. This fundamental truth impels the Church to train and teach her children as members of Christ and children of God. Recognizing that they are the lambs of the Good Shepherd in the true fold of His Holy Church, the divine seal and pledge of their baptism is to be impressed upon them. As babes in the Kingdom they are to be taught in the word the great and saving doctrines of the Gospel, and trained in the worship and duties of confirmed members of the congregation. Just as the young are taught and equipped in school, in college and in university, for the duties of manhood and womanhood in future life, so these children of the Kingdom are to be indoctrinated in the saving duties of the Gospel, familiarized with the order of worship harmonizing with these teachings, and inspired by the commands of the Saviour, and the knowledge and the needs of His earthly kingdom, to engage in the practical work of the Church. And in no less manner, to the unbaptized and wandering, this teaching service of the Church should come, telling pointedly and "face to face" the great love in God to sinful men. In this teaching service, the opportunity—the privilege—is blessed, to bring Christ to men through the divine Word—His means of grace and salvation. The very directness of this method makes it a mighty instrumentality to save men.

This conception of the Lutheran Sunday-school, this definition of its sphere, this brief statement of its great and all important work leads to the thought of the instrument by which the Church as teacher shall accomplish the true end of the kingdom. This topic denominates it literature, the literature of song in praise and worship, the literature of prayer and supplication, the literature bearing the divine truth of God's holy word and the literature of presenting the facts and knowledge of the practical things of the kingdom of God. The congregation in this teaching service of the Sunday-school differs only from the congregation in the preaching service by the fact that it uses not the sacramental word; further, that it follows the catechetical rather than the preaching method; and that the teachers, clerical and lay, are many, instead of one, and that one of the clergy. Therefore, at this service, three facts are emphasized: Worship, doctrine and Christian duties.

Is not this the same service as the Church in her fullness renders, save in the exceptions just noted? If the Sunday-school is the congregation training and teaching the young of the kingdom, how important, then, that this service, in its various elements, be just a miniature of the great congregation. Should not the songs of the Sunday-school follow the spirit and teaching of the hymns of the great sanctuary? Alas! how often the Sunday-school in its song and musical training unfits the children for the church service. The hymns written by our great hymnologists and the churchly and majestic music of their setting, comes to them with no impressiveness. Children in their worship are trained, the worship of the Sunday-school accomplishes this very end. Fed upon nothing but the religious ditties of the average Sunday-school hymnal, with their many departures from divine truth in their words and sentiments, and much of their music not far removed from the plantation melody or the popular air of the passing hour, it is not surprising that the divine words and the reverent and churchly music of the service is unappreciated. Thus, the young should be taught the surpassing beauty of the Kyrie, the Gloria in Excelsis, the Nunc Dimittis and the chanting of the Psalms, and, having these in early life in the days of their training, they will come to the church service after their confirmation with a full appreciation of the surpassing loveliness of the Church's worship. It will satisfy their spiritual hunger and edify them in their most holy faith. A Sunday-school—the Church—thus training her spiritual children, will find them always reverent and devout worshipers in the Church of their childhood. Mutations of time and the vicissitudes of fortune may cast their lots where there is no Lutheran Church, but their faithful training will abide with them. Yea, like the devout Jews of old, they will weep when they remember the songs of Zion. And then, in following our own historic order of worship, how it impresses the young, that, though the exposition of the Word is of the highest importance, yet the adoration and worship of the Saviour of children must have its due position in the children's service. The coming of children before God in the sanctuary to be taught by Him must be accompanied by the grateful remembrance of His goodness to them in the gift of His Son for their redemption. The literature used in the Sunday-school should have the end in view of training the children according to Scriptural principles how to worship their Heavenly Father in spirit and in truth. Thus the true Lutheran Sunday-school with its worship following the historic order will prepare and train the young to full appreciation of the blessedness of the matchless service of the great congregation. Yea, not waiting till they become confirmed members, but even when children in their parents' pews, they will swell the songs and the responses of the congregation in chant, in hymn, in anthem, in psalm and prayers. The congregations in which in the future they shall abide will have the great benediction of devout, reverent and earnest worshipers.

And, with still greater emphasis, the literature in the Sunday-school of a Lutheran congregation bearing the truth of God's holy word to the lambs of the flock will always be in harmony with the teaching of the pulpit of the congregation. It is to be taken for granted that the pulpit is faithful to ordination vows, faithful to the conception of divine truth as found in the great confessions. The literature used in our Sunday-schools should be for training and instruction, so that the children of the Church when they come to be men and women of the Church will have an intelligent conception of her teaching. Just here, it is all important in every Lutheran Sunday-school to thoroughly train and instruct in the Word, above all things. The Holy Scriptures should be given first place, and in a simple way exhibited to the young that they may be deeply impressed with the absolute scripturalness of the faith of the Church. It is a lamentable fact, how cloudy is the knowledge of God's Word among so many of the young. With so many aids and helps, yet how small a portion of divine truth is clearly known, so that as a result the young have convictions, the abiding possession of the verities of the ever blessed truth as it is in Christ. When it is considered how in this day innumerable views are held of the teaching of the Word, and then how these views are pressed by their various advocates, in private, on the platform, in tracts and leaflets gratuitously distributed, and in the current magazines and newspapers, views utterly at variance with the historic faith, if the young are to be held to the faith of the fathers, the Church must, by teaching, make a part of their intellectual being the divine plan of redemption. And the child thus taught is safely anchored by the word of God! Liberalism, legalistic narrowness, rationalism and blatant agnosticism and credulous and irreverent skepticism will fail to disturb them, much less to enlist them as disciples.

This instruction in the Word in the Sunday-schools must have as its rule and guidance the catechism. There must be harmony between the two, for the Lutheran Sunday-school without the catechism is without compass and cannot reach its true destination. The whole divine plan is joined together in a system in that little book. The doctrine of God the Father, God the Son, and God the Holy Ghost, the adorable Trinity, of sin and of grace, of conversion, of regeneration, of faith, of good works, of the Church, of everlasting life and death, of baptism and the holy supper, are presented as the Word teaches. If that little book is indoctrinated thoroughly into the hearts of the young, a strong and rugged faith and life and practice will be the result. The dangerous, angular, professing religionism of the times, so prevalent in all sections, will have no attraction to them. To know the simple truth of God gives rest to the soul. With the Scriptures and the catechism, should be, in teaching and instruction, the books to be distributed, week after week, to be read by the pupils. Alas! how careless and thoughtless the Church is in giving out in her name that which teaches the negation for which the Church is set to declare and defend. No book of un-Lutheran spirit should have the approval of the Church as the teacher of her Sunday-school work, that denies the faith or impugns or casts doubt on it, either by direct denial or the specious pleading for another teaching. The Church in her Sunday-school work should remember her obligation to the Lord and His truth, and in the teaching of the word and of the catechism and of the library should have but *one* teaching, the truth in Christ our Lord, as it is our heritage.

With literature for pure worship and pure teaching the office of the Sunday-school does not end. In the training of the baptized children, the work of the Sunday-school must be complete. These young Christians must be fully equipped, not one-sided disciples, but rounded and symmetrical, prepared for future service. Therefore literature must come into this work, instructing in the great practical duties of the kingdom. Literature telling of missions, home and foreign, and the duties of the young to them. Literature telling of the orphan, the aged, the sick, and sorrowful, and their duty to them. Literature telling of the cause of education and its relation to the future influence of the kingdom, and literature presenting the claims, the reasons and the necessity for the practical works given to the Church to do by the Lord. And this literature must be soundly scriptural, following the directions of Him "who went about doing good." It must avoid giving the cheap, worldly reasons and methods, avoid the penny-in-the-slot devices of modern churches, but have as its basis "a true fear, love and trust in God above all things," doing his will out of hearts full of faith and love.

The Sunday-school thus understood, as simply a teaching function of the Church, and the literature in worship, doctrine and practice used, to be after the same type and rule as the literature of the congregation proper, the question arises whether or not it would glorify God and advance His Church by having it common. Would it be a blessing to have every Lutheran Sunday-school using such a type of literature? The careful observer will notice the striking problems of the Church in this land. Here, as nowhere else, growing out of the brief history, the wonderful material development, the provision by the State for education from the primary school to the university, the cheapening of books, periodicals and papers, and the mixed character of our population, together with separation of Church and State with all it signifies, the Church must stand together. Subtle, yet all powerful, are these influences ofttimes against the truth and the teaching of the gospel. And, because of the great freedom of our institutions, the departure from historic teaching is ever arising. Here sects and isms spring up almost daily, with crowds to follow the leaders, until on every hand our children are beset by false and pernicious teaching. So much of it passes current with the name of the Church stamped upon it, calculated to mislead and deceive the young. How can they be retained in the Church but by thorough training and instruction? The necessity for every child of the Church to have a reason for its faith is apparent. They should be able to discern the departures from the truth, not alone in the influential denominations surrounding them, but even in the pulpit of their own Zion. Not only should this common training and instruction in the Sunday-school be for defence against the false and the partial truth from without, but primarily for the highest life of the Lutheran Church of the future. The Church, just as an individual, has its highest service in a positive rather than in a negative life. To combat error is of great importance and often a first duty, but richer is the life of the Church when she positively keeps the commands of her great Head, not alone in worship and doctrine, but also in her service for the world.

The Lutheran Church of the present is the product of the church life and spirit of the past generation of our fathers. To some extent the religious spirit of those about her has had a deep influence.

Looking at the conditions existing in our beloved Zion in the United States, though her growth and strides have been marvelous, and glad are her children for what she has accomplished, yet there must be keen regret at her losses, her lack of influence, and the meagerness of her accomplishments.

Can any other result be expected when the Lutheran hosts are broken into so many camps? And not only the many divisions among her followers, but the sad fact that these divisions signify an emphasis of one part of her doctrine and life, as over against the full consciousness and life of true Lutheranism. One synod or congregation stands for emphasis on worship, while another for confessional doctrine, and still another for service and practical duties. Among these divisions is seen imperfect, angular Lutheranism at its fullest. Is it not all the result of the training and instruction and influences of the past generation? Here is a synod of purest doctrine, venerating the confessions, yet it shows its appreciation of pure teaching by an offering of a mere pittance to the great causes of missions, orphans, education, etc., while on the other hand a synod of great practical godliness, its gifts ten or twenty fold greater, places little emphasis on doctrinal truth. What is the explanation? Is it not training? Pure doctrine does not militate against practical benevolence. It only shows that those people have been trained in but one sphere of the kingdom, they have but one vision and are unable to see the departments of the Church's life. Training in doctrine has been emphasized to the neglect of training in applied Christianity, while on the other hand training in applied Christianity is done at the expense of doctrinal truth. The trouble is the one idea among the divided sections of the Church, a failure to appreciate Lutheranism in its fullness and perfection. The hope of the future for the Church lies in the abolition of the one-idea Lutheranism, wherever it is found, and bringing the Church to the full appreciation of true, devout and reverent Lutheranism in worship, doctrine and applied Christianity. Training and instruction in this trinity of functions is our great need. Here presses home to us the utmost importance of common Sunday-school literature. Great is the power of family training, great the influence of the pastor's catechetical class; but with a full sense of these holy agencies, the Church training her children through the Sunday-school is a mighty power preparing for the future.

Common Sunday-school literature, emphasizing in due proportion worship, doctrine, and practical Christian work, would, if faithfully used, bring about a united Church, faithful in doctrine, worship and works. The outward unity of the Church would result from the consciousness of symmetrical, Christian life. This is the hope for the future, it can not be now. Those advanced in years in our congregations will not renounce or give up their training. The Common Service, the Common Book, the Common Ministerial Acts, the Common Translation of the Smaller Catechism, all have their influence toward this great end.

But, knowing that the fathers must pass away and that the children will take their places, no factor can be more powerful for the future than common Sunday-school literature. Fatal is the error of the Church if she realizes not the divine obligation to train her children; unfortunate for the Church, if they are not taught and trained in the same doctrine, worship and practice. They are the seed of the future Church. As the children are trained and instructed, so the Church will be within a score or more of years. If the Church in the various sections is to be close together in doctrine, worship and holy living, keeping her faith and blessing this great nation, then common Sunday-school literature is a necessity.

LUTHERANISM AND SPIRITUALITY.

BY EZRA K. BELL, D.D.

Spirituality is the realization of divine truth in the whole being of man. The truth of God is the essence of the spiritual as the great Teacher said, "The words that I speak unto you, they are spirit and they are life." The realization of divine truth which produces the spiritual, must be a realization by both the mind and the heart. The apprehension of divine truth intellectually and the statement of it systematically give us a confession of faith. The realization of it in the heart, gives us the active Christian life in conformity with the doctrine confessed.

The mere intellectual apprehension of divine truth produces a dead orthodoxy, and a spirituality without a confessional basis produces a vapid emotionalism subject to every wind of doctrine. Lutheranism, while laying great stress upon pure doctrine, lays equal stress upon purity of the heart. While making much of the truth she confesses she also places great emphasis upon purity of life. Lutheranism rightly apprehended is synonymous with spirituality. Lutheranism receives the divine word and has the Holy Spirit speaking that word to the heart. To be a Lutheran in fact is to be spiritual, for Lutheranism knows nothing but the divine word, and that word in the heart and life illumined by the Holy Ghost. When the Apostle spoke of some as, "Ye that are spiritual," he said no more than ought to be said of the Lutheran, who knows his Church and illustrates her doctrine in his life.

Muhlenberg and his co-laborers, who planted and founded our Church in this new world, were what their names imported. They were Lutherans. They held the Lutheran faith as set forth in the confessions of the Church. They were disciples of the famous pietists, Arndt, Spener and Francke, whose devout adherence to the Lutheran faith "was equalled only by the purity of their lives and the living power of their piety." Arndt had said of the symbols of our Church, "I have always voluntarily and considerately acknowledged the unaltered Augsburg Confession, and have no intention or thought ever to receive or disseminate any other doctrine." Spener said: "The symbols of our Church have *quod autoritatem*, a great, glorious, mighty and express authority. God has graciously guarded the authors of these symbols, that they mistook not in doctrine, but set it forth, and bore witness to that teaching which conforms to the divine word." Francke professed the most hearty acceptance of the symbols of our Church, and his solemn avowal was "I desire no other religion."

Muhlenberg and his associates followed in the footsteps of these illustrious men and laid the foundations of the Church in this country deep and strong in that true spirituality, which has its source in the pure word of God as illuminated by the Holy Spirit. They were commissioned by the most pious men of Europe to come to America and minister to the scattered flocks of the Lutheran fold.

Our people who preceded them were characterized by a spirituality that was not surpassed, if equaled, by any of the early settlers in this country. The first—the Swedish colonists "were of the same blood and faith as the noble heroes who a few years before had followed their great Prince in the defence of Christian liberty through the battlefields of Europe, and who like him at last lay down in victorious peace upon the plains of Lutzen. They brought with them the Bible with its sacraments, the Church with its ministry, the Augsburg Confession and Luther's Catechism." Of the next colonists it is said Wesley learned his first lessons in spiritual religion. It was his fortune to cross the sea with them, and after observing their piety, was himself convinced of the deep spirituality of their faith, and so influenced by it that he afterwards wrote in his private journal: "I went to America to teach the Georgia Indians the nature of Christianity; but I have learned myself in the meantime (what of all I least expected) that I who went to America to convert others, was never myself converted." Their own historian says: "In these strangers (Lutheran Colonists) the English Methodists beheld Christianity in a light more gentle, attractive and consoling than that in which they had ever before seen it."

There is nothing clearer in the history of our Church than that those bearing our name, who first planted our Church in America, were Lutherans to the manor born, holding tenaciously to the symbols of our Church and exhibiting a piety which presents one of the brightest pages in the early history of our country. Our fathers here in America professed a profoundly spiritual religion, and none of the other settlers exhibited a sweeter temper, a holier faith, or an humbler or more devoted service to the cross than they. They were pious souls, truly spiritual and thoroughly Lutheran.

But in America, Lutheranism found not only a new soil, but new environments. Other faiths had preceded and their votaries had come in greater numbers. While immigrations from Lutheran lands were less numerous, they were further hindered by the prejudices and persecutions of both Cavalier and Puritan. Moreover, as time wore on, two great religious bodies began more and more to influence Protestantism in America. These branches of the Reformed Church, the Calvinists and the Arminians, emphasized strongly their distinctive tenets and exercised a powerful influence in shaping the forms of religious thought and experience. Calvinism, starting in its theological system with the sovereignty of God, has emphasized the decrees of God, His predestination of elect and non-elect, producing that puritan type of religious life which predominated so largely in England and America a hundred years ago. Hyper-Calvinism produced a stern type of Christian life, a life conditioned more by fear than love, too ready to draw the sword against its foe, not ready enough to extend a fraternal hand to those who might have been its friends. The spirituality, hence, of Calvinism, produced a type of religious experience which lacked the deeper and finer touches of that fervid faith, which has its source and existence in the love of God as manifested in the gift of His Son.

Arminianism, on the other hand, ignored the decrees of God, and sought to establish a system of religious doctrine which should magnify the free agency of man. Making much of the reaction against hyper-Calvinism, and under a masterful and enthusiastic leadership, Arminianism swept over England and America. With a polity that solidified its gathering forces, and with a form of government evidencing greater strength than any known in Protestantism, it succeeded in making one of the most aggressive and powerful organizations the Christian Church has ever had. In this country Calvinism and Arminianism contested for supremacy. Fifty years ago votaries of the Arminian system believed with all the heart that Calvinism was synonymous with fatalism, and they opposed it as vigorously as they could have opposed the tenets of Rome. Calvinists, on the other hand, were just as sincere in the conviction that Arminianism was but another form of Universalism, and they opposed its progress with corresponding vigor. In the midst of this conflict the Lutheran Church prosecuted her work in this country. She came with her pure faith and her devotional treasures, expressed in a tongue that was foreign and unwelcome. As new generations came and the old ones passed away, they thought, and spoke, and read in the language which had no literature of their own faith. The Puritan published the books, and the Arminian furnished a large part of the preaching. Germany could not provide English preachers, and the American Lutheran Church had neither schools nor colleges of efficiency or renown. The Puritan protest against Lutheran forms of worship tended to modify the Lutheran service, and the mourner's bench contested for the place of the catechetical class and Lutheran preparation for confirmation. To render the development of true spirituality still more complex in the Lutheran Church, rationalism appeared very early in many Lutheran pulpits. The influence of the older rationalism crossed the Atlantic, and with the limited synodical oversight which many congregations had, there were ministers in German pulpits who declined the use of Luther's catechism, and rejected the Augustana, because of their intensely evangelical statements of Christian doctrine. Under such conditions, and with such environment, it is little wonder that, as English churches were organized, they should be influenced in doctrine and worship by the overpowering religious forces around them. It is little wonder that, during the period of transition, when the English tongue was displacing the German, that "new measures" should have been introduced, and a recension of the Augustana attempted. It is not surprising that there were leaders who, without doubt, sincerely thought that a Lutheranism modified by Puritanism and Arminianism, would best conserve the interests of the kingdom of our Lord. That experiment could not have been more honestly tried or more ably and earnestly advocated. But it is a matter of grateful import that many of these fathers lived long enough to be convinced that the spiritual life of Lutheranism could be developed best by declining Puritan innovations and Arminian extravagances, and by accepting without reservation the Lutheran system of faith and worship. It would seem in the providence of God that the attempt at recension should be an object lesson for all time, and thus prepare the way for a compact, conservatively aggressive Church founded upon the Word of God as set forth in our matchless Augustana.

The Lutheran Church, to develop the best spirituality, must always be herself. She need not go to others for either doctrine or forms of worship. Her own system of faith and devotion is at once symmetrical and profoundly spiritual. As our reverend Father who preached the Word at the opening of this Conference said more than thirty years ago: "Taking the deepest and broadest foundation of the Christian religion, and working ever from its inner essence and spirit, there is nothing good or praiseworthy in faith or practice which does not harmonize with her, or which may not be realized as her own proper fruit. She held and taught a sovereign salvation, by grace only, before Calvin was freed from the shackles of papal superstition. She confessed and believed that Christ tasted death for every man, before Arminius was born. She approved and practiced the holding of meetings for prayer and mutual edification, before there was a Wesley or any followers of his method. She had her liturgies and forms of devotion—the models and sources of the best that have followed —when England was yet in the arms of the papacy, and the English Book of Common Prayer had not been thought of.

She had her bishops before there were any Episcopalians so called, though ever denying that diocesan Episcopacy so called is at all necessary to the integrity of the Church. In government she prescribes for the pure preaching of the Word, but leaves all questions of outward forms to be relegated as the circumstances may render most convenient or desirable. And in all things she is as many sided as the graces of the Holy Spirit or the glorious character of her Lord.

The Lutheran system is deeply spiritual throughout. In its conception of the Word of God this is pre-eminent. It makes everything rest upon Holy Scripture. The ultimate foundation of our faith rests here. Individual errors or apparent contradiction cannot unsettle that upon which Lutheranism rests. As Luthardt says, "Our faith is not mere faith in the letter of the Scripture, but, above and beyond this, in the matter of which Scripture informs us. And this matter, if we would name it by a word, is Jesus Christ. We believe in Jesus Christ, not merely on account of Scripture, for rather do we believe in Scripture on account of Jesus Christ. It is true that it is the Christ of Scripture and none other, in whom we believe. But we believe in Him on His own account."

So too is our doctrine of justification deeply spiritual. Faith is an act of the human soul, and it is the gift of the Spirit of God. It requires total contact of the soul with the Holy Ghost. It is by faith that we obtain forgiveness; for, as Luther says: What thou believest that thou hast. Not that the reason of forgiveness lies in our faith, as though it were so meritorious an act, so good a work that God must reward it; nor in our love which proceeds from faith; nor in our repentance which begets it; it is not in us, but only in God and in the atoning death of Jesus Christ. It is grace alone, and nothing else, which induces God to pronounce our pardon and to receive us as His children.

So too is our doctrine of the Sacraments profoundly scriptural. In Baptism water is the means of purification, and the act of washing the act of purification. "Baptism signifies purification from sin—not only that we are to cleanse ourselves, but that God will cleanse us. But it does not merely signify this; it gives what it signifies; it lays the foundation of Christian life. A Christian life is a life of communion with God. The obstacle to this communion is the guilt of sin. Our first, our chief want, is the forgiveness of sin. Baptism is the sacrament of the cleansing of the conscience from guilt. But it is this for the purpose of uniting us with God. The bond of our communion with God is the Holy Ghost. The Spirit of reconciliation unites Himself with the water of purification, and baptism is the covenant of a good conscience with God."

This communion with God must become a matter of consciousness. And it is for this reason that we follow baptism by confirmation—not as Luthardt says, to complete baptism, for it is completed already; not to renew it, for it is a beginning once for all; but that the baptized may express, with his own mouth that confession of faith upon which he was baptized, that his covenant with God in Baptism may be the covenant of his conscious choice and that he may receive a blessing at the very time of his moral development and his moral danger.

Confirmation is connected with the first reception of the Lord's Supper. This sacrament is indeed a holy mystery, the highest of all exercises in which the soul can engage. It is so because the Master has put the formula in His own words—this is My body, this is My blood. Hence the form of celebration in the ancient Church was for the minister to say at delivering the elements to each individual: The body of Christ, the blood of Christ, the receiver answering: Amen.

The Romish Church and the Reformed differ from the Lutheran in the sense in which the sacrament is the body and blood of Christ, the former holding that the bread and wine are miraculously changed, and the latter that the earthly element is only a sign and pledge of an inward spiritual communion of believers with Christ. Our Church refuses in any way either to magnify or minimize the words of institution, and therefore takes Christ's words as they stand and as St. Paul understood when he said: The bread is the communion of the body of Christ, the cup is the communion of the blood of Christ. The sacrament seals the promise of the gospel. It individualizes, as Dr. Jacobs says, that promise with every giving of the bread and wine to the communicant. "Thus faith," as Dr. Jacobs further says, in his 'Elements of Religion,' "has offered to it its surest support; since it is the office of faith to change the plural pronouns of the gospel into the singular number. Instead of saying God loved the world, it says with Paul: Christ loved me and gave Himself for me; and instead of our Lord, with Thomas: My Lord and my God." For, as the Apology sayeth, Christ causes the promise of the gospel to be offered, not only in general, but through the sacraments, which He attaches, as the seals of promise, he seals and thereby especially confirms the certainty of the gospel to every one believing. Hence the Lutheran doctrine of the real presence of Christ is profoundly spiritual. Christ must come into direct contact with the heart. Our conception of His glorified humanity is so clear and profound and spiritual that we believe He can and does come into the heart in His whole personality and dwell there. Indeed we hold that the whole triune God is the inseparable companion of the believer. The Father, Son and Holy Ghost are present always. In the sacraments they are not only present, but are especially operative, bringing richest blessing to the heart of the believer. Here the mystical union of the believer with Christ reaches the highest culmination. That union, says Quenstedt, "is the real and most intimate conjunction of the substance of the sacred Trinity and the God-man Christ, with the substance of believers, effected by God Himself through the Gospel, the sacraments and faith by which through a special approximation of His essence, and by a gracious operation, He is in them, just as also believers are in Him, that by a mutual and reciprocal immanence or indwelling, they may partake of His vivifying power, and all His mercies, become assured of the grace of God and eternal salvation, and preserve unity in the faith, and love, with all the members of His mystical body."

Thus will it always be that Lutheranism, founded upon the pure word of God as expressed in her symbols, is in the highest sense spiritual in doctrine and worship. She need not go outside of herself for that which is most needful for the development of her best church life. True to the Word of God and Luther's doctrine pure, she will continue to be the greatest and purest religious force in the world. And it is a matter of great moment to our Church that there is good ground for the hope, that the future Lutheran Church of America will be the most spiritual in doctrine and worship since the days of the great reformers, who gave back to the Church the doctrine of justification by faith. Lutherans in America are to-day prizing their heritage as never before. The treasures of Lutheran spiritual lore are rapidly being translated out of the original tongues, and hence the present generations of English preachers, teachers and readers are enjoying privileges and making such use of them, as will tell mightily for the future welfare not only of our Church, but for the uplifting of all the religious forces in our country. Those who have not had enthusiasm for Lutheranism have for the most part never clearly apprehended the ground of our faith. There are men who have never read Lutheran books and whose studies have been exclusively along Puritan and Arminian lines. Such men may view the growing enthusiasm among our younger men with alarm and regard the increasing conservatism in our schools and of the press indicative of return to the dead things of the past. But the return is to the living things of both past and present, to a quickened apprehension of the spirituality which underlies, permeates and possesses the Lutheran system of doctrine and worship.

Lutheranism in America promises richer trophies than our Church has ever laid upon God's altar. Confessing the truth in Jesus as set forth in our confession, and emphasizing the life of God in the soul, with an apprehension of things spiritual at once clear and profound, our Church presses on, fair as the moon, clear as the sun and terrible as an army with banners! The aggressiveness of the Church of Luther, her steadfast cleaving to the Word of God in an age of doubt, her repudiation of liberalism in theology and her rejection of dead orthodoxy on the one hand, and of vapid emotionalism on the other, place her in line with the most spiritual forces of evangelical Christianity. The closing days of the nineteenth century find her apprehension of divine truth becoming clearer and clearer, while the realization of the vital principles which are the basis of Christian life, becomes more and more profound.

DEACONESS WORK.

BY W. H. DUNBAR, D.D.

Mr. Chairman, Fathers and Brethren:

Every one will concede that the importance of this subject of Deaconess Work necessarily gives it a place in any programme of religious thought in these days. Aside from this there is a sort of historical justice in placing it on the programme of this Conference. As we gather to-day in this noble institution some of us are reminded of another Conference which was held here over two years ago, when representatives of our general Lutheranism met face to face, clasped hands and sat together in fraternal fellowship and spirit to discuss matters pertaining to the Master's work in our beloved Church. That was the first Free Conference of Lutherans. The leaven has been working out results, and we rejoice to-day in this larger gathering and claim some credit for leading the way.

Since then one after another of our Motherhouses have been received into the General Conference of Lutheran Deaconess houses in the world. May we not indulge the hope that here again the Deaconess cause may lead the way and make possible a great Pan-Lutheran Conference in the Nineteen Hundreds, in some such capacity as this representing the more than 50,000,000 Lutherans in all lands?

Frances Willard is reported to have said that "no action more freighted with hope for humanity gilds the sunset glories of the nineteenth century than the establishment of the Order of Deaconesses." This is only a striking expression of what has become the growing conviction of every one at all interested in Christian work. The deaconess movement contains latent forces for service of which we have as yet formed no conception.

At the same time there are some important problems in connection with the work that remain unsettled. We are bound to recognize the fact that this movement needs to be rightly directed and properly developed. The Church is bound to face the problems involved in this development and needs to be guided by the Spirit to the right solution.

The time limit of this paper compels me to confine myself to a single phase of the very general subject assigned. What I have to say centers in the thought which might be tersely stated: *The Ecclesiastical Female Diaconate.*

Not a little has been written upon "The Female Diaconate of the New Testament." The study has been valuable, profitable and necessary. It has taken us to the right beginning of the work and has led us to catch its true spirit. The subject, "The Ecclesiastical Female Diaconate," is not taken as in any sense over against "The New Testament Female Diaconate." One who is justly regarded as of highest and soundest authority among us declares: "The New Testament Diaconate was intended to be the beginning and foundation of an Ecclesiastical Diaconate with ever-expanding powers of adaptation to the supply of the necessities for which it was devised." What is thus said of the Diaconate can be said of the Female Diaconate. "The Ecclesiastical Female Diaconate" then as growing out of the "Female Diaconate of the New Testament."

To make it more specific perhaps, and to give it a more practical trend, I might put the subject: "*The Church and the Female Diaconate.*"

In the discussion of this subject these questions arise: What is this Ecclesiastical Female Diaconate as founded upon the Female Diaconate of the New Testament? What is the proper relation to the Church of the Female Diaconate by a legitimate interpretation of or inference from Holy Scripture? And I think in attempting to answer these questions we will be forced to face these further questions:—What is the *wise and safe* course for the development of this work? What is the relation in which it will develop its *greatest usefulness?* Especially this: What is the *legitimate and correct adaptation* of this wonderful institution and its work to our American church life?

These are questions which interest me greatly, both as a pastor, and as one having officially some small part in shaping the course of development of this work. The questions are vital and have an all-important bearing on the correct settlement of all the problems involved in this work. They are questions proper for discussion at a Free Conference like this where no one is responsible for the views of any other, and all are equally interested in reaching correct conclusions.

My own mind was first led to an earnest consideration of this question in the preparation of a paper on "Parish Work in America" for the First Conference of Lutheran Motherhouses in the United States. The very decided conviction to which I was then brought was that what was probably necessary first of all and more than anything else, in order that the deaconess work might properly and adequately meet the needs of the Church, was a clear understanding as to and an emphasizing of the right relations of that work to the Church and of the Church to it.

The position I was then led to take was that, rightly understood, the deaconess work must be organically connected with the Church. Since then more careful study has confirmed me in this conviction. And observation has led me to feel that it is the only wise and safe position at least in this country.

It is probably known that this is the attitude of the work in our own General Synod for which I stand. The hope is entertained that no one will suspect me of being influenced by prejudice in my views by this fact. We are not ready by any means to say that ours is the model institution—that we have properly or finally solved all the problems. We are seeking for light, conscious of the fact that we are making our way through a new field.

It needs scarcely be said that in taking this position we *do not reflect in the least on those Motherhouses* that do not have such organic connection with the Church. It cannot be taken so. There are institutions of deaconesses whose main end is not training for parish work, but the blessed work of providing for the care of the sick and injured, for hospital service, for the Christian training of the young. We would not say one word to reflect on such work. After all it does not go to the heart of it. It is not properly the deaconess work of the Church.

The European Position not a Guide.

In taking this position it seems we are not in line with the development of the work in Europe. Pastor Goedel informs us that " while the German Motherhouses, without exception, stand in most friendly relation to their respective churches," while "they preserve their connection with it by appointing one or more chaplains belonging to the State Church by training and ordination, by acquiring for their institutions their parochial rights, by inviting into their management representatives of the church government, by reporting regularly to their synods, and, above all, by the ministrations rendered by the sisters to the individual congregations with direct subordination to the local pastorates; and while the Church in its turn reciprocates by extending to the Motherhouse the assistance and protection of the church government, and by the sympathy of most of its ministers; on the other hand, throughout Germany, and with the single exception of the London Diocese House, throughout Europe, none of the Houses connected with the General Conference up to the present time, are incorporated into the organism of the Church."

He further states that "it is the general opinion that this independence of the Motherhouses has really been a blessing, helping to develop the free ministry of Christian charity."

This opinion will hardly weigh with us in this country in favor of the independent Motherhouse. For the conditions are altogether different.

The conditions of *Christian activity* are different. Whatever may be the situation in Germany and in Europe, in this country there can hardly be said to be a call for a development of a free ministry of Christian charity outside the Church. The fact is that already outside independent charity is absorbing the resources and energies of our churches to the very great cost of our work.

It is also to be remembered that the *church life and organization* in this country is so essentially different from that in Europe that the argument from conditions there will not apply here. We can see reasons for keeping a movement free from the domination of a State Church which would not apply in the remotest way to a Church separated from the State as ours is and must remain.

The Only Safe Position.

When we consider the conditions of Christian activity in this country we are forced to the conclusion that the *only safe position* for our deaconess work in its relation to the Church is that of organic connection.

We cannot close our eyes to the fact that no institution possesses greater possibilities of creating wheels within a wheel, of forming tremendous circles of independent influence too strong to resist or control. This must be evident to any one who has had any connection with the work, and has watched it with any degree of thoughtfulness.

Much less can we close our eyes to the dominating place which certain independent religious movements have assumed in this country. Unchurchly as some of these movements are, it is not surprising to find that they have taken most of that which is good in them from churchly institutions. The very work in which our deaconesses are engaged brings them in contact with all these varied movements. The only safety in the midst of these conditions is to keep the movement and the work in direct connection with and under direct control of the Church.

The Position to Develop its Greatest Usefulness.

We cannot help but feel that in the line of this relationship lies the result of *greatest and highest usefulness* from the movement for the world and the race. I cannot take the time to develop this thought. It is self-evident. Believing as we do that the Church of Jesus Christ is the one institution divinely established for the promulgation of the Gospel, for the regeneration of the race and the redemption of the world, we cannot help but feel that this movement shall best serve its high and holy end by being, as it were, an arm, receiving its life from the Church, moved to action by the Church, and giving its service to the Church.

The Only Right Position.

But now, aside from the questions of safety, or wisdom, or usefulness, is the question of *Rightfulness*. What is the right relation from the interpretation of, or inference from, Holy Scripture? We believe that the conclusion of a careful consideration of this question will be that the separate position is not the right one— that the only right one is that of organic connection.

I regret that time will allow me only to touch upon a few of these considerations. For the sake of brevity and conciseness I will apply them to the *Female Diaconate in general*, the Office; to the *Deaconess in the Personal* capacity; to the *Work of the Deaconess*, the Service; and finally, to the *Motherhouse*, the Institution.

I.—The Relation of the Female Diaconate to the Church.

We have in mind now the Office. What, by direct teaching, or by inference from Scripture, is the relation of the Office to the Church?

In trying to answer this question a plain principle must be had in mind. I quote from no less an authority than Rev. Dr. Henry E. Jacobs, to set forth this principle: "In the study of all New Testament passages concerning the details of Church organization, as well as concerning the spheres of doctrine and worship," there is to be "carefully observed" "the law of growth." "All revelation has followed this law, and everything pertaining to the Kingdom of God on earth pursues the same course. We might as well expect to find in the New Testament a complete system of Dogmatics and Ethics, or an elaborate Church Service, as to find a Diaconate characterized by all the features and details of organization that has been found serviceable in the experience of the Church throughout succeeding ages." It is indeed true that "everything that is contrary to, or inconsistent with, Holy Scripture must be surrendered. Everything also that can not be found to proceed from Holy Scripture by a legitimate application of its principles must be repudiated. But we can not confine our teaching to the very words of inspiration without doing a great injustice to Him who has given these words to be the germs of the Church's faith and life, that shall bring forth a harvest until the work of grace on earth is completed. We can not force ourselves back into the moulds of the life of the Church of Apostolic times."

This same principle applies to the *Female Diaconate*. No advocate of the institution would claim that all its good features are to be found in the New Testament. Indeed, the institutional diaconate cannot be said to be found there. But the germ is there—that out of which it grew.

It is also to be borne in mind that all the features of the organized Church of to-day are not to be found in the *Church of Apostolic times*. This, too, has been subject to the same law of growth. The first idea of a congregation was that of two or three believers, gathered in the name of Christ. The germ was there. Out of this came the later conception of the congregation as any number of believers, and then of the Church as an organized body to which were committed certain clearly defined duties.

So the question resolves itself into this: *What is the Female*

Diaconate, and what is its proper relation to the Church as founded upon plain inference from Scripture? To answer this we must ask: Whence did the Female Diaconate *originate?* What was its *purpose?* What its *authority?* These questions open a wide range for discussion. We can only take conclusions. And for our purpose this is all that is necessary. We will take the conclusions arrived at with so much clearness by Dr. Jacobs in his paper on "The Female Diaconate of the New Testament."

What is the *Origin of the Office?* Dr. Jacobs says: "It was a true growth from the Diaconate, as the Diaconate itself sprang from the Presbyterate or Pastoral office." It would be profitable to follow this development as it has been so interestingly traced out by Dr. Jacobs. The very fact of this origin is enough to indicate its proper relationship to the Church.

What was the *Purpose of the Office?* Dr. Jacobs finds that "with the growth of the congregation, the work of administration, which, in the beginning, had been exceedingly simple, had grown to such proportions that, if it were to be efficiently rendered, a division and further organization of labor were necessary." Out of this necessity grew the Diaconate, to which were transferred certain official duties of the congregation. "With the growth of the Church it had been found, further, that there were spheres in its administrative work where even the Diaconate could not enter until its scope were enlarged so as to admit of the work of the women." Hence came the Female Diaconate.

What was *its Authority?* Dr. Jacobs says: "The Presbyter . . . became the mouthpiece of God in so far as He was the mouthpiece of the congregation of believers to which God had given the authority to speak in His name." So naturally comes the next statement: "So the work of the Diaconate was also a purely representative work." The same follows of the Female Diaconate.

So we must come to the very natural conclusion that there can be no true diaconate, male or female, unless organically associated with the Church, in its nature gaining its power and authority from the Church, in its work subordinate to the Church, and in its results serving the Church.

And this leads us to some practical conclusions with reference to

II.—THE RELATION OF THE DEACONESSES THEMSELVES TO THE CHURCH.

This may be inferred from the relation of the Female Diaconate,—the Office. There is, however, more direct light.

There can be no doubt but that the office of the diaconate of women is mentioned in Romans 15: 1, 2. Phœbe was "a deacon of the Church." There is only one other passage in the New Testament which can fairly be said to refer to the subject in any clear or direct way, 1 Tim. 3: 11. But these are sufficient to establish the fact of the office existing, and from them may be inferred what is to be the relation to the Church of those holding the office.

"Phœbe was a deacon or *servant* of the Church." The deaconess is to be a *servant* of the Church, giving her energies and service to the Church. This idea belongs to the very spirit of the Female Diaconate.

"Phœbe was a *deacon* of the Church." That is, she held an *Office* to which she was set apart by the Church at Cenchrea. "It is not an office which she has assumed for herself, or one transmitted by external succession from other deacons; but the congregation at Cenchrea has called her, and set her apart to the work. She thus becomes, and remains even while at Rome, an officer of the Cenchrean Church." This the true deaconess must remain in her relation to the Church.

In this office the Deaconess must be regarded as *A Minister of the Church*. She is not primarily either a nurse or a teacher. In both these offices others might take her place and fill it just as well as she can. Her ministry is not a ministry of the word or sacrament, but a ministry of mercy, a ministry of the Church, for the Church and by authority of the Church.

And this suggests some thoughts as to

III.—THE RELATION OF THE DEACONESS WORK TO THE CHURCH.

This work was not in the New Testament and can not now be a mere philanthropic work. It is not to be a mere work of charity in ministering to temporal needs. Its end and aim is at once deeper and higher, viz., to save souls lost in sin for Christ. This is the end; the others are means. As the work fails in this it loses its commanding position, and the deaconess becomes no more than a professional nurse, or an ordinary parish visitor, or a mechanical agent and tract distributer. This is not her work as a minister of the Church and in her high office.

This work must have the *endorsement of the Church*. This is recognized even in the work in Germany where there is no organic connection. They are careful to secure parochial rights. In this country with our different form of free church organization this must mean a much more direct control.

Furthermore the work must be done under the *immediate direction* of the minister as the head of the congregation in which she serves. This is self-evident. Without this the work might easily become, and probably would soon become, a disorganizing factor in a congregation. The very work of a deaconess gives her a ground of vantage. Her influence in a congregation may become simply enormous. This too is recognized in the work in Germany. We are told that the services are rendered "with direct subordination to the local pastorates."

It is understood, however, that this relation *does not limit the sphere* of activity to mere congregational work. Phœbe was sent to Rome. So our Deaconesses are sent to the Foreign Mission fields. But it is to be observed that it is still the work of the Church.

We can, on the other hand, find no authority to make this high calling subserve the ends and aims of independent religious movements outside the Church. Experience has already taught us that this is a diversion of this force against which we must guard. Our Deaconesses must not be allowed to become the agents for the furtherance of this or that popular religious or moral movement in these modern times.

Just a word as to

IV.—THE RELATION OF THE MOTHERHOUSE TO THE CHURCH.

The idea of the Motherhouse must be very firmly fixed, and the Motherhouse must be regarded as the great centre of all Deaconess work. From this must emanate the general rules for the conduct of the work. To this the Deaconess must be subject. This is absolutely necessary in order that this work may become of permanent value to the Church.

But on the other hand that Motherhouse must be very closely related to the Church,—gain its headship from the Church, and be responsible to the Church. We believe that this will be the ultimate position of the Motherhouse in the proper development of the work. It is to be a training-school, not for nurses, not for skilled teachers, but with a distinct reference to spiritual and church work. It stands, therefore, in its own distinct place just in the same relation to the Church that a Theological Seminary does. An independent Deaconess Motherhouse would appear to be in an abnormal position,—just as much so as an independent Theological Seminary.

The limit of time has compelled me to present many of these thoughts in the crudest possible way. I have only been able to suggest some of the thoughts that come to us in connection with this phase of the work. Slowly and surely we are moving forward in these last days toward the settlement of some of the greatest practical problems of Christian work. In all the quickened activity in the religious world there is none so full of promise as the restoration of the Female Diaconate. If it be properly directed we confidently believe it will bring forth the richest and most abundant fruits unto a golden harvest. The Church needs it. The need is felt everywhere. The closer we can bring the movement to the Church, the more closely we can identify it with the Church, the richer the results for the Church and for the Deaconess' work.

I should have liked to have said a word upon another subject closely related to this. To my mind the time is at hand for action on the part of the Church looking to the restoration of the New Testament Male Diaconate, or rather for a careful study of the subject with a view to adapting it to the needs of our modern Church-life. The demand is pressing. No living man can do the work at present laid upon him and expected of him in a large city or country pastorate without being hopelessly inefficient in some or in all, or becoming a premature physical wreck. No man can bear the strain of being preacher, pastor, executive officer, social leader and meeting the expectation of his people to be a success in them all. We need men trained specially for parish work as our deaconesses are trained. Dr. Edward F. Williams, in his excellent book on "The Christian Life in Germany," has a most interesting chapter on the movement in this direction in that country. It is probable that nothing would serve the ends of such a conference as this better than to propose a joint commission of all Lutherans to consider the establishment of a great Training School for Deacons in this country.

We had brought before our mental vision last evening a beautiful ideal; but even as our hearts thrilled with joyful pulsations at the very thought of the great University of a common Lutheranism in this land, the shadow of present conditions, the result of past mistakes and misunderstandings, was flung over the brightness of our hopes. May it not be that in line of this movement, untrammeled by the prejudice of untoward circumstances, is the hope, not of organic union, but of united action on the broad and deep foundations of God's Word?

THE BEGINNINGS AND SOME PRINCIPLES OF THE DEACONESS MOTHERHOUSE.

REV. W. A. PASSAVANT, JR.

Kaiserswerth on the Rhine has always been a Roman Catholic town. Its old Romanesque church of the twelfth century contains in a reliquary the bones of St. Suitbertus, a native of Ireland, who first preached the Gospel in 710. On the banks of the river still stand the ruins of the palace from which the young Emperor, Henry IV, was carried off in 1062 to a vessel belonging to his wily guardian Hanno, Archbishop of Cologne. In 1600 there was but one Protestant in the town, and he, a pastor Sondermann, was in prison for preaching the Gospel, where he perished miserably by a true martyr's death.

Hither, in the latter part of the last century, the starting of a silk factory attracted a number of Protestant families. Two little congregations, a Lutheran and Reformed, struggled for existence until the Union in 1817 which blended them in one and made the united congregation part of the Established Church of Prussia. To this parish, Theodore Fliedner, a young candidate of theology, just about to seek an appointment in a high school, was chosen pastor. The salary was $135 a year and a debt of several thousand dollars rested on the property. But he joyfully accepted the proposal as a call from God, and three days before his twenty-second birthday (January 18, 1822) Fliedner entered Kaiserswerth on foot.

As his parish was very poor and in debt, he visited Holland and England to gather funds and collect a small endowment for its support. As it was small he had time to interest himself in the forlorn prisoners in the jail at Düsseldorf, six miles away. Their condition of spiritual neglect pierced his heart, and their position when discharged appealed keenly to his sympathy. The condition of the hospitals also lay heavy upon his thoughts. The attendants were incompetent, brutal, and often worse, and no regular provision was made for the sweet consolation of the Gospel at the bedside of the sick and dying. He opened a little house in his garden, 10x10 feet in size, for a woman discharged from prison who wished to lead a Christian life. Others came, a larger house was filled—but the helpers!—Ah, here the great crying want that meets every merciful agency and institution even yet, stared him in the face. There were none.

All about him open doors to rescue the fallen, care for the sick and teach neglected children, invited his entrance, but little or nothing could be done. "Did not," he says, "such abuses cry to heaven against us? Did not that terrible saying of our Lord apply to us: 'I was sick and in prison and ye visited me not?' If the Church of Apostolic days had made use of Christian women, under the title of 'Deaconesses,' and if for many centuries the Church had continued to appoint such Deaconesses, why should we longer delay the revival of such an office? The disposition to active compassion for the suffering of others, says Luther, is stronger in women than in men. It is only necessary that this inborn gift should be aroused and cherished in such women to render them suitable for the office of Deaconess, and there must be institutions erected in which they can be trained for the care of the sick, the destitute, or the criminal." "The quietness of retired Kaiserswerth would be very advantageous," he thought, "to such a training school, and God could send thither the needful money, the sick people and the nurses too."

In vain Fliedner pleaded with neighboring pastors of richer and more influential congregations to begin the work. The Lord had selected him, and when in the spring of 1836 the largest house in town was offered for sale, he bought it with not a dollar for the first payment. Soon after Gertrude Reichardt, a young woman of proven Christian character, offered to come on the 20th of October as the first probationer. But so great was Fliedner's ardor to begin, that *the first Deaconess Motherhouse in the world was opened October 13, 1836, without a deaconess.*

The ground floor was arranged for the expected patients: "One table, some chairs with half broken arms, a few worn knives, forks with only two prongs, worm-eaten bedsteads, and other similar furniture that had been given to us. In such humble guise did we begin our task, but with great joy and praise, for we knew, we felt that here the Lord had prepared a place for Himself." The hospital received its first patient October 18, 1836, and she was a Roman Catholic, an earnest of the Christ-like charity that to-day welcomes to thousands of deaconess institutions through the world the sick, distressed and outcast without distinction of creed, nationality or color.

*   *   *   *   .*   *   *   *

Ten years have passed, and a young American clergyman of twenty-five is walking the streets of London. A sudden shower drives him into the shelter of an open doorway, whence he discovers before him a stately building erected by a pious Jew to perpetuate the virtues of his deceased wife. It bore upon the memorial tablet over its chief entrance the simple .inscription : "Within the orphan shall find compassion." With deep emotion Dr. Passavant, for it was he, examined the beautiful edifice, made himself familiar with its management, and when he turned away there had been formed within him a resolution to begin a like institution in America, for Christ and the Church. It was the turning point in his life. By walking from the meeting of the Evangelical Alliance, to which he was a delegate, to his stopping place he saved a shilling. It was laid aside as the beginning of a work of mercy.

A few weeks later he reached Kaiserswerth and saw with amazement how wonderfully God had blessed the deaconess cause. The Motherhouse already numbered 108 sisters, 62 being upon 19 outside stations. The Dresden Motherhouse for Saxony had been founded and preparations were making to begin a Motherhouse in London, to which five sisters had been sent the previous year for the newly established German Hospital.

An earnest plea was entered for deaconesses for America. Rev. Passavant also left a sum of money that chosen sisters might be especially trained, and he exacted a promise that they be sent over within two years. But 1848 was the year of Louis Napoleon's *coup d'état*, and of universal political agitation and revolution throughout Germany; and though the house was rented for the expected deaconesses and stood vacant for eight months, they did not come. It was not until 1849 that Theodore Fliedner arrived in Pittsburg, assisted in the dedication of the hospital that had been opened in January, and on July 17th solemnly installed the four deaconesses he had brought with him in *this first Protestant Church Hospital in America*. The seed had been transplanted and the friends of the cause looked to see a flourishing Motherhouse after the pattern of Kaiserswerth arise on these shores. The outlook was promising. Probationers presented themselves, and on May 28, 1850, Louise Marthens was solemnly consecrated the first American deaconess. But she never wore the deaconess habit; and though the Institution of Protestant Deaconesses of Allegheny Co., Pa., was chartered in the same year, no other deaconess was consecrated under its auspices until 1891—an interval of forty-one years.

*　　*　　*　　*　　*　　*　　*　　*

Just here a question suggests itself that has been often asked:

Why was it that Dr. Passavant, though rightly denominated "the Pioneer of Deaconess work in America," so signally failed in this first attempt to establish a deaconess Motherhouse and a growing Sisterhood? A number of surface reasons can be given which would seem to indicate that the project *was premature and under the existing circumstances doomed to disappointment.*

1st. The whole subject of the wider spheres for women's activity was just beginning to be agitated. The training of women for nurses had only been attempted a few years before in London at the suggestion of Elizabeth Fry. But the training school had not been a success and a world of prejudices, religious, social, professional, hedged in those who longed to give their sympathy, service and life to the sick and suffering. Not until Florence Nightingale—and she voluntarily took her training at Kaiserswerth, amid the horrors of that winter of '54 and '55, in the military hospitals of the Crimea—broke down this Chinese wall of stupid prejudice and exhibited nursing as an art peculiarly suited to women's deft fingers and delicate intuitions and tact, was it admitted that woman could honor her sex and bless the world as a Christian nurse.

2d. It must be remembered that there were comparatively few hospitals in this country of any kind, and the Lutheran Church had neither hospital, orphanage nor asylum in which to employ deaconesses. Nor indeed had any other church save the Roman Catholic. Dr. Muhlenberg's appeal for funds for the founding of St. Luke's in New York—the first institution of the kind in the Episcopal Church, though not successful, until five years later, really grew out of the Pittsburgh hospital. Where there is no demand for workers and no field for them, few will respond.

3d. The Lutheran Church fifty years ago was exceedingly deficient in its facilities for female education. How could the deaconess cause appeal successfully therefore to its untrained and uneducated women? Says Dr. Passavant in the *Missionary* of 1852, upon this very point: "We have seven theological seminaries, four classical schools, and five colleges for the education of our young men, and two female seminaries *on paper.* It shows the wrong estimation we have put upon female character, and the slight value we attach to female education. The undeveloped talents and capacities of the female mind among us are too great for our feeble words to describe. All the elements of greatness, goodness and truth are here; but in how many instances are they yet in the quarry! There are endowments that would give the Church characters like those of Phœbe, Persis, Mrs. Fry and Miss Dix—splendid for their noble forgetfulness of self, and their sublime consecration of body and soul to the relief of human woe. Our present policy is neither scriptural nor hopeful. It is alike unjust to the female sex and to the Church of Christ."

4th. Nor were the principles or methods of the female diaconate at all understood. It is true the visit of Theodore Fliedner and the establishment of this first deaconess hospital excited wide interest. Both secular and religious papers commented upon them, and for the most part favorably. Fliedner made several addresses in America, and appeared in person before the New York Ministerium, which he addressed in the English language upon the object of the founding of the Kaiserswerth Deaconess Institution and the urgent need of the Synod's coöperation with the recently established branch at Pittsburg. Resolutions of sympathy for the deaconess cause were unanimously adopted, and the Synod resolved that "we await with deep interest the result of the effort made in its behalf at Pittsburg." Similar resolutions by the Pittsburg Synod were alike effective. *They all waited.*

In the meantime the Motherhouse was dominated by the Hospital, ever a wretched method of beginning. Its forty beds made it not a Motherhouse, but a workhouse. The exertions of the Sisters in caring for 917 patients through the first four years, during which cholera broke out in and an epidemic of small-pox devastated the city, left no time for recuperation, self-culture or spiritual refreshment. Dr. Passavant himself could give little of that personal attention to the inner life of the sisters nor the systematic training of probationers that is essential for a Motherhouse. In 1850 he projected and carried out the plan of establishing four branch missions from his church—itself still burdened with $16,000 of debt. With Prof. Reynolds he spent weeks that summer in Illinois and Wisconsin in the interests of the Norwegian and Swedish immigrants, and to save them from the unscrupulous proselyting efforts of the Episcopal Church. The German and English work of his own Synod, the establishing of the Orphans' Home in 1851, the erection of the new hospital building the same year, and the additional work on the *Missionary* left the infant deaconess community without adequate supervision, and often without a head. Disintegration could not fail to follow.

5th. But there were sinister influences at work hostile to the movement. The political world in the United States was agitated at that time by passions that religious bigotry and intolerance intensified to fever heat. The large emigration of Germans after the revolution of '48 and the incoming of many Scandinavians, together with the aggressiveness of Roman Catholicism in the decade before, created apprehensions of grave perils to American institutions in timid minds. Anti-Popish riots in Boston and Philadelphia led to bloodshed and a frenzy of hostility to everything that seemed to indicate the faintest similarity to anything connected with the Roman Church. The hatred of and agitation against foreigners reached its climax in the organization of the "Knownothing Party," and the putting forth of their candidate in the presidential election of 1854. The tide of prejudice was so strong that the deaconess "habit" was permanently laid aside, and more than once the sisters were assailed by the public press. The charge was that they were Roman Catholics in disguise and had taken vows of celibacy. These continual misunderstandings and concessions to blind and unreasoning prejudice could not but have "an injurious effect both upon the Institution and the Infirmary under its care."

After this short resume of the attempted beginnings of the Deaconess work in the United States it may be well to point out briefly a few of the principles that seem to be essential to a successful Motherhouse in this country. I do this with considerable diffidence knowing that upon these points there are perhaps differences of opinion.

I. The Deaconess Motherhouse we believe to be a product of the Holy Ghost, working in His Church through the Word, and a visible realization of the plan of the Church's Head. The Church is a community of believers in the Holy Ghost—the communion of those being sanctified. This "communion" is invisible. But through the Word—which is the voice and potency of God—individual believers are not only invisibly united to their Head, Jesus Christ, but are visibly united in the unity of doctrine, symmetry of life and beauty of worship in the external Church. Creeds and confessions, church government and machinery and the blending of music and art in divine worship are the flowers and fruits of this "seed of the kingdom." All of which, however, is conditioned and safeguarded by the Lutheran principle "that what is not against the Gospel is for it."

Now that there *has been* and *is* a constant development of the rich fruitage of the Spirit's presence and activity through the living Word in the Church, *is a fact of history and our own daily experience.* The simple creed formula of the early Church, "Believe on the Lord Jesus Christ and thou shalt be saved," has expanded into the matchless fulness of the Augsburg Confession. The simple community life of the Apostolic congregations has grown into the vast and complex machinery of our Episcopal, Consistorial and Synodical governments and the multiform activities of mission, educational and merciful boards and organizations.

If there be direct Scripture warrant for the office of the female diaconate (and that among us is settled beyond dispute), then the direct sanction of God for the communities of Levites, those servants of the Old Testament Church, His evident blessing for sixty years upon the communities of Deaconesses, these servants of the New Testament Church, their marvellous adaptability to the relief in Christ's spirit and in the name of His Church of the mass of misery and degradation existing in our enormous city populations, *and their ever strict adherence to the historic and scriptural traditions of the office as a ministry of mercy and not a ministry of the Gospel,* all warrant us in claiming for the Motherhouse a divine sanction. It is the legitimate and logical product of the Word. It need no more trace its model or parentage to the Order of the Sisters of Mercy than we need seek the origin of our theological seminaries in the College of the Propaganda at Rome.

II. It must, for its healthy life and development, be in direct connection with the Church. Theodore Fliedner soon recognized this necessary connection, and a few years after its founding, applied for parochial rights for the Motherhouse congregation. It is to-day a parish of the Prussian Church. At no time during his many and long absences did he fail to have a pastor take his place as the spiritual head, as the Augsburg Confession was the doctrinal standpoint of the community. Indeed, the Kaiserswerth General Conference, recognizing the dual character of the Motherhouse as a congregation of believers and as a Christian family of women, requires, as a *sine qua non* of admission to its membership, that the applying Motherhouse must have both a Rector and a Directing Sister. The pastor thus becomes the external bond between the Motherhouse and the Church. He is subject to its discipline. He is guided by its teachings. He reports to its Synods, and he seeks, by stimulating a deep interest within the Sisterhood for the Church's history, missions and literature, to make the connection close and living. In fact, the great object of the pastor should be to interest every sister in the progress of the kingdom of God upon earth.

This connection is further evidenced by the fact that the Church's means of grace, the Word and the Sacraments are relied upon to do all the work of unifying, controlling and sifting out the sisterhood. The inner relation in which the probationers stand to Christ, before they are admitted as Deaconesses, presupposes that they have subordinated their wills to the will of God. Now the supreme lesson of the Motherhouse training is: That the most holy is the most Christian. That it is not what she has, nor even what she does, which directly expresses the worth of a sister, but what she is. This must always be the criterion which is least deceptive: "By this shall all men know that ye are my disciples, if ye love one another."

And that Word must permeate the whole house. In the thousand worries of the work, the discouragements, temptations and disappointments, it must be her stay and refreshment. The pastor, with a deep knowledge of human nature, must apply the Word with tact and tenderness. It was to a woman that Christ once said: "The water that I shall give thee shall be in thee a well of water springing up unto eternal life." Here is the secret of the strength, and cheerfulness, and quiet peace that the true Deaconess distributes as she goes about her work in hospital, asylum, prison or parish. Ever as she goeth through the valley of Baca (weeping) she maketh it a well, and the gentle rain of God's Word filleth the poor, dusty, broken pools of many a wretched life. *Yes, the pastor is and must be the master—for he is the shepherd of the flock, the ambassador who stands for the King.*

III. The Deaconess Motherhouse should be not only in doctrine, but in spirit, Lutheran. If the reason be sought why the Motherhouse did not for years flourish outside of Lutheran countries, we find it not in the character of the Germanic nations, but in the distinctive spirit of Lutheranism as over against the Reformed type of religion. Prof. Amiel in his "Journal" thus pictures Calvinism at Geneva: "Our Church ignores the wants of the soul instead of divining and meeting them. She shows very little compassionate care for her children, very little wise consideration for the more delicate griefs, and no intuition of the deeper mysteries of tenderness, no religious suavity. Under a pretext of spirituality we are always checking legitimate aspirations. We have lost the mystical sense. And what is religion without mysticism? A rose without perfume!" On the other hand, the Lutheran Church, by the very necessities of her sacramental doctrines, has developed a churchly symbolism that is ever becoming more rich and suggestive. This she largely inherited from the Latin Church, and the treasures of her undesecrated old churches and cathedrals, the priceless gems of prayer and praise from the early and middle ages set in her beautiful liturgies, the very form of her chancels and the robes of her clergy, all mark the continuity of her history far back of the Reformation. We are not fearful then of churchliness in the Motherhouse. Our sisters wear their simple habit. They bear the plain silver cross upon their bosoms. They have no desire to borrow either from the High Church sisterhoods the veils, the girdles, the scapular or the crucifix, nor to seek their model of dress, demeanor or work from denominations that have neither the historic precedents nor scriptural foundation for their peripatetic evangelists. The Lutheran Motherhouse, reflecting the rich churchliness that ages of growth have gathered about the kingdom of Christ, can be made the House Beautiful, where not only the words *repentance* and *sanctification* are often on the lips, but adoration and consolation are part of the beauty of its holiness.

IV. The Motherhouse should adapt its training methods to the American character of the probationers. "As in a Gothic building each constituent part from the largest window down to the smallest rosette in the ornamental carving represents the spirit and form of the entire structure, so each member of the sisterhood should contain in herself the ruling principles and methodizing habits that characterize the whole body." The purpose is to have each one do her work, whether at the Motherhouse or on the most distant station not as *hers*, but as the work of her beloved Lord and Master, Jesus Christ. Now, obviously, the training of Deaconesses, as well as procuring probationers, will not be entirely alike in Germany and the United States. There there is a homogeneous population; here a medley of nationalities. There a certain type of woman exists, created by uniform environments and similar education. The standard type of American woman is not yet evolved. In Germany not only is there an innate sense of the duty of subordination to authority, fostered by the religious training in school and Church, but that recognition of the right of others to command is part of the military discipline of the nation. "The powers that be" both in the family and in the State expect and require instant obedience. Here parental authority is often unknown, and the unsettled term of office of the "powers" in Church and State, together with the insane idea that every American is born a sovereign, unsettles or destroys subordination. There the Church doctrine is accepted without question by pious souls. Here the woman is trained in a spirit of independence of human authority in matters of religious concern, and whether in destructive criticism of her pastor's last sermon or of the Mosaic record, she claims and jealously guards her inherent right to speak her mind.

In a word, the intense individuality of the American woman

has to be reckoned with in the training of the Motherhouse. She is willing to devote herself to the humblest work, to sacrifice everything, to endure hardships, but she wants to work and suffer in her own way. She is pious and conscientious, but if matters do not suit her, and things are not to her taste, it is hard for her to submit.

Perhaps I have shaded the lines a little, but the picture will be recognized. Such characters, with force, originality and resourcefulness, when made true handmaidens of the Lord, will become as irresistible a power for the Church as were our troops before Santiago for their country, of whom a foreign attache remarked, "Every one of them would make an officer." But will not the hard and fast methods of the German probe-saal only irritate and discourage such probationers? Can they be won to the work by the enforcement of petty rules and exacting customs that may have been successful in entirely different environments and with other material, but which must ever be foreign to American girls? The principles of the female diaconate must be and remain the same the world over, for they are scriptural, but their application may be modified and adapted to varying circumstances and places without destroying in the least the Motherhouse idea.

REMARKS.

Dr. SPAETH said:—In earlier days there was great antagonism to the deaconess movement, not only in the secular press, but also in the Lutheran church papers. This was especially true of the paper edited by Dr. Benj. Kurtz. It is a great cause for congratulation that the General Synod has now taken up this work. There is a difference in the conditions existing in Germany and America. In Germany home and foreign missions, for example, are supported by private individuals. Here the church organization has taken charge. There should also be a Board for deaconess work. But be careful not to forget that after all this work must be in the sphere of mercy. The work is not spiritual in the sense of saving souls by teaching, but to relieve the minister in the pastoral work. However there can be organic connection with the Church without the control of a Board, as in the case of the Philadelphia Motherhouse.

Rev. FRANK P. MANHART, pastor of the Motherhouse in Baltimore, said:—It may be well to look hurriedly at the possibilities for the development of deaconess work which the Lutheran Church in America presents. Many parts of our Church are known to be in active sympathy with deaconess work, and it may be hoped that all soon will be.

In a very general way deaconess work is classified as:—Nursing, teaching and parish.

As nurses, deaconesses may work in hospitals and in institutions of various types. They also find much to do in the way of private nursing in homes. Our Church now has in the United States 18 hospitals, and 18 homes for the aged and asylums, and 44 orphanages. Besides, some deaconess work is done in hospitals that are not strictly under church control. A moderate estimate of possible demands for nursing sisters working with other deaconesses in stations, in private nursing and in institutions of various types, would be that 2,000 nursing deaconesses could find fields of labor within our Church.

As teachers, deaconesses should be found in all of our 44 orphanages. There is also for them a great field of usefulness in schools for little children, or in the Christian kindergarten. The kindergarten is sometimes used as an un-Christian or even an anti-Christian school. The Christian kindergarten uses some kindergarten materials and methods, but dominates all with Christian truth. The child is not simply like a plant in its beginnings needing only a good environment to reach perfection. It needs regeneration. The Christian child is dedicated to Christ in baptism. This, then, is a basis for Christian nurture. The Christian kindergarten takes children from the ages of three to seven, and by rightly teaching such Bible stories, Christian hymns, prayers and Christian truths as are specially adapted to their state develops them, in their most important pedagogical period, in the nurture and admonition of the Lord. Besides, in many parishes and with other sisters in stations, many other teaching deaconesses could be found eminently useful. Certainly the possibilities are that 1,000 deaconesses might thus be employed.

As workers in parishes, deaconesses are prepared to serve as aids to the pastors in all the varied ways that it is fitting for a Christian woman, who is educated, trained and consecrated by the Church, to work. The parish work is the crown of the female diaconate. Here is her widest field. Here the most varied talent and the fullest culture and training find ample room for exercise.

Surely in individual parishes and in a completely organized system of stations, covering city, village and country parishes, our Church could well use 3,000 deaconesses.

The number of deaconesses of the Kaiserswerth type at work in the world exceeds 15,000. Exclusive of America, there are then 15,000 deaconesses working among 50,000,000 of Lutherans. In America there are a few more than 200 working among a Lutheran population of 7,000,000. As everywhere in Europe the demand for deaconesses is far beyond the supply and every Motherhouse is anxiously desiring more, six thousand seem a moderate estimate of the number of deaconesses who could be wisely used by the Lutheran Church in America, having in mind only its present numbers, life and work.

Dr. DUNBAR said:—Probably the necessity of being brief has compelled me to be so concise that in some of my statements I have failed to be as clear as I desired. This is especially true with reference to two points. In saying that the Motherhouse should be under the direct control of the Church I did not intend to reflect on the Drexel Home. We, in our own work, are too greatly indebted to this noble institution to have anything but the kindliest feeling for it and the most profound regard for its work. Again in speaking of the deaconess as a minister of the Church, I may not have made my meaning sufficiently clear, by failing to emphasize the distinction between the ministry of the word and sacraments and a ministry of mercy. I regard the deaconess as a minister of the Church, but only in her appointed office and sphere, and to perform the service of a deaconess.

Dr. V. L. CONRAD said:—Allow me to call attention to the suggestion of Dr. Dunbar on the enlargement of our deaconess work. I presume all who are here present have read the recent discourse of Dr. Da Costa, of New York, in which he arraigns Protestantism as a failure and flings into the faces of us Protestants the terrible fact, that out of 70,000,000 of our population, only 20,000,000 attend the churches, and 50,000,000 are outside and do not attend them.

Now we know that Sunday bicycles and newspapers, Sunday football and theatres, Sunday races and other demoralizing sports keep thousands and thousands out of the churches on Sunday who would otherwise attend, and human depravity in general does the rest.

Now in order to bring these 50,000,000 of outsiders into the churches, we need a reinforcement of lay gospel-workers, who are competent to impart religious instruction and are adapted for the work of seeking these outside multitudes *individually*, in their homes and elsewhere, and like deaconesses win their confidence, and with the offices of kindness and the benevolent ministrations of religion, induce them to attend the churches and thus bring them under the influence of the gospel of Christ.

We need such lay gospel-workers to supplement the work of the pastors in all our large congregations, in our cities especially, as a part of the regular working force of the Church. Without such lay workers, the irreligious masses will not be brought into the churches, their numbers will continue to increase, and the churches will continue to fall behind.

Rev. PASSAVANT said that the recent disclosures in a certain publication concerning sisterhoods in the Church of England reminded him of a story told of Dr. Krauth, when one night after the family retired they heard a great uproar and found him calling out, "There's a man in the house." Upon investigation it was learned that it was now after midnight and he was twenty-one years old. Every motherhouse should have a "man in the house." His presence as the pastor exerts a healthy evangelical influence.

F. A. KÄHLER said:—In reference to the remark that a priest of the Protestant Episcopal Church had flung at Protestantism "the fact of its failure" I would beg to suggest that we are perfectly willing to meet facts, but must respectfully insist that they shall not be taken from the devil's factory of fiction. We have even great happiness in standing by the comparison which the Lord of nations has in these last days, in solemn judgment, made between Protestant and Roman Catholic. There are countries where the Roman Catholic Church has had the inheritance of Empire and the traditions of the Church untouched by the Reformation, such as Italy, Spain, South America, Mexico, Cuba and the Philippines. Compare with them England, Germany, Scandinavia and the United States, and where has God set the seal of His approval? Arguing from "the fact that Protestantism is a failure" recalls that other priestly argument: "Say we not well, thou art a Samaritan and hast a devil?"

LUTHERAN ESTIMATE OF ORDINATION.

BY REV. J. A. W. HAAS.

Ordination is a segment of the larger doctrine of the ministry. This determines ordination and is in turn determined by it. Therefore the value of ordination has been differently estimated, according as the ministry has been conceived of, either as the transferred exercise of the general priesthood of individual believers or as a service divinely given to the whole Church with the means of grace for their administration, or as an office of divine institution not merely for the administration of the means of grace, but also for church government. The first conception has been developed in antithesis to Rome, and in it Lutherans have agreed with the Reformed. But in its baldness and lack of connection with the means of grace, it becomes essentially Reformed, makes the ministry an organ growing out of the congregation, which ill befits the divine origin of the ministry, and ought consistently allow only sacrificial service. In it the main accent is placed on the vocation, of which ordination is the attestation. Apparently it is in harmony with the Augsburg Confession (Article XIV), where the ministry is allowed no one, "except he be rightly called." But the call is there used in a wider sense to include ordination, which is used interchangeably with call by Luther and Melanchthon before 1535. (Erl. Ed. 31, 348; C. R. III, 236; XXI, 103.) The adherents of the doctrine of transference should have the ordination performed, as ordered in the 18th Article of the second Helvetic Confession, namely, by the lay-elders of the congregation, for whose Lutheran legitimacy Walther contended. This would be the attestation of the spiritual priests properly and directly, though it is nowhere the practice of the Lutheran Church and never has been. Its constant usage of ordination by the ministry alone increases the incongruity of transference with the central place of the means of grace in the Lutheran system, particularly in the doctrine of the Church, which is so closely bound up with that of the ministry.

The position diametrically opposite, which makes the congregation the object of the office, and the ministry the divine self-perpetuating office of shepherd, is in antithesis to Reformed conceptions. It ought consistently, as Vilmar, give ordination a high sacramental character. But whether it does so or not, it tends to narrow down ordination to laying on of hands, and unwittingly creates an order (ordo). It has thus become Roman, must needs emphasize a succession not merely spiritual, and is really inconsistent with the Lutheran practice of election by the Church.

The mediate position emphasizes the separateness of the office and its connection with the means of grace over against the Reformed, as well as its purely administrative character and its perpetuation by the election of the whole Church in all its members over against Rome. This accords most fully with the Smalcald Articles (Power and Primacy of the Pope, II, 66 ff.), which properly understood claim ordination as the prerogative of the whole Church. "Where there is therefore a true Church, the right to elect and ordain ministers necessarily exists." And the words of Peter, "ye are the royal priesthood," are applied thus: "These words pertain to the true Church, which since it alone has the priesthood has the right to elect and ordain ministers." Their office as divine is not injured by the democracy of an atomistic spiritual priesthood, nor by the aristocracy of a self-generating priestly order. Ordination will then be the public approval of the call by the Church, but it will also include the separation for the ministry, with invocation of blessing and consecration under divine approval. These features form a sufficient reason why ordination is not repeated, without gravitating in the least to any "character indelibilis," or leaving it actually unexplained and inconsistent, as does the theory of transference.

The scriptural basis of ordination cannot be derived from any institution or act of Christ. His breathing upon the Apostles (John 20: 22) was a special transmission of His Spirit and an actual proof of the forgiveness of sins in Him to fit the Apostles for their special foundation-work. As the ministry is no continuation of the Apostolate, so this afflation has no bearing on the rite of ordination. This is simply an Apostolic institution, and was used as well for the Seven (Acts 6: 5), as for Barnabas and Saul (Acts 13: 3), when separated for their call, and also for Timothy (1 Tim. 4: 14; 2 Tim. 1: 6). In the same manner Paul and Barnabas appointed elders upon the vote of the Church. (Acts 14: 23). Here, as in Acts 13: 3, fasting marked the importance and solemnity of the occasion. It prepared for prayer (Cf. Mark 9: 29), but was no integral part of the act. The accompanying rite was the laying on of hands with prayer. Laying on of hands was an Old Testament and general religious form to express the imposition, impartation and communication of something, e. g., sin and transgression (Ex. 29: 14; Lev. 4: 4; 16: 21; Num. 8: 12), guilt (Lev. 24: 14), thanksgiving (Lev. 3: 2), blessing (Gen. 48: 14), life (in burnt-offerings, Ex. 29: 15; Lev. 1: 4; Num. 8: 12), office (Deut. 34: 9). Christ uses it at times (Mark 6: 5; 8: 23; 10: 16; Luke 4: 40; 13: 13), but not often, nor always when requested (Mark 5: 23), perhaps because it was sometimes conceived of magically, and not as by the mothers (Matt. 19: 13) combined with prayer. Blessing, healing, life, were expected from Christ by laying on of hands. The value was that of Christ's person, and the action symbolized a real gift imparted by the word. What Christ did, God did. His power in Christ was presupposed when Christ gave the laying on of hands for healing to His disciples (Mark 16: 18). Paul thus uses it (Acts 28: 8), as did also Ananias upon special divine commission (Acts 9: 12, 17). The Apostles can also give charismata with it (Acts 8: 17; 19: 6). Thus the charisma of Timothy given by prophecy *with* (meta) laying on of hands, as the accompanying rite, is also spoken of as imparted *through* (dia) laying on of hands (1 Tim. 4: 14; 2 Tim. 1: 6). This agrees with Christ's mode, the word and symbol are together. It is this reality of the divine gift through the word which justifies the remark of the Apology: "But if ordination be applied to the ministry of the Word, we are not unwilling to call ordination a sacrament. For the ministry has God's command and glorious promise (Rom. 1: 16): 'The Gospel is the power of God unto salvation to every one that believeth.' Likewise (Is. 55: 11): 'So shall my word be that goeth forth out of my mouth; it shall not return unto me void, but it shall accomplish that which I please.' If ordination be understood in this way, neither will we refuse to call the imposition of hands a sacrament" (Art. XIII, 11). Chemnitz (Examen Decret. Conc. Trid. III, 3) approves of this, and explains that sacrament is here used in a wide sense. He is thus not in conflict with Gerhard (Loci, XII, 159), who thinks of the sacraments in the proper and limited sense, when he says of the laying on of hands, "not as though it were any sacramental symbol instituted by

Christ." Frank (Sys. der Chrl. Wahrh. II, p. 308) is in line with Chemnitz when he holds that a real blessing is given in the laying on of hands. "But not according to the manner of the proper sacraments is the impartation of the gift bound to the outward act. He, who rightly called, and belonging to the gifts which the exalted Christ promised His Church (Eph. 4: 8), extends his hands in prayer to Him, who has called him, will not remain unblessed if perchance the laying on of hands would not be given him when entering into office. Many of these acts, as this appears most clearly in absolution with laying on of hands, are only special combinations and applications of the effect, which takes place generally through the divine word, in a single significant action instituted for this purpose. From this effectiveness of such actions they can be better conceived of." This realism of a divine gift was apparently not held by Luther. From his treatise to the Christian nobility (1520) and his "Babylonian Captivity" (1520), through the tractate "Das eine chrl. Versamml. od. Gemeinde Recht u. Macht habe, alle Lehre zu urtheilen u. Lehrer zu berufen" and his "De instituendis ministris ecclesiæ," etc., sent to the senate of Prague (both 1523), to the polemic "Von der Winkelmesse u. Pfaffenweihe" (1533), and often elsewhere, he declares the right of all believers to the office because of the spiritual priesthood (Erl. Ed. 40, 170 ff.; 47: 161), and sees the consecration (Weihe) in the call. "Ordo est ministerium et vocatio ministrorum ecclesiæ." Ordination because of the prayer and the promise (Mt. 18: 19) is effective, but it is only like a notary's seal or the confirmation of marriage by a pastor. (Köstlin, Luther's Theol. 2,539). Nevertheless Luther emphasizes the divine institution and call (Erl. Ed. 31: 219; 40: 171). In part this counterbalances his combative position against the hierarchy, in which as well the ministry as ordination received a low value in the transference theory. But the truer constructive thought of Luther appears most fully in his Ordinations formular, which is the basis of most later orders. (Erl. Ed. 64: 290 ff.). It begins with the invocation to the Holy Spirit and a collect. Then the word of promise (1 Tim. 3: 1 ff.; Acts 20: 28 ff.), which is sacramental, is read, followed by a short statement of the duties of the office, ending with the question to the candidate and his reply of acceptance. Thereupon the sacrificial prayer, which seeks sacramental blessing, is recited with laying on of hands. The office is then given, and the ordinand dismissed with the benediction: Benedicat vobis Dominus, ut faciatis fructum multum." Some orders as that of Lüneburg (1598), Calenberg, Wittenberg (1565), Osnabrück, simply adopt this form. The orders of Mecklenburg, Pomerania (1563), Hoya, Hildesheim change it somewhat. The Pomeranian Agenda (1569), the Lüneburg (1643), and the Ostfrisian K. O. unfold more fully some features indicated in Luther's form, e. g., the separation for the ministry, the laying of God's Word upon him, etc. (See Kliefoth, Liturg. Abhandl. I, p. 462 ff.).

Melanchthon at first, in opposition to Rome, holds it possible to enter the ministry without ordination (C. R. III, 184). But later he accepts its necessity as a public confirmation of the call (C. R. XXVIII, 524), and, like Luther, will allow it to the episcopate if this be evangelical (C. R. V., 585, 596). But it is not to be placed with the sacraments instituted by Christ (C. R. IV., 422). In the Loci (3d stage) Melanchthon, in consonance with his position in the Apology, gives ordination a sacramental import, and says: "Christ the Priest places his hands on them (the ordinands), i. e., chooses them by the voice of the Church, blesses them and anoints them with His gifts, as it is written, He ascended, gave gifts to men, Prophets, Apostles, Pastors, Doctors, whom he adorns with the light of doctrine and other gifts." (C. R. XXI, 852) (Cf. also C. R. XXII, 52, the German translation of the Loci.)

It has often been claimed that the controversy of Frederus disproves such high estimate of ordination, but this is rather a misapplication of its result. The opposition of Frederus to ordination, seconded by Æpinus, was really brought about by his own peculiar position, in which his ordination was several times prevented by political complications. Stralsund would not have him ordained by Knipstroh, the Superintendent of Pomerania, because the Pomeranian Duke might deduce therefrom a claim of Church authority. Again when Frederus was called as Superintendent to Rügen by the Duke of Pomerania, he was not ordained because the Duke feared to so far take away the rights of the Danish Bishop of Roeskilde, Palladius. Knipstroh simply introduced or installed Frederus. Finally Frederus defended his non-ordination, and made necessity a law, even though he was ordained by Palladius (1551) after deposition from his superintendency and his professorship in Greifswald for his obstinate rejection of ordination. Knipstroh, whose position the Greifswald Synod (1556) and the Wittenberg Faculty sanctioned, rejected Frederus' restriction of ordination to laying on of hands, claimed prayer and other features as its content, and held this whole ordination to be confirmed as God's order. It was "ordinatio apostolica," "not necessary for salvation, but only for the preservation of Christian teachers and the office of the Church."

Chemnitz in his Loci (De Ecclesia), but most fully in the Examen. Decr. Conc. Trid. (III, 2) adds to public approbation as parts of ordination: (I) the admonition to devote oneself to the ministry (se destinari, addici, et quasi devoveri ad ministerium et cultum Dei); (II) the public and solemn protestation of the Church before God, that in election and call the form and rule, prescribed by the Holy Spirit, was kept; (III) the approbation of God (ut illo visibili ritu significato Deum approbare vocationem, quae fit voce ecclesiae); (IV) the offering and presenting of the candidate to God, that He may bless him and bestow upon him grace (quia persona illa, quasi offeretur Deo, ut sisteretur in conspectum ipsius, additis supplicationibus, ut Deum gratiam et benedictionem suam, illi largiri dignaretur).

Gerhard (Loci, XII, 159) uses the very order and repeats the very words of Chemnitz; and Hollaz (Examen., 1339) combines these elements into one definition.

But John Matthesius speaks most fully and beautifully in his sermons on Christ (1579, fol. 111, quoted in Kliefoth, Liturg. Abhandl. I., p. 414): "With such act and prayer of the churches the Son of God has always been present and still is, for He sends His laborers into His vineyard, and is therefore ascended into heaven, that He might give gifts, and order the churches, although He does so now mediately through the elders and appointed Superintendents. And as He has anointed His prophets and apostles visibly with the balsam of His Spirit, and invested them with glory and power from on high, thus He is always effective in this order and power of keys, in the holy ordination. For St. Paul clearly testifies, 1 Tim. 4 : 14; 2 Tim. 1 : 6, that Timothy had received the gift of the Spirit in his ordination, and asks him to give heed to it, awaken it with prayer, study, work, for God had given him (Paul) and Timothy the spirit of power, love and reproof."

It is evident, then, that ordination, which follows the election, call and examination, and is followed by installation, ought, in the Lutheran system, be not only the *attestation* and *confirmation* of the call by the whole Church, but also the *consecration* by the divine word and prayer, which consecration consists in the *separation* from other duties, and the *putting of the word of promise upon* the ordinand, to whom, in the *sight* and *presence* of God, the seal of divine *approbation, blessing,* and the *Holy Spirit* are given for the office of administering the word and the sacraments, *committed* to him by the *voice* of the Church.

LUTHERAN ESTIMATE OF ORDINATION.

BY PRES. J. R. DIMM, D.D.

According to the Augsburg Confession, Art. 7, let there be:

1. "A congregation of believers among whom the gospel is preached in purity, and the holy sacraments are administered according to the gospel."

2. Let there be the *want* of a presbyter, an elder, a bishop or a minister—for these terms are scripturally synonymous—and we have the conditions demanding the call and ordination. In the 14th article of the Confession we have the following language: "Concerning church government it is taught that no one should teach or preach publicly in the Church, or administer the sacraments without a regular call." Now it is known to the student of the Confession that the Reformers included in the terms —" regular call " (rite vocatus)—the whole process of transfer

from the common walks of life to the full exercise of the ministerial office. We are, therefore, led to ask:

I. *What Constitutes the Regular Call—rite vocatus?* This entire transfer is divided into *three* successive steps of advancement.

1. The *internal* call, which, if genuine, is immediately from God. This needs to be carefully examined and fully guarded; for it may be merely a subjective impression resulting in a preference, over other occupations, for entering the ministry. If genuine, it is the communication of God's will to the individual by the Holy Ghost. It is a deep conviction and a heartfelt sense of obligation to preach the gospel for the salvation of men. It attaches to certain individuals and continues, if not consummated, for years. It is that which Paul, after his enlightenment, felt when he said—"Woe is unto me if I preach not the Gospel."

Aside from this internal immediate call of the Holy Ghost, conscientiously felt by the individual, all the other steps in the process *may* be originated by men. Without this call in its genuine form, the candidate lacks the true spiritual animus, and his entrance will result only in producing a mercenary ministry, entering the office and rank for personal gain. There may be a modest person of excellent talent, who, receiving the internal call, smothers it up within his own bosom. Such a one may feel too timid to make it known lest he be derided by his neighbors for his pretensions. On the other hand, there may be others who are evidently lacking the necessary intellectual qualifications, but who imagine they have the inward call, and announce themselves as candidates. Hence there is a necessity for another agency in the process—(1) to encourage the timid who are divinely called, and (2) to restrain the pretentious who are self-deceived. That is—

2. *The External and Mediate Call.* Now whilst every call that is genuine is primarily from Christ, the mediate is administered by the Church, *i. e.*, the whole body of believing Christians. It consists in her recognition of the validity of the internal call, and the encouragement and support given to the candidate in his preparation for the ministry.

He is now put upon a course of trial in the process of his education under the auspices of the Church. During the years of his development he will disclose his character—of what sort it is—and prove his talents or the want of them. He is now under the supervision and observation of the whole Church, in the persons of the professors, the pastors and the laity, during a series of years. If all this proves satisfactory to the teachers, preachers and laity, the candidate receives the approval of the Church, and by rite of some synodical body he is admitted to the next step in his ministerial progress. This constitutes the external, the mediate call—the call of the Master through the Church—to enter the holy ministry. Here the united judgment of the pious laity may correct any mistake previously made. If it be doubted that the Church has the right, by divine authority, to make such call, we may answer in the affirmative and found the claim on *two scriptural considerations.*

The *first* one is, that to the Church was given the power of the keys—Potestas Clavium. It was done in the words in Matt. 16 : 19, "And I will give unto thee the keys of the Kingdom of Heaven, and whatsoever thou shalt bind on earth shall be bound in heaven, and whatsoever thou shalt loose on earth shall be loosed in heaven." Also, John 20 : 23, "Whosesoever sins ye remit, they are remitted unto them, and whosesoever sins ye retain, they are retained." Now, as there is much mystery in regard to what is meant by the power of the keys, we are glad to have a definition of the same, so far as human testimony goes, in the 28th Article of the Augsburg Confession. Here the Confessors, in speaking of the power of the clergy, say: "The power of the keys or of the bishops, according to the Gospel, is a power and commission from God to preach the Gospel, to remit and retain sins, and to attend to the administration of the sacraments; for Christ sent forth the Apostles with the command : As my Father hath sent me even so send I you ; receive ye the Holy Ghost. Whosesoever sins ye remit, they are remitted unto them ; and whosesoever sins ye retain, they are retained. This power of the keys, or of the Bishops, is to be exercised and carried into effect alone by the doctrine and preaching of the Word of God, and by the administration of the sacraments to many or few persons according to the call. For by this means are conferred not temporal, but eternal blessings and treasures, as eternal righteousness, the Holy Spirit, and eternal life. These blessings cannot be obtained otherwise than by the office of the ministry and by the administration of the holy sacraments."

In the appendix to the Smalcald Articles we find this language: "This, moreover, must be confessed, that the keys belong and were given, not to one person only, but *to the whole Church*, as it can be sufficiently proved by clear and incontestable reasons." For precisely as the promise of the Gospel pertains, without limit, to the whole Church, so the keys pertain to the whole Church, without limitation, since the keys are nothing else but the office through which the promise is imparted to every one that desires it. It is evident, then, that the *Church, in effect, has power to ordain ministers.*

Christ, in Matt. 18: 18, uses these words: "Whatsoever *ye* shall bind," and "Whatsoever *ye* shall loose," etc.

These words declare and specify to whom He gave the keys, namely, to the whole Church. The power of the keys, therefore, authorizes the entire body of believers to participate in the external and mediate call.

The *Second* Scriptural basis upon which the whole Church takes part in the call is the accepted doctrine of the universal priesthood of believers, 1 Pet. 2: 9. Also, 1 Pet, 2: 5, "Ye also, as lively stones, are built up a spiritual house, a *holy priesthood to offer up spiritual sacrifices,* acceptable unto God by Jesus Christ."

Luther, in his exposition of the 110th Psalm, says: "If we have become Christians . . . then we have also received the right and the power to teach and confess the *word* that He gives us before all, every one according to his calling and place. For although we do not occupy a public office and calling, yet every believer may and should teach, exhort, comfort and rebuke his neighbor through the Word of God, whenever and wherever that may be needed."

Now this personal privilege and duty is not to be exercised publicly by every one; but by uniting their franchise in certain individuals selected for the public service. This makes it not only the privilege, but the duty of every church member to take part, by his vote, in the call of those who are to be set apart for the public preaching of the Word and the administration of the sacraments. This is productive of law and order. All believers thus unite in the priestly functions through their representative, and officiating pastor who fills the ministerial office by delegated authority. The whole Church thus preaches the word to Christians and a sinful world through the agency of these representatives whom they have chosen, under the guidance of the Holy Ghost, out of the ranks of believers by the mediate call. But with Gerhardt we may say: The mediate call, no less than the internal and immediate, may be considered divine: For 1. It is referred to God as its author: Jer. 3: 15; 23: 4; 1 Cor. 12: 28; Eph. 4: 11. 2. It is based upon the authority of the Apostles: 1 Tim. 4: 14; 2 Tim. 1: 6; 2: 2; Acts 20: 28. 3. The mediate call is attended with precious promises: 2 Cor. 3: 6; Eph. 4: 12.

The third step of advancement is—ORDINATION.

Ordination is defined as the sign and seal of a man's divine call to the ministry. It is not the call itself. It is the ratification of the same. It does not confer the essential qualifications nor the divine authority of the ministerial office. *That* comes down from God through the internal immediate call, and through the external mediate call, made through the Church. The latter is in recognition of adequate, mental, moral and spiritual gifts in the candidate proposed.

Then comes ordination to consummate and complete the "rite vocatus." What, then, is included in ordination?

1. An *examination* of the candidate. The subjects upon which examination is had are determined by the various Synods who hold the door of entrance to the ministry. They vary but little in the different bodies. The principle involved is the same in all, that is, to guard the entry into the sacred office against unqualified persons and to protect the Church against imposition.

2. This examination is executed by properly authorized and thoroughly qualified men. It is the privilege of the whole

Church to examine the candidate. But as this is inconvenient, if not entirely impossible, the duty is performed by representatives who are chosen by the membership for their qualifications and fitness. These examiners must themselves be ordained presbyters, elders or ministers, whose immediate appointment is made by the Synod.

3. *A report is made to the Ministerium.* This report must be made so that the Church through its ministers may intelligently and finally decide that the candidate is worthy and well qualified to perform the solemn and responsible work of the sacred office.

4. *Consecration by the Laying on of Hands.* Gerhardt (12 b. 145) says that "Ordination is a public and solemn declaration or attestation through which the ministry of the Church is committed to a suitable person, called thereto by the Church to which he is consecrated by prayer and the laying on of hands, rendered more certain of his lawful call, and publicly, in the sight of the entire Church, solemnly and seriously admonished concerning his duty." Appropriately is the laying on of hands retained and the anointing rejected. For although the $\chi \varepsilon \iota \rho o \theta \varepsilon \sigma \iota \alpha$ is not a sacramental symbol appointed by Christ Himself and commanded to be employed in this rite, yet it is retained—*first,* because it comes down to us sanctioned by the practice of the Apostles (Acts 6: 6; 1 Tim. 4: 14; 2 Tim. 1: 6), and *second,* because it carries with it most useful and solemn admonitions. "Ordination is nothing else but *the public and solemn confirmation of a legitimate call,* that all may know that this person has not taken violent possession of ecclesiastical office nor crept in otherwise, after the manner of thieves and robbers, but has entered by the true door. . . . . Ordination is not indispensably and absolutely necessary, ... for it is *neither divinely commanded,* so that it cannot be omitted, nor *is its influence so great,* as is pretended by the papacy, so that it cannot be omitted without great danger; nor *does the efficacy of the office depend upon ordination,* as though the gospel could not be savingly taught without it; but it is an apostolic and ecclesiastical custom which recommends the servant of the word and admonishes him of certain most sacred duties." (Baldwin.)

Thus we have shown that the divine call to the ministry—

1. Originates from Christ Himself the author and head of the Christian Church.
2. The call is, *first*, internal and immediate—known only to the person himself.
3. Its validity is tested by the judgment of the Church, and this, when the call is approved, constitutes the *mediate* call.
4. *Ordination* is the consummation and ratification of the entire divine call to the holy ministry.
5. The laying on of hands, according to Apostolic custom, is performed by the whole Church through the Presbyters or Pastors by delegated authority.

II. *What is the essential import of Ordination?* It conveys nothing *ex opere operato*. Though numbered among the seven, by the Romish Church, it is not a sacrament, because not established by direct divine command.

When united with self-consecration, on the part of the candidate, and entire devotion to the service of God in the sacred office, it conveys special and peculiar blessings. Among these is the gift of the Holy Ghost, not in the degree bestowed upon the Apostles, yet in a degree above that in confirmation. So that we may affirm that the gifts of the Holy Ghost, necessary for the discharge of the sacred duties of the ministry, are conferred and increased. Nor is it affirmed that the bestowal and the gifts are to be "ascribed to the laying on of hands as a sacramental symbol, truly so called and divinely appointed; but to the prayers of the Church and the Presbytery to which the promise of hearing have been made." (Ghr.). Ordination carries with it the office and authority:

1. To teach.
2. To preach publicly.
3. To administer the sacraments—Baptism and the Lord's Supper.
4. The function of remitting sins.
5. The function of retaining sins.

These last two may require explanation. They are contained in the commission to preach the Gospel to every creature. (John

20: 21; Mark 16: 15). They are not unmeaning declarations, but real powers. "They are put into execution only by teaching, preaching the Gospel and administering the sacraments; and that whether to many or to single individuals."

The power is delegated, and therefore entirely depends on Christ. It must be exercised only in His name. No mistake can possibly be made. "No absolution is ever announced that does not depend on a confession; and as absolution always, either silently or expressly, presupposes a condition of contrition and confession, that which is declared by the voice of the minister to the contrite believer is confirmed by a merciful God as certainly as if Christ Himself were to say to the penitent, 'Thy sins are forgiven thee.'" (Baur).

The special gifts which are conferred by laying on of hands, may further be defined. In 1 Tim. 4: 14, Paul says: "Neglect not the gift (χάρισμα) that is in thee, which was given thee by prophecy, with the laying on of the hands of the Presbytery." Olshausen says that "the χάρισμα denotes the gift of the *divine Spirit* which qualifies him for the Gospel—for the work of an evangelist (2 Tim. 4: 5), and of which he had to make use at present in the service of a particular church." On the two words "in thee" (ἐν σοί) we have an explanation in 2 Tim. 1: 6: "I put thee in remembrance that thou stir up the gift of God which is in thee by the putting on of my hands." Here the gift is represented as a spark of the spirit lying within him, the kindling of which depends on the will of him on whom the gift is bestowed. The connection of the bestowal of the gift with the laying on of hands, depends upon the meaning attached to the preposition—μέτα—in the Greek text. Liddell and Scott in their lexicon say that before the genitive μέτα means "in connection with" and "by means of." So reading it, whatever is meant by "the gift of God" in 2 Tim. 1: 6, was bestowed "in connection with," and by means of "the laying on of hands by the Apostle Paul."

Now as to the laying on of hands in general. We have examples of two kinds:

1. That to set apart individuals for some *particular* work.

In Acts 13 : 3, hands were laid on Paul and Barnabas by the prophets and teachers at Antioch, in order to separate them for the work to which they were called. "So, they being sent forth by the Holy Ghost," departed on a long and successful mission.

In Acts 6 : 6, hands were laid in prayer by the Apostles on the newly-elected deacons, in order to impart to them the gift of the Spirit for their ministry. In every case it is an appropriation of the gift of the Spirit in prayer, through the instrumentality of others, for a definite object, for a *work* which is undertaken, or a service which is entered upon, whether this service be marked out in a standing office or a limited mission.

2. That to set apart common Christians to a spiritual life in God's service. Such was the case in Acts 8 : 17–19 : 28. Here were converts to Christianity upon whom the Apostles laid their hands, and they received the Holy Ghost. It was for no special calling or definite sphere of duty, but for the general calling of the Christian spontaneously to serve God and to testify the new life of the Spirit.

Therefore Ordination, with the laying on of hands and prayer, accompanied by self-consecration on the part of the candidate, confers the gift of the Holy Ghost in proportion to the degree of submission and devotion, and in degree adequate to the discharge of the divine commission.

The question, whether ordination performed by a heretic is valid, has been answered in the affirmative. The decision has been based on the words of the Saviour, Matt. 23 : 2, 3 : "The Scribes and Pharisees sit in Moses' seat ; all, therefore, whatsoever they bid you observe, that observe and do. But do not ye after their works."

III. What is the status of him who has been ordained to the ministry, but receives no call to take charge of a pastorate ? We would answer, though the ministry is not an order, but an office, the ordained remains a minister. He may not for years receive a call. Yet while he enters into no business permanently, but awaits an invitation, and stands ready to serve when opportunity offers, his ministerial standing is maintained, and that for an indefinite time. Otherwise we must conclude that the call of a congregation makes and unmakes the minister, and not the call of the whole Church completed by ordination.

IV. The Lutheran estimate of ordination includes also the question, What is the status of him who, having been ordained, and having served for years as regular pastor, yet, by want of a call, or by disability, has been permanently retired, possibly much to his regret? In *our opinion* his ministerial standing is maintained to the end of life, unless he voluntarily propose, for the sake of entering business, to lay it aside. In that case he may so do by asking the Synod that ordained him to take back his ordination papers, and relieve him of the responsibility. This relegates him to the rank of an ordinary communing member of the Church and of that congregation to which he belonged before his ordination.

REMARKS.

Dr. WOLF maintained that the individual congregation and not the Synod or Ministerium had the exclusive right of calling a man and thereby making him a minister. He did not believe in a special grace or charism being conveyed by the laying on of clerical hands. The Church of Würtemberg did not practice ordination before A. D. 1855. As that country had great and effective preachers, some of them having a world-wide fame, it was never realized that their ministrations were in any way defective for want of ordination.

He challenged the right of any body of men to ordain a candidate until he presented a call from some congregation, or, it may be, a mission board. And the churches sometimes assert their sovereign right as over against a self-perpetuating ministerium. The latter may place their label on a man and say he is a preacher, but the people say, We do not want him, and his ordination goes for nothing. He knew of preachers ordained without a call, and they never received a call. By what right are such men called preachers, ministers? They preach not, they minister not—why do they bear the name?

He also claimed that when a man ceased official ministrations he practically ceased to be a minister. It was anomalous and disorderly for such men to claim the right of voting at Synods, as though their ordination gave them an inalienable right to shape the Church's legislation and a perpetual share in her government. In a number of

Synods those who have retired from the active ministry nullify the votes and defeat the views of men who are braving the heat and burden of the day. For this there is no warrant in Lutheran polity or in the Scriptures. It is the idea of a hierarchy, a clerical aristocracy, which is a remnant of the pretensions of the Romish clergy. Lutheran theology recognizes no distinction between a layman and a so-called clergyman, unless the latter fills the office of preaching the Gospel and administering the sacraments.

Dr. Seiss said there was danger of being led into extremes on this subject, both on the side of hierarchism and on the side of irresponsible individualism, one being about as unscriptural and faulty as the other. To the sentiments voiced by his friend, Dr. Wolf, he could not subscribe. He did not believe that a little company of laymen, of their own movement organized into a congregation, and without a pastor, is the true and only source of a rightful call to the ministry, or that with them rests the inherent and exclusive divine prerogative to make and unmake a minister of Christ. Where there is no other help or recourse, no one disputes their right and duty to appoint one of their number to exercise the ministry for them; but that is a wholly abnormal case. It is also a blessed thing that Christ has promised to be wherever two or three are gathered together in His name; but that does not signify that He has authorized them to create and ordain a ministry in the face of the Church around them. The promise holds the same, although the two or three may be women; but where has Christ made it the right and duty of women to ordain ministers for His church?

A proper call to the ministry is necessary to the rightful exercise of its functions; but I challenge the doctrine that that call must be by some individual local congregation, and that this must needs precede ordination. Individual congregations may say whom they will accept as their pastors, and their voice and choice in the matter are not to be suppressed; but that does not mean that the right of ordaining ministers rests with them, apart from those already in the office. Christ ordained the twelve Apostles, not in the name of subsequent congregations, but in His own name. There is no instance in the Scriptures of any called and acknowledged minister of the Church who did not have commission, authority and ordination from those already ordained. A congregation is not in normal condition without a pastor, and a congregation out of normal condition cannot rightfully represent the Church, and so is not in condition itself to exercise all the rights and prerogatives of the Church, especially that of constituting and ordaining a ministry for the Church. Our doctrine is, that it is the right and power of the Church to appoint and ordain ministers for the Church; but no individual part has this power to exercise it separately, except by the common consent of those with whom it stands connected. The Synod, made up of ministerial and lay representatives of the churches, surely has in it all the rights and prerogatives of the Church at large, and certainly to a less questionable extent than a pastorless individual parish. And whatever part the Apostles allowed in the selection and recommendation of public servants of the Church, they were always strict in reserving to themselves, or to those already in office, the right to confirm or ordain those to be entrusted with sacred functions; while Paul gives it as a sad day for the Church when the people, after their own lusts, heap to themselves teachers, having itching ears.

Luther was as radically anti-hierarchical as any one could well be; yet he was particular to insist that, where things are normal, the pastors or bishops already in office shall participate in the induction of every new candidate into the ministry. Our theologians have always held that to the ministers belong the examination, ordination and inauguration of ministers. All the theoretical talk of the divine rights of individual congregations to call and constitute pastors, has everywhere been set aside in Lutheran practice. It is an ultra-congregationalism which must needs breed disorder in practical working, which never has been accepted by our Church, here or in Germany, and against which I enter my solemn protest. Our system is Synodical, and congregations united in Synod are certainly as divinely competent to call, approve or ordain ministers for the Church as any one of them in separate isolation; for what one church alone can do, surely many pastors and congregations together can.

Dr. G. W. Enders said: "Mr. Chairman—I should like to inquire which was first, the *congregation* or the ministry? Did the *congregation* first exist and then call and ordain the *minister*, or did the minister first preach the Gospel and gather and organize the congregation? Our Lord called, qualified, authorized and ordained his disciples as ministers to preach the Gospel and administer the Sacraments, and so create and organize the Church. How could the church or congregation call and ordain the ministry when there was no church? The church in her entirety calls and ordains men properly qualified for the office of the ministry, and the local or territorial church or congregation calls such as are properly authorized and ordained to local service in the bounds of such congregation. If every congregation of a handful of Christian people had the power to ordain whomsoever they deemed fit to be their minister—and also the right to *dismiss* him and so *disordain* him at their pleasure—where would this theory lead and where end? In utter disorder and confusion. To the Church as a body belongs this authority. If only individual congregations have the right to ordain, then had India still to wait for Father Heyer—and Muhlenberg in Africa were still a heathen desert. But Father Heyer was ordained and sent to India, and there he created a church. Rev. Morris Officer was called and ordained and sent to Africa, and there he organized a church. So our Mission Boards now send properly qualified and ordained ministers into Home Mission fields to gather and organize congregations, and these congregations, when so properly organized, may call a minister into their service. No congregation in Egypt called and ordained Moses. Jonah was not ordained by the Church of Nineveh. Paul was not called and ordained by the Church in Rome," etc., etc.

Dr. Horn said: There are two principles which have ruled in the Church from early time which will relate to this question, and will help to decide what is meant by *the congregation*, when we say that the congregation has a right to ordain. One is, that the congregation at any particular place never was to choose and ordain its pastor without the assent and coöperation of other churches. As early as the Nicene Council it was the rule that no bishop should be ordained without the coöperation of three neighboring bishops. The people whose pastor he was to be gave their consent, but the choice was usually under the presidency of a neighboring bishop, the representative of another "local church." No "local church" was to act in entire disregard of the whole church. Again, as early as Leo the Great it was forbidden to ordain a man *sine titulo, i. e.,* "at large"; a bishop could be ordained only to a particular pastorate. The impression had been made on him by Dr. Dimm's paper, that the effect of Ordination was made to depend in too great a degree on the subjective spiritual condition of the candidate. The Holy Ghost was poured out on Christ, the Head of the Church. If a man is called by God through the Church to any office in it, in virtue of the call (which any ceremony can only bear witness to), the charism that answers to that call, which is needed for the fulfilment of that office, is given, to be accepted and used, or to be rejected, just like the grace offered in the Word and the Sacraments.

Rev. Haas said: The central point is the doctrine of the ministry. I cannot accept the theory of Hoefling and Walther, nor can I go as far as Kleifoth and Loehe. I would rather in general side with Philippi. The ministry is given to the Church with the means of grace. The Church fills it, but does not create it. The Augsburg Confession (Art. V) connects the ministry with the Word and Sacraments. Christ brought the ministry and gave special foundation work to the Apostles, for which He gave them His Spirit (John 20: 22). The apostolate was not continued. It ceased. But the ministry was continued in another form. The Apostles and their helpers appointed elders, i. e., ministers upon the vote of the Church (Acts 14: 23; Tit. 1: 5).

Dr. Dimm said: The objections of Dr. Wolf were fully answered by the very able reply made by Dr. Seiss. Dr. Wolf's thought of conflict, between the introduction and closing paragraphs of the paper, was caused by a misapprehension of our use of the words. In the introduction we use the words "congregation of believers" in the sense of the whole Church in general, borrowing them from the symbols. In the latter part of the paper we use the word "congregation" in the sense of a local subordinate organization of Christian worshippers, in number from "two or three" upwards.

Now, if we admit that these few people, according to opinion expressed here, are a congregation that have a right to select a man as their bishop or pastor, either of their own number or of others, and thus make him a minister, the Synods that represent the whole Church will be bound, whatever his natural and acquired qualifications may be, or the want of them, to ordain, consecrate and set apart such man to the holy office. This view is defective in theory, contrary to good judgment and the teaching of experience, and impossible of successful execution in practice.

STANDARD OF MINISTERIAL EDUCATION.

BY W. E. PARSON, D.D.

This subject is directly related to every phase of the life and work of the Church. Whatever the Church counts vital must be advocated and promoted by her preachers. The foreign field and the home, the various doctrinal, liturgical, educational and missionary interests, concerning which we are met to confer, the founding of schools, the endowment of college and seminary, the defence of the larger cause of Christianity in its contentions with error, must rest chiefly with the ministry. Any inadequate or cheap methods of bringing men into this office; any lowering of the standards of requirement must soon react disastrously upon the Church herself. We assume, therefore, that this topic is inferior to no other in its bearing upon the varied interests of the Church.

And by the Church we mean, in general, that body as defined in the seventh article of the Augsburg Confession, in terms the broadest and most liberal to be found in any creed-statement of Christendom, viz.: "The congregation of saints in which the gospel is rightly taught, and the sacraments rightly administered."

In particular, we mean now by the Church that body in whose interests we are assembled; for the furtherance of whose doctrines we are all fellow-laborers; and for the union of all whose forces in one grand forward movement for Christ and for the only saving truth of the gospel, we all must most devoutly wish and pray.

In taking up this subject for discussion we are oppressed by the embarrassment which is created by the difference between the ideal minister and the actual result as turned out by the schools or admitted by the Synods.

Bishop Potter, of the Protestant Episcopal Church, has recently said (speaking, of course, for his own clergy), that he had listened to many extemporaneous sermons that were "*vulgar and ungrammatical.*"

One of the leading dailies of this city (Philadelphia *Press*, December 13, 1898), on the question whether there has been a decadence in church interest, speaks of "those installed into the ministry who are not sufficiently educated in theology to hold sway over congregations."

Because the standards have been set low we are open to such criticism in all the churches. Yet we bless God that a rusty wire does not break the communication, that the word passes on even out of an unworthy mouth. The Scripture ideal is so high, the work so exalted, the end so holy that instinctively we shrink back to ask: Who is sufficient for these things? There is no other comfort can come to one who feels his inefficiency, but that which Paul took to himself in thinking that the treasure was in an earthen vessel that the excellency of the power might be of God and not of us. The entire time allotted to this paper might be used in setting forth the strong characteristics with which the Bible invests the man of God who is thoroughly furnished. "He shall purify the sons of Levi" was the Old Testament declaration. Christ, the ideal beyond all human attainment, was seen in prophetic vision by Isaiah, who declared, " Righteousness shall be the girdle of his loins, and faithfulness the girdle of his reins." Paul shows us the ideal minister; *negatively*, "not as one that beateth the air;" "not a novice;" "not as many which corrupt the word of God;" "not given to wine, no striker, not greedy of filthy lucre, not a brawler, not covetous;" "and the servant of the Lord must not strive;" but, *positively*, "be gentle unto all men, apt to teach, patient; in meekness instructing those that oppose themselves;" "ambassadors for Christ;" "stewards of the mysteries of God;" "faithful and able to teach others also;" "he must have a good report of them which are without;" "an example of the believers, in word, in conversation, in charity, in spirit, in faith, in purity;" "a pattern of good works; in doctrine showing uncorruptness, gravity, sincerity; sound speech, that cannot be condemned;" "that he may be able by sound doctrine, both to exhort and to convince the gainsayers;" "being ensamples to the flock, that when the chief Shepherd shall appear, he shall receive a crown of glory that fadeth not away."

Such a picture of the ideal preacher is both encouragement and discouragement. It is high, we can not attain unto it. Our gifts are few, our abilities straitened, and we cry with Moses— "Who am I, that I should go? I am not eloquent."

The restriction imposed by a limit of time allows only this passing reference to the standards which might be erected through application of these Bible principles.

It is said that Origen once in Jerusalem was urged by the pastor to preach, and that he simply read from the fiftieth psalm:

"What hast *thou* to do to declare my statutes, or that *thou* shouldest take my covenant in thy mouth?" Then sitting down he burst into tears, and all the congregation with him. That feeling must often overcome the faithful minister.

As I understand the subject, "Standard of Ministerial Education," we are to look at it rather from the academic side. The topic belongs to the educational interests set forth in the call for this Conference. We might change the form of the subject, expressing it interrogatively—What Educational Standards guide in determining the fitness of candidates for the holy office of the ministry? We assume that the spiritual qualifications are met. The question of zeal is settled. We are only concerned now about the knowledge, so as to avoid the possibility of supplying the Church with a class of teachers who "have a zeal of God, but not according to knowledge." Their race increases rapidly enough, with all the caution we can exercise. Surely we need make no provision for adding to their number, either by abbreviating the required course of study, or, which is the same thing, by lowering the standard of educational requirement.

We must recognize at once the practical difficulties in the way, making it almost impossible to enforce a uniform standard, arbitrary and absolute. Rules, when too rigid, become inoperative. There must be some flexibility. The various fields of usefulness in the Church will allow that there should be a varying product by the modification of our standard, when we have once agreed upon it. As you do not cut a granite rock with a razor, you may find a place of eminent usefulness for one whom the schools were not able to sharpen. The law of survival of the fittest must work, as it does in the other walks of life. In the legal, medical, and scientific professions, the standards are set, with examinations and conditions hedging off the entrance. There must always be a working out of the problem of individual fitness and success, by use, by application of theories learned in the schools, by experience, by mistake often, by contact with men.

Some of these principles apply here, in so far as the ministry is a profession or calling with a human side to it. We can only hedge the human side, and set up our standards to be applied so far as fallible men can successfully or reverently set limits to the methods by which the ministerial office is perpetuated. We must recognize, also, that there are certain qualifications which cannot, in the nature of things, be developed until the work of the ministry has actually been begun. The qualities that make leadership, sympathy, and the tact which knows how to deal with human nature, upon the possession of which so much depends, must come to their ripest usefulness in the progress of time. These things cannot, therefore, be made factors in the requirements set down in advance. Indeed, if we look at these elements, we shall find that they all belong to a class of *desiderata* which the schools cannot supply. Pastoral theology may tell how to proceed in a given case, but the *manner* cannot be taught in the lecture-hall. Homiletic may lay down the rules for the making of a sermon, but the true preacher is in a sense superior to homiletical rules. For sermonizers, like poets, are born, not made.

Assuming now that the standards we are to discuss are educational, chiefly, we come upon two main questions for our consideration:

First. What are these requirements without which the candidate should not be received?

Second. How shall the standards be applied, or by whom be enforced?

In answering the first question, in order to reach a determination as to the required grade of educational equipment, we can dismiss all consideration of the moral and spiritual fitness of the candidate. These are factors unconnected with the educational, and can be determined separate and apart, even in advance of the entrance upon an academic course—certainly before the theological course of study is concluded.

Supervision of the educational preparation must run back over the years of student life, else no standard could fairly be applied. We must give notice that we expect such a grade of attainment in certain specified branches, in which examinations will be conducted. It is too late to announce your standard when the candidate is under examination. The work has been done. Can your candidate meet the test now to be applied? It is too late to ask how you will plan your house when the builder is about to hand you the keys. You are to move in on the morrow, and *as it is*, you must occupy it.

Let me indicate some of the most important elements in the educational requirement in order to meet the standard of an ideal minister of the Gospel. The standard ought to be set so as to require a thorough knowledge of the language in which the candidate proposes to preach. Yet it is a lamentable truth that our colleges and seminaries graduate men who are very deficient in the fundamentals of education. How to correct these defects that run so far back into the course of *preparatory* training is one of the chief difficulties in the way of enforcing an absolute standard.

Several of our district Synods in the General Synod have wrestled with this problem, and are now making the experiment of dismissing from their funds all the candidates who fall below an average standing in their studies of 85 per cent. There are difficulties in the way of an enforcement of such a rule. One difficulty is found in the fact that a student, though dropped from the Synod's funds, when falling under the required percentage, may not have reached the low grade which would cause him to be dropped from his class by the college authorities. We may then have the anomalous condition of things, that a student, dismissed from the list of the Synod's candidates for the ministry, is going on with his work in the college, having an honorable standing and a notation in studies that will advance him to the next class in the next year. Or, we may confront this other embarrassment, that students thus blacklisted might leave the institution and Synod in which they have been so dealt with, going to another college having no such rule.

One of the General Synod institutions has now a number of students who have come into her classes under just such circumstances, having been crowded out of another institution in the same general body by the application of such a notation standard. All these things are elementary. Yet we are convinced that a large number of our divinity students would be likely to fail here rather than in History, Dogmatic or Homiletic. Indeed, we might fairly assume that the usual curriculum of the theological seminary would be required in the making of any standard. Hence we indicate a few things outside the usual course.

The candidate for ministerial orders ought to know the Bible both in his own tongue and in the original language of the Scriptures. He can not know his English or German Bible properly unless he is prepared to receive the benefit of the Hebrew and Greek research which *others* have made, if he does not himself enter upon such research. Misquotation of the Scripture is almost a sin against the Holy Spirit. Any candidate who cannot quote his English Bible correctly should be reckoned as falling below the required standard. He ought to know his own creed. He ought to know it well enough to be a walking rebuke to the superficial criticism of our time against creeds. He ought to stand in his place to declare that a creed is as necessary, in its way, as the Scripture itself. For a man might announce his acceptance of the Bible, yet we could not know whether he were orthodox or heretic. But if he will show us his creed we can identify him. A man without a creed is a river without banks—in other words, a swamp.

We, who hold the first creed of Protestantism, both in the order of time and of merit, can say this with an emphasis which will hardly be found among the adherents of any other form of Christian faith.

While other creed-bonds are loosening, in the skepticism of the times, our own devotion to the Augustana grows with the growth of the years, and the new century will likely see the Church of the Reformation outstripping in numbers and influence every other organization in Protestantism.

In illustration of the loosened hold which others have upon their own creeds, let me cite a recent example. Dr. Gordon, of the New Old South Church, Boston, in an address delivered at the Jubilee Anniversary of Plymouth Church, Brooklyn, said, that Calvinism, as an adequate interpretation of the ways of God with men, or even as a working philosophy of life, was gone. Her followers, he declared, are waiting for another theology to fill the vacant throne, and are lamenting that no contrasted conception of equal thoroughness and vigor has yet come.

Doctor Gordon's entire address, when closely scrutinized, becomes exceedingly instructive. It shows us the unsatisfying nature of any system of doctrine which fails to make Christ its centre. As his address declares—"the righteousness of God must come to sovereign expression in the incarnation." Does he not know other creeds? Can he not see in our own earlier, Christo-centric statement of Protestant doctrine a "contrasted conception" of even *greater* thoroughness and vigor than Calvinism ever showed; finding, as Calvinism did not, a sovereign expression of the righteousness of God in the incarnation?

Whatever standards we establish for entrance upon the duties of pastor and preacher in our Church, we can never omit insistance upon a knowledge and full acceptance of our standards of doctrine.

How shall they hear without a preacher, who knows the history and doctrine of the Church he serves?

Take another instance from the ranks of our own ministry in illustration of the need of this knowledge of his own creed.

One of our doctors, who essays to instruct others, has frequently declared in public print, where it may have done some mischief that it is not fundamentally laid down in the Augsburg Confession that salvation has its source in the paternal love of God; and has urged that it might be well to revise our creed, at least to that extent.

Our Calvinistic brethren when, some years since, they were debating the revision of the Westminster Confession of Faith, seriously proposed to add such an article to their creed—the form of which was actually submitted by the late Doctor Schaff—affirming the divine goodness, and declaring that redemption took its roots in the love of God. That was all right for Calvinism, to balance up against its harsher declarations respecting election, reprobation and infant damnation. But the Augsburg Confession has no such gaps, and we do not want to be mortified by seeing one of our ministers, who comes so near to the required standards on other lines, sending it out to the world that there is nothing in our creed teaching that redemption is based upon the paternal love of God. How could such a glaring error be made when the very first article of the Augsburg Confession declares our faith in the *infinite goodness of God*; the third article speaks of our consolation, defence and protection against the devil and the power of sin; the fourth article teaches that we obtain the forgiveness of sins *through grace;* the fifth article assures us that we have a *merciful God,* through the merits of Jesus Christ; the twentieth article declares: "He that knoweth that he hath the Father merciful to him through Christ, this man knoweth God truly;" the twenty-seventh article teaches us "to trust assuredly that God is pacified toward us, for Christ's sake, to ask and certainly to look for help from God in all our affairs." Indeed, the whole scheme of salvation, as set forth in our most remarkable confession, moves to its consummation in an atmosphere of the goodness and paternal love of God, coming to sovereign expression in the incarnation. This much each preacher must know of his own creed.

The ideal preacher ought to know *other creeds.* While he may not wisely give his strength to *antagonizing* them, he must know their history and doctrine in order to defend his own. There are great questions astir, especially in our age, all of which run back in some form into the religious life of the people. The ideal minister must be fitted to take his share in the discussion and settlement of those problems. He may not be able to solve them all. He could not hope for the wisdom needful for that, even at the end of his ministerial life. We could not fairly expect it of him at the beginning. He must feel enough moved by the *Zeit-geist* to do his work with freedom to himself and the largest helpfulness to his parish; yet not with any sense of suffocation through the multitude of heresies and fanaticisms which becloud the ecclesiastical sky in these last days.

The age is materialistic, and the multitude perverted to every kind of fantastic teaching, hence the ideal minister must know the isms and schisms that abound to set men on their guard. In other words, he must know the errors that are arraying themselves against the truth, just as the entomologist must impale the repulsive as well as the beautiful. He ought to know general literature; politics, in a good sense; philosophy, sociology; in addition to the usual routine of study in the theological seminary, he should know of the best of scientific study, the poets and the book of human nature.

When one of these modern, shallow advocates of that unphilosophical moonshine called *Christian Science* is met, let the preacher quietly quote his Bible about the *"oppositions of science, falsely so called."* If that is not enough, let him open his Shakespeare and ask the question which the Bard of Avon asked, with one of these pestiferous troublers in mind:

> "Who can hold a fire in his hand
> By thinking on the frosty Caucasus?
> Or cloy the hungry edge of appetite,
> By bare imagination of a feast?
> Or wallow naked in December's snow,
> By thinking on fantastic Summer's heat?"
> —RICH. II., ACT. I., SC. IV.

One of the topics of this Conference deals with Modern Religious Issues. These the preacher must be prepared to meet, and his standard of equipment ought to be such as to qualify him fully on such lines. His intellectual culture must bring him abreast of the times, without allowing him to degenerate into a humanitarian fanatic, a temperance crank, a sociological bore, expending all his intellectual acumen on penology, charity organization, reform movements or allied topics, to the detriment of his chief work.

All these things, with others which the time would fail me to tell, enter into the creation of a standard by which to measure the fitness of a prospective candidate for the holy office of the ministry, whose usefulness is likely to be commensurate with his ability to meet the requirements.

If it be true, as one of the writers on homiletics has said, that every sermon is only worth the effect it produces, then it must be further true that every preacher is worth only the effect he is able to produce. There must be *the man behind the sermon*—the man behind the pastor—with a knowledge of *this* world, as well as a *specialist's* knowledge of spiritual things. The message must convince, if not immediately of the truth of the message, at least of the truth of the messenger, so it can be said of the minister now, as was said of Basil, that his preaching is like the thunder and his life like the lightning. If we have made only the *human side* perfect we have not completed our work. We may have been guilty of *unintentional Simony* in supposing "that the gift of God may be purchased with money" expended on education, and other things connected with a purely material equipment.

The bird with one wing can only flutter to the ground, with difficulty preventing flight from becoming a fall. So by our human preparation alone we can not soar into the realms that will give us a vision of the King in His beauty. We have always in our Church striven to rightly co-ordinate these human and divine factors. We hold to the somewhat old-fashioned notion that the call to the office of the ministry is a *divine* call. We have never held to the fanatical and suicidal theory that one so called of the Holy Ghost does not need any other outfit; that no standards are to be set up, no tests of fitness applied.

There remains time for the briefest possible statement as to the second part of the topic: How shall the Standard be applied; by whom be enforced? There are two points, in our existing machinery, at which to apply our theory, so as to bring the candidates approximately up to our standard. The relation of the Synod to the schools is involved in this matter. The Theological Seminary (with its feeders) and the Synod must co-operate to enforce the requirements. It is doubtful whether it is possible to fix a grade in scholarship, or a per centage rating, in a course of study, that will secure the desired results. There are many men of many minds, and some rather dull students have been preachers of great power, and instruments under God of infinite good. But of one thing we are convinced, that no educational machinery should be set in motion for turning out a partially-prepared ministry. Synod should never let down in its requirements, by partial examinations, by the questionable system of licensure, or by the reprehensible practice of *ad interim* licensure.

The Synod, in our system, guards the door. She assumes the responsibility. Her authority is absolute. All else is preparatory, whether the school be academic or theologic; or, as may happen, the candidate be self-taught. The Synod of Maryland has recently enacted a rule that all ministers from other churches shall undergo the same examination as the regular applicants for ordination.

General Conclusions.

1. There should be a stricter supervision by the Synod of the young candidates for the ministry in the early stages of their education. If the Standards are to be advanced, the beginnings must be made at that end of the line.

2. This more rigid supervision (during the academic course) of students in preparation for the ministry, at the Synod's expense, should result in better material, stimulating the dull, encouraging the diligent, dropping the incapable, unspiritual or vicious.

3. Our denominational colleges should be guarded by the Synods against any lowering of the standard of admission to the several classes, under the mistaken desire of gaining an increased registration. This can readily be done in all colleges under the control and government of the Church.

It is not possible if the college is a close corporation, without synodical representation in its Board, and, therefore, to all intents and purposes, an *undenominational institution*.

4. Examinations should be carefully conducted, under the eye of the Synod's Committee, in the years preceding the close of the theological course.

5. The same or equivalent standards should be agreed upon in all the theological schools of our general bodies; and as far as possible in our Synods, to be enforced by their examining committees, and endorsed in final action by the Ministerium.

6. No candidate for the ministry, dismissed from one school or rejected by one Synod, should be accepted by the schools or synods of any other co-ordinate body, unless by mutual agreement.

This has happened, not as between Council and Synod, but as between the several theological seminaries of the General Synod. As one of the practical forms in which the matter of co-operation can be further applied, we make these two suggestions.

7. In general, we would recommend synods to more carefully guard the entrance door rather than the exit. Our government military and naval schools are more particular in the reception of candidates than at any other point. We shall find one sure method of raising our standard if we fix our attention here. We shall produce a race of preachers to each one of whom we may justly apply the words of Tennyson:

> "Thou art no Sabbath-drawler of old saws,
> Distill'd from some worm-canker'd homily."

STANDARD OF MINISTERIAL EDUCATION.
BY REV. F. A. KAHLER.

We consider the subject under two questions, which we endeavor to answer.

A. What is our standard, and why must it continually come before us with new interest?

B. What is the shaping element in education, which fixes the standard for the Christian ministry?

A.

Our standard, as compared with that of any learned profession, must be equal to the highest, and with advancing learning in the university our standard must keep rising. This demand is recognized, and many of the noblest efforts are made to satisfy it, in establishing Christian schools, colleges and theological seminaries, in giving munificent endowments and in sending forth choicest literature.

(1.) Our standard must grow broader in scope. There are always new branches of learning and investigation, and the minister must feel the touch of intelligent sympathy with the students of each branch. Our whole commission is to make all nations Christ's disciples, students, followers, teaching them to observe all things that He commanded. As divinely sent leaders of men's thinking, we must be acquainted with their forms of thinking and channels of thought. The guides of students must have some knowledge of their absorbing studies. To reach men we must know them, and to know them we must know their mental world. That world is expanding, and our standard must grow broader.

(2.) Our advancing standard must keep its height. The exalted proportion must not be disturbed. We dare not sacrifice in altitude what we gain in latitude. We dare not try to level God's mountain merely to make its base broad. There is a difference between a pile of stones and the Cathedral of Cologne. True, education is broad, but it has something more than expanded flatness. The mathematical plane is an imaginary thing, and it should be left such. We have no yearning for mere spread materialized. If education is not elevating it is not education. Philistines are always ready to make raids into God's holy hills. This leveling age would grade down Calvary for rapid railway transit, and use the pattern of the Cross for telegraph poles. Sinai was made holy and full of dread by the giving of the law to Moses. Some of the learned of our day can take that law and with irreverent hands run it into ingenious patterns of the striped and ring-streaked, and substitute for all its exalted Mosaic solemnity and awe kindergarten mosaics of glaring polychrome. Some keen and intellectual students seem to value only the parchment of the law of God and to use that only for a strop to put a finer edge upon the sharp instruments of their incisive criticism and to be satisfied and to expect the world to be so. In our standard we need something higher than that spirit, though it flatly calls itself high.

(3.) Furthermore we need a higher grade of manly development in every direction of discipline. (*a.*) Even in physical discipline. The demands upon our strength are more exacting than at any previous age. Close communication with all parts of the world gives greater complexity and wider reach to all branches of the work that we are to grasp and hold and hallow. We cannot keep pace with the march of life without great physical strain. Our standard calls for well-trained physical frames. It is true that athletics have turned out circus performers and professional nothings, but they have also made heroes who hunted down the inquisition on San Juan hill and scattered its wrecks in Manila Bay and along the smoking shores of Cuba. If the brutal prize ring basely claims for physical strength and prowess the first place in manliness, does the class-room not grossly err in giving them scarcely any place? Surely athletics can be used to educate the physical strength of the servant of God and leader of men to endure hardness in the campaign for expanding the kingdom of our Lord.

(*b*) There is need of larger mental discipline. Specialization of work has brought a larger amount of information, and while we do not need to know more of the truth of God than our faithful fathers knew, we must know more things in order to do as effective service as they did in preaching the truth to men. If Thomas had been the only kind of doubter the field of apologetics would have been closed the week after Easter.

(*c*) We need a larger moral discipline. The greater diversity of attack upon our faith and the more subtle ingenuity of insinuation from all sides of learned skepticism and unbelief absorbing and distracting the mind call for more unswerving fidelity and tenacious and obedient firmness in faith than ever before.

(*d*) We are justified in demanding more from applicants for ordination and in making a more select choice for the special work of the ministry. For this reason: In the development of the diaconate a larger variety and scope of work will be found for many useful servants of Christ. Not every one who wishes to give all his strength to this service, need on that account be set apart for the ministry in the stricter sense. Work in the Church schools, in Sunday-schools, in colleges, in larger parish work, in institutions of mercy, and medical missions, calls for many consecrated men. The question has been raised whether we are in want of more men in the ministry; there certainly can be no question that we need more thoroughly trained, fully disciplined and learned manfulness everywhere. Learn from the wisdom of the world to specialize. Our standard must call for specialists in the ministry. We must bring power in order to wield power in the Church. Masterful thoroughness commands the influence and standing which whimpering incompetency demands and never gets.

Moreover, there can be no doubt that a system whereby young men leaving the seminary could serve for some years as assistants to pastors of experience in large charges would add immensely to the effectiveness of their service.

We therefore maintain that an efficient ministry demands the highest standard of education and must keep step with the advance of general learning.

B.

Our second question is: What is the shaping element in education which fixes the standard for the Christian ministry?

What is the heart of Christian education and what must be regarded and maintained as the first and all-influencing element in ministerial learning?

The positive assurance of divine revelation. To the commissioned teacher, sent out by the order of his Lord with a specific message to lead and change the world, all knowledge arranges itself clearly under three subjects:

(1) God. (2) Man. (3) Things.

The conscious personal Creator, the conscious personal creature who responds to the will of the Creator, and the subordinate world, all made for man, given to him, forfeited by him, ruined with him, to be restored to him according to the revealed plan of the Creator, who is Redeemer.

1. Of God the eternal, unchangeable, we know. As Christian believers we start with absolute certainty. We have immovable and unshadowed infallibility. We have knowledge, not theory, not supposition. Our knowledge is not the presumption of man's finding out, but the gracious revelation of God. He has declared it, He has sealed it. We know the truth. We are called to the truth. We are baptized into the truth. We rest in the truth. We live by the truth, and we are sent by Him who is the truth to give the truth, the gladness of the world. This truth is simply the will of God. In creation, through all history to the final purpose we know the will of God. That is the truth of the world. That will of God was fully revealed and fulfilled in Christ, therefore He is the truth. We know the whole world; we may not have accurate knowledge of the details of a single atom in it, but we know the whole as related to God, to us and to final destiny.

"This is life eternal that they should know Thee the only true God and Him whom Thou didst send, even Jesus Christ."

"Christ is made to us wisdom."

"In whom are hid all the treasures of wisdom and knowledge." "When He, the Spirit of truth, is come, He will guide you into all truth."

This Spirit is come; Pentecost is here.

We have the word of the Spirit, the truth of God in Christ.

2. Of Man we know God's record and God's will. We know man's creation, fall, redemption, sanctification, and final glory. In his changing and unstable life, we know the highest possibility, fixed by the Unchangeable. It is the revealed purpose of God. In that we know the truth in man, and concerning man. We may know all else about him; not knowing that, we do not know the truth. We may be ignorant concerning a thousand things about man, but knowing God's will concerning him in Christ, we know the truth. You know your friend. You do not know the hairs on his head, or the bones in his body, but you know him. The scientific fraternity of the whole university may devote a lifetime of busiest ingenuity in profoundest learning in accumulating most interesting and useful facts about him in zoology, ethnology, genealogy, physiology, chemistry, anatomy, biology, psychology, philosophy, history and literature, and yet all that accumulation will never make up your knowledge of him. They know truths about him. You know God's purpose with him; you know the truth about him.

3. In the confused and broken realm of things we know the truth. We see a meaning in them only as we discover the will or purpose of God. God is all in all. If we know God's will and order in the chemical combinations, we know the beautiful truth of chemistry. If we know God's will in the order of the worlds in their inter-attraction, motion and relation, we know the truths of astronomy. If we know God's will in the processes of life, we know the truth of biology. We know that the great truth of the world is one. There is one will of God controlling in the one plan or type running through the universe. Men may call the broken suggestions of God's will in things truths, but it is the one will or purpose that is the truth. The glittering mountain-top reflects the sun from unnumbered facets; the ocean throws back myriad flashes of his out-poured radiance; every crystal, prism, leaf or blade, flower or stone, gives some new pic-

ture of His work; yea, even the muddy little pool grasps the image, and claims to hold the King of our world; but none of these, nor all of them together, make up the sun. No more can all the gathered little truths of human learning in things make up the truth of the whole will and purpose of our God. "Hath not God made foolish the wisdom of the world? For seeing that, in the wisdom of God, the world through its wisdom knew not God, it was God's good pleasure, through the foolishness of the preaching, to save them that believe."

We know that truth is personal. The secret of the world is what the personal God purposes in the world. This will has a personal object. It is directed to a person, man. It shows itself in things, but it shows itself to man. Can person ever find truth in things that will satisfy person? You may apostrophize beauties and powers in nature, but that means only addressing in them, or through them, a fancied or a real person The soul of man finds rest only in person that answers to its personal cry. "As the hart panteth after water brooks, so panteth my soul after Thee, O God. My soul thirsteth for God, for the living God." Not for an abstraction called a truth, but for the living Reality, the Truth. And behold the blessed assurance of the word, "God so loved the world that He gave His only begotten Son," that is personal, and ultimately "He shall see of the travail of his soul, and shall be satisfied." When man gains his full rest in the living Truth—the living Truth, even God the Saviour, shall be satisfied, and in some sense have rest in him.

Distinctively Christian education starts with these fundamental points in our standard: (1.) Christian revelation gives us the truth. We know and are to teach the origin and destiny of the world. (2.) All learning about the world and things in the world must subordinate itself to this truth.

What learning, without the revelation of God, can do for man we have discovered in the history of Babylon, Egypt, Greece and Rome, and we keep learning the same sad lesson as universities try to get from under the influence of the teaching that gave them birth.

Paul met the learning of the day among the Greeks, the reach for something new in the field of guessing, trying to piece together the sun out of mud-puddle reflections. How did he meet it?

"The unknown God, Him declare I unto you." No theory, but a certified declaration. Something new? Yea, verily, something renewing, regenerating in the field of certainty. "I determined to know nothing among you but Christ and Him crucified." Ministers in Paul's line must be certain, and they must make others certain. Paul told Timothy: "I know whom I have believed," and taught Timothy to know and to bring the world out of the darkness of guessing into the light of knowing.

Our position is that religious conviction must shape all our teaching. To prepare our ministers we must have in our schools teachers who themselves are thoroughly convinced of the truth, not beating the air. Therefore while our liberal education will include a wide knowledge of all the range of human studies in the university course, the ministerial standard will always classify all this knowledge under the certainty of the knowledge we have from God concerning the sum of all things. The seminary idea must stand above the university idea, as life stands above physiology, anatomy and chemistry.

This may at first appear to be very close to the hierarchical rule of doing all judging and interpreting by the appointed authorities. When we discarded the idea of papal infallibility we surely did not mean that we have something less. Equally certain it is that we did not intend to accept the infallibility of private judgment in all teaching, making every person a pope, multiplying the papal absurdity by the myriads of the human race. Nor did we intend to accept the infallibility of the brilliant specialist with his generalizations in learned guesses of theory. The infallibility of the professor's chair is only a little more presumptuous than the infallibility of the papal throne. The infallibility we accept is that of God's revelation in His Word. Accepting that, we teach it and we train ministers in it and send them out to teach it, and do not send them out unless they solemnly vow that they will teach it. Of course that binds them, but it is to the solid truth that makes them free. The force of gravity binds you to the earth, but only to give stability to your free action and firmness to your freedom. Is there less liberty in the sturdy march of the conquering hero than in the aimless, aerial bobbing of the thistle-down?

We are bound, not by the fetters of slavery, but by the bonds of saving love; not tied down to the narrow, but held up to the infinite, our liberty safe, and our field unbounded. The danger we fear in the rocking and swaying standards of varying university education, is that even Christian men may be made uncertain of the one thing sure.

As men awake to the folly of claiming infallibility for any thing of human invention they ridicule the teaching that unerring truth can be had from any source. Every subject is to be left open. The ideal cap of liberty is Sam Weller's hat, all open. Because somebody's roof leaks everybody's house must be torn down. The ideal palace is the open air.

On that fatal night there was something open in the dam on the Conemaugh, and Johnstown was swept away. It is the indeterminate, the undecided, the indefinite in the education of our day that leaves the flood-gates of destruction open. When men of brilliant gifts and abundant reading can be caught in the muddy flood of Spiritism, Christian Science and Theosophy some things in their education have been left open that should have been closed. "Professing themselves to be wise, they have become fools," and are wretched slaves, and ye plain believers "shall know the truth and the truth shall make you free," and ye are to make the world free, even the learned world.

REMARKS.

Prof. J. R. DIMM, D.D., after the reading of the two papers on "Standard of Ministerial Education," said:—

1. The Synods, by their power of ordination, hold the door of entrance to the Gospel ministry.

2. The Synods alone can and do set and maintain, as far as it is, the standard of ministerial education.

3. Colleges have more trouble with Synods, in keeping up the standard, than they have with the students.

4. Colleges often incur the displeasure of parents, pastors and educational committees, when they report to them the delinquencies of beneficiaries.

Rev. Prof. J. FRY, D. D., said:—I look at this matter in a practical way, and my experience as a teacher has convinced me the most serious lack with many applicants for admission into the seminary, is in their primary education. Even in the matter of correct spelling, and the formation of sentences according to the common rules of grammar, some are surprisingly deficient. The lack is not so much in their college studies as in their primary instruction, and the question is not so much what shall be the standard of admission into our theological seminaries, as into our colleges. Reference has been made to the importance of their familiarity with the Augsburg Confession, but we find that many who come to the seminary are not familiar even with their catechism, and cannot give the proper answer to such questions as, What is Baptism, or, What is Luther's explanation of the second article of the Creed? Something should be done to correct these defects in early education before they are admitted into college classes.

Dr. SCHOLL said:—In all the learned professions the demand is for thoroughly qualified men. Our best institutions have learned to place the emphasis at the right point. Some time since a gentleman of more than average ability, who had already taken the degrees of A. B. and M. D. in institutions of good standing, sought entrance in the Johns Hopkins University with the view of taking a post-graduate course in medicine. He could not matriculate because he had failed to take the elementary course in chemistry and biology and was accordingly referred to the under-graduate department of the University for the acquisition of those branches of learning.

Here we have a good example to follow in the matter of ministerial education. We cannot be too careful in laying the foundation. The standard for admission into both college and seminary needs to be raised. The times demand it, and we cannot afford to be indifferent on this point if our men are to maintain a creditable position in the ranks of the Gospel ministry.

Rev. W. A. PASSAVANT, Jr., asked whether it was not time for the Lutheran Church to adopt a system of beneficiary education in her institutions in which merit alone should be the gauge. He advocated scholarships established by the Synods, to be dispensed by the Synods or the faculty, and on the basis of an educational test or examination. He saw no reason why men should be pushed into the ministry.

Dr. SCHANTZ objected that as long as the Synods had no such scholarships, it could not dispense them. He maintained that unworthy and incapable men were being dropped, that the standard had been raised, and that students should receive no assistance prior to the sophomore year.

Dr. CHAS. S. ALBERT said:—After having listened to the sharp criticisms of the intellectual standing of the ministry, we feel that it would not be fair to close this discussion without emphasizing the other side. We are inclined to be optimistic in this matter. The papers of marked ability, the presence of so many intelligent listeners of our ministry indicate the high standard of ministerial education prevailing with us. Our knowledge of our younger ministers convinces us that an unusual number of able and scholarly men are being nurtured, who will be leaders of whom we need not be ashamed at no distant day. There is an intellectual quickening, the thrill of which is felt throughout our whole ministry. There is a demand by our laity for the literature of their Church, because they are alive to its greatness and the richness of its truth. This demand must accrue to the intellectual stimulation of our ministry. Such people will demand thoughtful and scholarly preachers who in turn will be inspired to do better work, because of the recognition of their labors by their people.

Dr. KROTEL added a word in the same strain. He recalled the state of affairs in the Church fifty years ago and took courage. Wonderful progress had been made. He believed in beneficiary education. Fault may often be found with our institutions, but they have done a great work. We may learn a lesson from Uncle Sam. He supports two institutions, one at Annapolis and another at West Point, and has a large number of beneficiaries, and though often blamed for extravagance, the standard insisted on is high and we have to thank him for training so fine a race of beneficiaries as that which recently gave us our victory over Spain. The fault lies not in the beneficiary system, but in the standard. Keep up the standard.

Dr. PARSON suggested that the only way in which to raise the standard was to move back and begin early.

Rev. F. A. KÄHLER repudiated the idea that the standard of education in the ministry was lower than that in the other learned professions.

Rev. KÄHLER said: My paper was not calculated to call forth discussion. The purpose was simply:

First, to restate a few of the reasons why a minister must not be satisfied with anything short of the highest standard of education, compared with the standard of all the learned professions of the university; why our standard must continually rise; and why we must be more rigid in our demands for a learned ministry.

Secondly, to show that the claim for knowledge received from revelation is the highest. That we have authority for *knowledge*, where human investigation apart from revelation has only *hypothesis* or changing theory. That the seminary is above the university. That Christ's messengers are to lead the university to knowledge, not to be led by the university to theory. That Paul came to Athens not to learn from the teachers of the world, but to teach the ignorance of the greatest human learning, the wisdom of God's revelation in Christ.

THE LUTHERAN CHURCH AND MODERN RELIGIOUS ISSUES IN GERMANY.

BY A. G. VOIGT, D.D.

Religious issues are not identical with religious problems. Many problems are investigated without ever leading to controversy. Germany is the country for the discovery of theological problems, and for their solution.

The Church in Germany has also great practical problems to solve, which are closely akin to the religious issues. What is the proper attitude of the Church towards abnormal social conditions? What shall be the method of counteracting the great estrangement of the masses from the Church? Should "evangelization" be encouraged? What attitude shall the Church take towards the intruding sects? These, and similar practical questions, are of no less importance to the life of the Church than the existing religious issues. But it does not lie within the scope of this paper to discuss these practical problems.

We are to limit ourselves to the religious issues. By religious issues we understand those great agitated questions which involve either the being or well-being of the Church. These issues are essentially the same in Germany as in England and America. For they arise from the relations of Christianity to modern life and thought, which are essentially the same in spirit and tendency in Europe and in this country. If there is any difference in the relation of the Lutheran Church to modern religious issues in Germany and in this country, it is the degree to which the Church has been affected by the modern spirit in the two countries. The living issues of to-day in Germany may become ours to-morrow. This is where our interest in this matter lies.

It is not easy to single out particular issues in the religious life of Germany, for the conflict rages through the whole field of religious thought. There is really but one great issue for the Lutheran Church, and that involves the whole system of faith. If the modern spirit prevails in theology, even the Small Catechism will have to go out of the Church. This is an age of reconstruction in theology. The issues are not concerning the correction or clearer definition or fuller explication of particular parts of Christian teaching. The whole conception of Christianity is to be revolutionized.

It may sound like an exaggeration, but we think close reflection will sustain the assertion that the issue which modern thought has pressed upon the Church is greater than that of the Reformation. It is not attended by so great an agitation of men's minds. For the change in thought that is in progress has been proceeding more quietly and gradually. Nevertheless the revolution in Christian thought that is now confronting the Church is vaster than that of the Reformation. The reformed theology of the sixteenth century allowed a large part of the traditional dogma of the Church to stand intact. The product of the religious thought of the preceding centuries, as it had crystallized in the great dogmas of the divinity of Christ, of the trinity, of the person and natures of Christ, and of the vicarious atonement, was accepted by the Reformers, and has been transmitted in the Lutheran Church to us. Now all this is to be changed. Since the days of Schleiermacher a reconstruction has been gradually going on, which does not stop even at the simple basis of Christian faith in the Apostles' Creed. When, a few years ago, the heated controversy concerning the *Apostolicum* blazed up, the mind of Germany was awakened to the vast extent of the religious change in progress. And when now it is unhesitatingly argued that the Lord's Supper was never intended to be observed as a rite in the Church, it is manifest what a break with the whole course of religious life, from the beginning of the Church, is being consummated. It is reconstruction from the bottom. The foundation stones of traditional Christian belief are torn up, either to make room for something else, or, at least, to be relaid in different order.

If we are not mistaken in our analysis of present trends of thought, there are three factors especially at work in producing the gradual transformation of religious views in the present age: 1. Aversion to intellectual religion; 2. Subjectivism; 3. The scientific spirit.

To speak of an aversion to intellectual religion in this intellectual age may sound paradoxical. But the fact remains. Schleiermacher properly interpreted the mind of the nineteenth century when he declared religion was feeling. Whether it be because the age has been intellectually overstrained and seeks relief in religion in another direction or whatever the cause, there is a very decided tendency to value that alone in religions, which bears directly on the feelings and the will. The religious spirit of the times is ethical, and not speculative or mystical. Hence we observe the inclination to eliminate or at least reduce the intellectual elements of religion. Our dogmatic, it is said, must become shorter. Hence the strong opposition to everything "metaphysical" (as it is termed) in Christianity as a product of Greek thought and not of genuine Christianity as originally given. Hence also the constant charge of intellectualism against old Lutheran orthodoxy.

Co-operative with this anti-intellectual tendency is the prevalent subjectivism, which estimates religious truth by the standard of personal experience. Hence so much is said about *Werturteile*, judgments of value. That which we recognize as of religious value in our personal experience is to be accepted as the truth. Whatever does not come within our personal experience is to be treated as unessential or problematic.

And with this subjectivism concurs the predominant method of science. Modern science demands facts, and facts are furnished by experience. Hence the disposition to limit the sphere of knowable truth to experience, and to pass by, if not to deny, that which is transcendental. In accordance with this method of science theology is likely to become a science of those peculiar facts of inner experience which are denominated "religious." In order to estimate the facts of experience, science labors to discover certain relations and connections between them, which it calls laws. The one kind of connection between facts that is of special interest to science at the present time is that which tells how things came to be as they are. The genetic and evolutionary method of science applied to Christianity most seriously affects its historical basis.

Now this entire modern way of looking at things is at variance with old Lutheran orthodoxy. The traditional dogma of the Lutheran Church was developed under the operation of none of the three factors just traced. The old orthodoxy was strongly intellectual. It estimated truth not by inner experience, but by the objective revelation given in the Bible. Its method was not genetic, but rather that of tabulating articles of belief.

Here now we have the conflict between the traditional and the modern. It is a conflict that ploughs far below the surface to the subsoil of religion. Shall the traditional be maintained just as it has come down to us, without any correlation to modern thought? Some would perhaps fain do so. But they are few. Or shall the traditional be wholly cast aside and a "new dogma" be evolved? This has been demanded by some. Or shall the issue be met by concessions to the modern spirit and by partial reconstructions of the theology of the Church? This is the course of the large majority of conservatives. The last is the way not only of reason, but of safety. It must be confessed there is some reason in the anti-intellectual, ethical religious tendency and in the subjectivism of the age, and there is real progress in knowledge in modern scientific methods. Moreover, it is not safe, but very perilous, to defend untenable positions.

Passing from these general considerations on the tendencies of the age to special phases of religious controversy, we observe that the realistic, not to say materialistic trend of thought makes the very existence of Christianity an issue. The danger here is not so much from direct assaults upon Christianity as from a process of disintegration and undermining. Much of the hostility to Christianity is probably unconscious, but this makes it none the less dangerous. The predominant interest in natural science, the assumption that material things are the only realities, at least the only realities we can know anything about, and the excessive valuation in practical life of the goods of this world all tend to produce an indifference to the spiritual truths of Christianity and an alienation of both cultured and uncultured classes from the Church.

Professor Lemme, the writer on Apologetic in the new "Real

Encyclopædia," edited by Hauck, says: "If ever a time stood in need of a thorough apologetic, present-day Christianity has that need. For it must carry on the conflict, not only with the extra-Christian religions, but it sees a new heathenism arise in its own midst to an extent never seen, and with intellectual resources never witnessed before."

When we now inquire, How is Christianity prepared to meet this issue that involves its very existence, we cannot answer in any triumphant mood. Modern theology is weak against anti-Christian forces, because it has adapted itself to the empirical and agnostic philosophy of the times. In order to win back the alienated classes, there is a disposition to follow them in their agnostic trend of thought and to remove, as much as possible, the antagonisms between the religion of Christ and the culture of the age. Where does the most recent apologetic of Christianity take its stand? The writer just quoted gives us the answer: "It lies in the nature of the modern tendency in theology that it surrenders the objective theoretic proof for the truth of Christianity, and confines itself to this, to offer Christianity to the moral and intellectual needs, under certain subjective presuppositions given in the intellectual life of Christendom; or it retires to the position that in spite of modern science religious faith in God can still be maintained."

We have called this concession to the empirical philosophy of the age an element of weakness in modern theology. On the other hand it is a source of strength in traditional Lutheranism that it defends Christianity on the basis of objective facts given in a revelation. It presents something to be believed, and not only something to be inwardly felt and experienced. Christianity cannot be maintained upon the sole ground that it is a matter of personal inner experience, and that this is its vindication. Every illusion is also a matter of personal inner experience. The historical and metaphysical basis of Christianity, which the Lutheran Church never will surrender as long as it is true to itself, must furnish the guarantee of victory over the empirical philosophy of this century.

The effort within the Church to adapt itself to the prevalent thought of the age has raised an issue as to what is genuine Christianity. The traditional dogma of the Church is believed by many to be no true representation of it. Hence an undogmatic Christianity or a new dogma is to satisfy the mind that takes no interest in the traditional teaching of the Church and to bring to it the genuine original Christianity of Christ without accretions and malformation.

In order to bring this genuine Christianity to light not even the teachings of the apostles are to be received as genuine presentations of the religion of Christ without scrutiny and qualification. Not only the accretions of the traditional Church dogma, but the personal views of the apostles are to be peeled off in order to get down to the genuine Christianity of Christ. But the process of sifting and scaling is not to stop even at the acknowledged words of Christ. Out of His accepted sayings His consciousness is to be analyzed, and whatever in it is found to be merely a belief or view of His times, is also to be peeled off.

An illustration of what this process of penetrating to the kernel of the real religion of Christ involves, is given in the article on Demoniacs, by Joh. Weiss, in the new " Real Encyclopædia." He says: "Jesus believed not only in the existence of demons, but also in the possibility of exorcism like His contemporaries." But when the writer declares his judgment on demoniacs, he says: "For the biblicistic orthodoxy the insuperable difficulty exists of perceiving that the men of the New Testament, especially Jesus, stood on this question at the religious and scientific standpoint of their time, from which we have been forced away by the world-picture of modern natural science." Then we learn: "Inasmuch as we theologians are no competent judges of the existing psychical facts, we must accept instruction from the physicians." From this it appears that Jesus also was "no competent judge of the existing psychical facts," and that His "self-consciousness" is to be regulated and corrected by modern science.

Now whatever corrections in its traditional theology the Lutheran Church will accept, it will not suffer corrections in the religious teaching of Christ, nor even of His apostles. Nor, knowing that its old dogma is based upon the writings of the apostles, will it ever cast it aside for a new dogma. But meantime the controversy between old faith and new faith (for such it is, and not only a controversy between old theology and new theology) must go on in the Lutheran Church; and to maintain itself and its old dogma the Church must bring its theology into right relations to the advancing historical and scientific knowledge of the age. Here is the source of difficult questions that must be met in the spirit of fair and honest inquiry. It should be remembered that it is not the wish to change the confession of the Church, that has begotten the modern attempts to reconstruct the system of faith. It is the desire to bring that confession into correct relations to modern thought and knowledge. The sincerity of the effort, of course, does not correct its errors. Nor should the errors of many deter the Church from performing the necessary task of proving that in the light of modern knowledge its system of faith preserves and presents the truth of genuine Christianity. Rocholl says, truly, in a recent essay: "Theology must keep in touch with the general science that surrounds it."

The issue as to what constitutes genuine Christianity is almost the same as the issue concerning the "historical Christ," of whom so much is now said. It is fondly believed that this is the Christ whom our age needs and will accept. But it is a grave question whether even the most modernized Christianity will be acceptable to the modern spirit of the large numbers who have been alienated from the Church. A still graver question is whether with the "historical Christ" the essential truth of Christianity is not sacrificed. We remember what Luther said of the Christ of Zwingli's Alloeosis: "I would not like to be a Christian after him." The same can with propriety be said of the "historical Christ." What is the "historical Christ?" It is not easy to define, because the thing itself is somewhat vague. Is it the Christ of the Gospels? By no means. For this Christ is to stand independent of whatever criticism may make of the Gospels. To get at the idea of the historical Christ, we must first cut off all that is not historical, that is, all that pertains to pre-existence and post-existence. Now whatever idea of the person of Christ the modern theologian forms of Him within these historical limits, that is the "historical Christ." The Lutheran Church must have something more than the "historical Christ" as the foundation of its faith. For this reason conservative Lutheran theology has for years waged unceasing warfare against the "historical Christ," and has stood out for the pre-existence of our Lord with all that it involves of metaphysical theology.

Inseparably connected with the controversy about the "historical Christ" is the issue as to the basis of Christian certainty, and the principle of Christian knowledge. Old Lutheran theology answers: The Bible. To our orthodox fathers the authority of the Bible was absolute; its declarations were the source of saving knowledge, and guaranteed the certainty of Christian faith. But now we are to learn that this was not the Lutheranism of Luther. For, as Harnack says, "this is the greatest reform which Luther instituted, both for faith and theology, that he made the historical Christ the only principle of the knowledge of God." The historical Christ is thus brought into opposition to the Bible as the source of Christian knowledge.

But even among those who oppose the school of Ritschl there is a want of agreement on the question: What is the ultimate ground of Christian certainty? It is now generally recognized in Germany that the method of Christian faith is not first to become convinced by intellectual arguments of the truth and divine character of a book, and then to submit to all its statements. Nor was this the method of the seventeenth century orthodoxy, although for the sake of antithesis the matter is so represented. But it must be conceded that the older orthodoxy did not value Christian experience as much as modern theology. It is now generally acknowledged that Christian faith lives not by what a person knows is stated in the Bible, but by the amount of truth inwardly appropriated in inner experience. It is a merit of modern theology that it emphasizes the importance of actual living faith. In this there is general agreement, but in regard to the basis of Christian faith and knowledge there is a want of agreement. The conflict here is between three different views.

1. Many hold fast simply to the old orthodox position, that the

ground of Christian certainty and knowledge is to be found in the declarations of the Bible.

2. But most modern theology is troubled by a distinction between believing in the Bible and believing in Christ, whom the Bible declares. A dictum of Schleiermacher is regarded as fundamental. He says: "Respect for the Holy Scriptures cannot be the basis of faith in Christ; rather this faith must be presupposed in order to concede a special respect to the Holy Scriptures." There is a false antithesis here, for Christ cannot be believed in except through the word which declares Him. Nevertheless, this dictum is accepted by conservative Lutherans, who try to combine the authority of the Scriptures with inner experience as a double ground of certainty. They argue from the experience of faith back to the Bible as the producing cause, or, if not directly back to the Holy Scriptures, at least to the Word of God, which is in the Church, and which, in its primary and normal form, is authenticated in the writings of prophets and apostles.

3. But those who follow the teachings of Ritschl try to build up the whole structure of Christian faith on the foundation of an inner experience of Christ, thereby escaping from the principle of authority altogether; or if, like Kaftan, they recognize the necessity of some authority, they discover it not in the Scriptures, but in an ideal Christ.

The dangers of this third view, and the exaltation of inner experience, also contain a warning for those who combine inner experience with the Scriptures as the ground of certainty and the principle of knowledge. Kuebel was not far wrong when he characterized the exaltation of inner experience into the position of an authority as *Schwarmgeisterei*. The position is, in fact, akin to the teaching of the fanatics of the Reformation period, who relied absolutely upon their inner revelations. A Christianity that has nothing under it but an inner experience has poor underpinning. Nor can there be any assurance of the reality of the operations of the Christ of history upon our hearts unless, at the same time, the history of Christ is assured to us, and this throws us back again upon the Scriptures. Christianity based upon the Bible will, of course, be necessarily exposed to the attacks of adverse criticism. But this danger is nothing compared to the immense peril of a Christianity that has only a subjective foundation. Christianity is a historical religion. If the history is unfounded, the religion founded upon it cannot and does not deserve to stand. Not what we experience inwardly, even under the influence of the Word of God, but that Word of God itself as the producing cause of our faith, is the ultimate source of our Christian knowledge and certainty.

The question as to the seat of authority necessarily leads to the issues presented by modern criticism of the Bible. One school of modern theology would fain make the preservation of Christianity independent of the results of criticism. Let criticism eliminate whatever it may, it is fondly hoped that enough of the picture of Christ will remain to produce the overwhelming, inspiring impression which is the experience of faith. But conservative Lutherans are not so sanguine. Shortly before his death Dr. Frank expressed his apprehension : "The possibility seems not to be excluded that by critical investigations the evangelical picture of our Redeemer will be so much dissolved and decomposed that what remains of it will be no longer adapted to let Him remain the centre and foundation of our faith." The controversy about the Scriptures involves several points, their historical correctness, their inspiration and their normative authority. Lack of time forbids us to dwell upon these points. We limit ourselves to a few brief general remarks. On all the points mentioned there is a general weakening on the conservative Lutheran side. Yet it may safely be asserted that positive Lutherans will not surrender the vital positions connected with the historical accuracy, the inspiration and the normative authority of the Scriptures. But meanwhile there is great uncertainty as to the method of defence. It is not a sign of strength that there is a general disposition to fall back upon the so-called testimony of the Holy Spirit as the ultimate defence of the Bible. But this is in a line with the prevailing subjectivism. The battle is one of historical criticism and it must be fought to a victory by historical criticism. It is a more hopeful sign that theologians like

Professor Kœnig point out the necessity of bringing forward the external arguments for the genuineness and authenticity of the books of the Bible.

It is characteristic of modern theology that it turns its attention almost exclusively to Christ. It is but natural, therefore, that the traditional and modern spirit should clash in regard to the central doctrines of christology and the atonement. The old doctrine of the two natures in Christ is a stumbling block to modern thought and is set aside. Christ is regarded from the point of view that in Him is a self-revelation of God. Is He then Himself God? It is hard to tell. He stands in unity with God, but this unity is one of will, not of essence. The pre-existence of Christ is virtually denied. The atonement is ethically conceived. His life and death are valued not as a vicarious offering making a reconciliation with God, but as an exhibition of the love and forgiveness of God. Man is saved by faith in God, and Christ's life and death are the divine means to awaken this faith in man.

The issue here presented is one that can be triumphantly met as long as conservative theology takes its stand upon the New Testament. For it will require more ingenuity and critical acuteness than even German theologians display to get the truth of the essential divinity of Christ out of the Gospels and the doctrine of the vicarious atonement out of the epistles.

And on the whole the lover of old Lutheran theology and faith need not be discouraged. The existing religious issues make us concerned, but not despondent. Much injury has been done to the faith of the Church, for the new religious views are not confined to the universities. The modern spirit has also invaded the pulpits, the catechetical instruction and the homes of the laity. But the old faith still has its able defenders. And a still mightier conservative force than the learning of theologians is to be found in the devotional literature which the people read and use in church and home, and also love. The liturgies of the Church, the hymns, the prayer-books and the postils are all saturated with the old theology. And above all, the Bible is still in the hands of reverent people.

THE LUTHERAN CHURCH AND MODERN RELIGIOUS ISSUES IN AMERICA.

BY T. E. SCHMAUK, D.D.

"The Lutheran Church" is the Church that clings to salvation by faith alone; and to its corollary that each individual is responsible unto God for himself; to Scripture as the one rule of faith and life, the one determiner of theory and practice, the one test of doctrines and methods; to Jesus Christ as the Son of the living God, manifest in the flesh for the removal of the sin of the world by the redemption of the cross, and as the centre and the radius of Scripture; to the Law which commands and condemns, and the Gospel which offers grace and pardon; to the Word and Sacraments as the only means which the Holy Spirit uses to convince of sin and work faith; and to a life of daily repentance and faith. Wherever men together cling to these things, there is the Lutheran Church.

"Modern religious issues in America" are such important positions or problems in theology and church-life, or in the mental attitude of thinkers towards either, as the present age has brought into prominence in our land. By implication in the terms, it is clear that in this paper the Church is to be dealt with in relation to issues that come to it from without, and that internal issues, such as the race and language question, the question of fellowship between various bodies of Lutherans, the questions of the Four Points, of a Common Service, the Luther League question, etc., are excluded, except in so far as they have lines of contact with more general religious issues in America.

Few or none of the latter have originated in our Church. They have sprung up, as a rule, from the wayside seeds of radicalism. For many of them no church is responsible, but they have germinated outside the pale, and are a product of the course of history and of the times. The Church is not to be held to account for their presence, little as is the Sower for the presence of the tares; but she is responsible for what she does with them. Modern issues that have not been imported from other lands come to us largely from the New England, Presbyterian and Methodist Churches, and from our American types of culture, literature and government. For in America, as in few other countries, issues spring from the current fund of public thought, and in turn quickly react on it.

I.

Underlying the issues of present day theology, there is one fundamental question. The Lutheran Church says, Scripture is the only rule of faith and life. But nearly all other theology is asking, Where does Reason come in?[1] The question presents itself to us in very different aspects from those in which it appeared in the rationalism of the last century. Since then the heart of every great contemplative soul-seer, from Goethe to Tennyson and Browning, has brooded over it; the soaring wings of a latter-day philosophy have extended, the keen eyes of a latter-day science have examined it.

The whole problem entered American theology by way of reaction against the pressure of the teaching of Jonathan Edwards. After some preparatory periods, an American rebellion of reason was developed in a wide and revolutionary way by Emerson, and in a more limited theological sphere by Horace Bushnell. Under its general influence Longfellow, Channing, Whittier, Holmes, Bryant, Stedman, Warner, Elizabeth Stuart Phelps and a host of essayists and modern religious society novelists have contributed to the diffusion of liberal ideas.

Since the middle of the century the modern inductive method of research, the general mechanical and biological doctrines of La Place and Darwin, and, to some large extent, especially within recent years, the transplanted results of German philosophy, have affected American religious thought and theological culture, and added additional elements to the problem. In the general American mind the backbone of the old Calvinism is effectually broken. It is a dead issue.

[1] This question is as old as the Garden of Eden, where God laid down the first rule of faith and life; and Satan for the first time volunteered its solution in saying, "Your eyes shall be opened, and ye shall be as gods." The question has come up in some form in every age, the Scholastics elaborating it specifically in their discussion of the relation of *credo* and *intelligo*.

Following the rebellion against *dominant types* of American doctrine, there has come rebellion against the *source* of doctrine. The more recent extension of the domain of Reason by European critics to the source of authority itself, the Scripture, has led American liberal theology and literature to a criticism of the rule of faith, and, with the facts just mentioned, brought about the leading general religious issue and condition in the cultured American mind of to-day. It is not necessary to detail the rise of this movement of Higher Biblical Criticism which has taken possession of all Germany, much of Holland, a great part of Scotland and even conservative England, nor to state how it was brought over and is being disseminated here, particularly through such schools as Union Theological Seminary. It is sufficient to say that the old style of Biblical scholar and critic, represented, for instance, by Ezra Abbott and the writers of Smith's "Dictionary of the Bible" of a quarter of a century ago, has been supplanted; and present-day Biblical theology, as represented in both the great new Bible dictionaries summarizing the learning of this epoch, is a theology mainly occupied with showing that the Bible cannot be the only and infallible rule of faith. It would be well worth while to examine the compromise of the English half-way school, which is trying to maintain, in criticism, about the same position that the Ritschlians have set up in doctrine, namely, that their critical results do not interfere with their piety, devoutness, Christian faith and orthodoxy.

The Lutheran Church in this land is almost the only great united and uncompromising foe of such negative critical issues. Lutheranism, if orthodox, must be such a foe because of her formal reformation principle. But when our Lutheran Church is asked to meet the issue in a theological and scientific way, how shall she do so? When we are asked, "Where does Reason come in in the theological handling of the Scripture?" what shall we say?

Mere general statements on the untrustworthiness or the sinfulness and blindness of human reason, however true they may be, and however satisfactory to true believers in the Word, are neither justifiable nor prudent as a matter of argument against the springing up of this modern American issue. In the judgment of the writer there is something better to be said.

Scripture, though the only rule of faith, is not the only rule nor the only source of knowledge. It was not intended so to be. Reason is the rule and one of the sources of knowledge. As in all other complementary spheres, so there is constant interaction, reinforcement, and mutual dependence in these two spheres. Faith, coming by hearing, rests on knowledge, and knowledge is nothing if it does not rest on faith. Faith is needed as a principle in all knowledge, and reason is needed as an organizer and tester in all faith.

Knowledge is of less account than faith, because *knowledge fails in all the great and supreme finalities*, whereas it is here that faith helps. In matters of faith Scripture is the only reliable and authoritative source of knowledge, and it is the only rule and standard of test. But in matters of faith reason also is employed, and is necessary as an organ and instrument. Now it is the instinct of reason to discover, experiment and construct wheresoever it is employed; and to be so confident of its method, materials and results as to proceed in the sphere of faith, independently of the rule of faith; and it is this constant self-confidence of reason, cropping out everywhere in faith and knowledge and life, that leads the Christian theologian, notably if he has such a profound personal spiritual insight as Paul and Luther had, to disparage and distrust reason. The philosopher's temptation is to disparage the rule of faith. The theologian's temptation is to develop the materials of faith by the method of reason, and call the whole "Faith" Logic, the organ of reason, is supreme in its own sphere, and is infallible as a method, but always fallible and partial in its application. Facts, the material of reason, are often not what they seem, as the testings of science show; and few combinations of fact and logic, *i. e.*, knowledge, are strong enough to exclude the possibility of error in them. They appeal to us in part by faith. Conversely faith always appeals on the basis of some knowledge. The basis of knowledge in Faith (*i. e.*, in Scripture) is *subject* to the same laws and tests of knowledge as elsewhere; but it is not to be *subjected to the same theories*, if those theories are in conflict with the rule of faith. The thing to do is to hold to the rule of faith on the one hand, and not to despise what seem to be the facts on the other, but knowing the fallibility of our powers of investigation and witnessing the changeableness in science from age to age, trust to an unseen harmony in both. This, it appears to the writer, is the true attitude for our Church in all the critical problems of the day, and especially in reference to the negative or the half-way theories so universally seeking introduction under the name of the Higher Criticism of the books of the Bible. It is an attitude which all thinkers must assume in reference to many of the paradoxes of knowledge and of life in general. It is scholarly, honest and orthodox.

II.

As a result of the critical spirit, it is a significant fact that the theological issues of our day are not those of a creative epoch. There is no great breaking up and bursting forth of fountains of life and soul and spirit. Not the heart of our theologians, but their eye and their hand seem most active. Things are looked at from without rather than lived through from within. The issues are those of the bearing of facts on theories, of intellectual speculations, of doubt, of order and externals, of works.

There is no great and absorbing controversy on doctrine. None of the old types of intense emotionalism are dominant. There is no universal wave of revivalism or pietism sweeping the land. Writers are not discussing the nature of the operations of the Holy Spirit, nor the questions connected with conversion; nor are the motives of eternal life and death put forth with overpowering earnestness in the pulpit. The great Methodist Church is relegating many of her early historic and essential features to the background, and in some parts is substituting a Pelagian culture as the best order of religion. Large parts of the great Presbyterian Church are at sea on the critical question, and know not how to choose between the old spirit of legalistic adherence and the new one of critical examination.

Puritan, Presbyterian, Reformed and Methodist are yielding in externals to the Festival and Liturgical idea. The Episcopal

Church is desirous of becoming the Church of the American nation, and as heretofore is broad enough to receive distinguished orthodox and unorthodox into the one fold. The Roman Church is pleading in national matters with sweet reasonableness, that its affinity for the American patriotic spirit and institutions may be evident to all. The Second Advent doctrines, especially as they are connected with Seventh Day Baptist teachings, are vigorous and seem to be making some progress.

A sober view of religious issues in America, however, does not justify German historians and theologians in describing America as a hot-bed of religious wildness and fanaticism. It is well to recognize the truth that in general and on the whole America is a conservative and not a particularly fanatical religious country. To speak of "Sectarian America," as is often done in discussions of American religious issues, seems to the writer to be unjust to our land. Scotland gave us the half score branches of Presbyterianism. England furnished most of the Baptists and the Puritans. From her we have the Salvation Army and similar types. Germany sent us the Dunkers and Schwenckfelters and Moravians and Amish and Mennonites. Not merely the wild theological, philosophical and anarchistic, but a large majority of the religiously fanatical, unorthodox and sectarian ideas have come over to us from Europe to become less wild here. If there were no State repression there, we Americans might probably be speaking with some justice of the old country as "sect-cursed Europe." And it is a marvelous testimony to the general conservatism of America that in spite of the fact that the State Churches of Europe, in their unwillingness to grant every man the right to worship God according to the dictates of his own conscience, have driven to America many whom state intolerance has brought to the borders of revolution, nevertheless throughout the country the spirit of religious extravagance is not dominant, but is ever growing weaker and weaker. We should recognize that America is not a particularly fanatical religious country.

But on the contrary the general religious situation, under the stimulus of what may perhaps be called a journalistic or newspaper pulpit and religion, is one in which the Church is regarded rather as an influence on society than as a communion of saints or a peculiar people; the Scripture is looked at as rather an inspiration than a rule; Christ is considered as rather an ideal than a Redeemer and Judge. Every man holds religious views absorbed from philosophy and literature, rather than a faith grounded on and ruled by catechism and creed. There is a widespread feeling that a simpler religion of the future is developing. This general way of regarding the whole subject of religion becomes evident in the addresses of prominent men at public conventions; in what is taught in schools of lower and higher and of technical university education; in the instruction of some departments in such colleges as Harvard, Yale, Columbia and Princeton; in the teachings of such reflectors of public opinion as *The Harper's* and *The Century Magazines, The Forum, The Outlook, The North American Review, The Review of Reviews,* and *The Literary Digest.*

The issue then is one of a civilization weakening widely in its positive faith, willing to regard fundamental religious doctrines as open questions, active in works of education and mercy; of an age in which a luminous haze of universal charity, "gorgeous as the dying rays of sunset," diffuses itself throughout all the air. Expectation of future judgment, of hell, and even of heaven, are sublimated almost to vanishing.

What shall the Lutheran Church do in such surroundings? Shall she tone down her teaching of salvation by faith alone to a harmonious resonance with such universal sentiment? Shall she loosen her hold on Scripture as the only rule of faith and life? Shall she give up her Lord and Christ, in His person, work, and offices, and deal with Him and with them as an open question? Shall she widen out the nature of the Gospel and the Word, and attenuate sin, and humanize the means of grace, to fit the religion of the day? Not if we can help it. By faith the fathers of every age held to their treasure of salvation in by-gone days, even amid the greater darkness of the Old Testament, as we are told in Hebrews 12, and by faith we shall be able to hold to Word and Sacrament until the world is overcome.

The Lutheran Church in her innermost nature and fibre is

altogether against the spirit of such a civilization as we have just delineated. If there is any strength in her strength, and she is to be strong in her own strength, she cannot yield to it. Our Church's *faith* is her only power and treasure. Give up this, and all is gone. None who have ever strengthened weakness, have done so by making themselves like unto it. If to become all things to all men, we give up the one thing needed to save some, we rather lose than gain.

But what is the Church to do? To shut itself out from present-day civilization? It could not if it would, and it ought not if it could. To day's problems are our problems. Their weaknesses are our weaknesses. Their burdens are our burdens. Their powers of fascination are our temptation. Their strength is our rod of chastisement. To ignore them, means death to us, no less than to compromise with them. We cannot remain in our citadel with the enemy tampering with our fields and our water supply. We are to go forth and meet the influences of the day. We are not to despise what good they have to offer us; and we also are not to be beguiled into becoming like unto those affected by them that we may sail smoothly in the broad current of the majority.

Faith more than theirs, patience more than theirs, large heartedness more than theirs, a humble willingness to learn from adversaries more than theirs, a better use of our reason, an equal skill in method, will finally give us the victory. For they who believe what they know, and who know what they believe, are always in the end more powerful than they who do not know whether they know or whether they believe.

III.

As we pass from the general issues of the modern theological situation to the special and more practical religious issues of the day, we meet first of all as a prominently discussed American problem, a question that probably will come up in many aspects in various papers presented at this Conference.

With the advent of large views and easy toleration of adverse systems, the feeling always grows that it is a discredit, if not a disgrace to the Christian faith, and a practical argument against its divine character, that Christendom is divided into so many churches each holding its own narrow and peculiar views on minor points so tenaciously, and each so jealous of the other in competing activities, that the force of unity and the exercise of Christian charity are altogether lost. There is probably no theme which is touched on in a popular way by the average critics of the Church more frequently than this one.

There is no one who has been more anxious or more zealous in attempting to gather the scattered forces of Christendom into a visible unity under a single head than the present Pope of Rome. This has been his dream and his hope for years. In his view these divisions are the natural and necessary result of the individual-responsibility principle of Protestantism, and he is most earnestly desirous of bringing Congregationalists, Episcopalians, Presbyterians and all others back into the Roman fold. Then Christianity would have but two sects at least, the Roman and the Russian.

Some of the leading Protestant agitators in America, who are not altogether prepared for a return to a visible unity under the Pope, have been urging that all the small denominations gather and merge themselves into four or five representative Protestant types, and that all the various divisions in the large bodies come at once into organic fellowship relation with each other. It has been notably a powerful independent religious journal in New York which, assuming a quasi-Papal prerogative for American Protestantism, has been telling the various religious communions that they must do this, and that they have neither reason nor right to refuse. By one of the curious instances of the laws of extremes, it is thus the leading independent paper of America which is endeavoring to compel denominations of America to give up independence. A third and curious proposition made to Christendom to unite, is known to all as the Lambeth Proposals of the Episcopal Church, and needs to be only alluded to here.

The Lutheran Church disposes of this whole issue in its most essential points by the fundamental teaching that the true unity of the Church is a unity of spirit, and not a unity of government; that the "One Holy Church" is the congregation of saints which is to continue forever, and which is to be found wheresoever under any name the Gospel is rightly taught and the sacraments are rightly administered;[1] and that no human government, rites, or ceremonies, instituted by man, are essential to the true unity of the Church, or necessary to salvation.

She admits the advantages of external unity, and has suffered from the lack of it. She realizes that an organically united church can throw weightier power, in influence, in training, in finance, against the world and against unbelief. She knows that there is economy in concentration of interests in these days, and that the Church's educational and publication spheres would be served with better qualities at lower rates. The Church cannot help seeing, furthermore, that much misspent energy now wasted in denominational rivalries, would be conserved by greater unity. Her young people, also, are much attracted by the fact that size and number and influence make the Church popular and seem to draw in followers.

And we confess that the Church ought practice as fully as she realizes, and that she ought realize more fully than she does, that it is a scandal for any part or the whole of the body of Christ to hold jealousy or hatred toward any neighbors, to engage in earthly methods of unlawful competition, or to alienate members from the vilest sect in earth by means that would be considered disreputable in business. The Church should see that she ought fear and love God and not unlawfully entice a person away from another church, even if she thereby intends to save a soul. This latter is Jesuitism. And furthermore certain agreements to these effects ought be entered into where necessary by even the most hostile churches.

The Lutheran Church appreciates in full also the glories of a common service and a common praxis. But she appreciates in addition that these are the blossoms, and not the root of a vital unity, and that they are valuable chiefly as they are the outbreathing of a common doctrine and common faith. She holds that it is not a scandal on Christendom, but a righteous thing, to have the Church divided so long as convictions and spirit are

[1] Aug. Conf., VII.

diverse, and faith and doctrine are divided. She holds that doctrine ought hold together and rule any church body, and not a form of government or practical expediency. This is only another way of saying that, in her judgment, men ought be true to their principles, and not be asked to compromise them.

She does not consider that it is charity, but weak sentiment, as a rule, to admit to pulpit and altar those who believe differently, and intend to continue believing differently, from what she does. She does not consider that a failure to admit them is any personal disparagement of them, or any judgment upon their Christian character; and she herself would not desire to be found in pulpits or at altars where what she prizes is missing. She could quote with approbation a large part of the words of Dr. Hodge, found in a letter written as early as 1839, and now in the archives of the Gettysburg Seminary, in which he says, " I cannot see that external union is of any great value among Christians, except so far as it is the expression and evidence of internal union. The Scriptures enjoin on all the disciples of Christ τὸ αὐτὸ φρονεῖν, which, of course, includes a great deal. Where this is, there is true union; and external union should be carried just so far as it can be without endangering this spiritual union, which is of so much more importance. . . . It is, I think, going the wrong way to work to bring people externally together before, or to a greater degree than they are in harmony as to views and feelings. All such attempts have not only hitherto failed, but have ultimately widened the breach."

Though the Church cannot unite, yet much can be done, even where there is open hostility to remove the stigma that often attaches itself, and sometimes justly, to religious and theological controversy. Even the nations of the world, when they are not at war with each other, have some sense of justice, charity and honor respecting each other, and enter into and regard agreements that strip the war of its most inhuman and unchristian features.

Armies are not permitted to glut their passions, unnecessary destruction and rapine are prohibited, prisoners of war are exchanged, prisoners are permitted to receive home mail, flags of truce are respected, the Red Cross is protected, the dead are not robbed but decently buried, and are allowed to be reclaimed, and a multitude of minor annoyances are borne calmly in time of tension, every resource of diplomacy being exhausted to maintain the public peace.

If the world in its warfare can create such a series of important and restrictive understandings, and hostile nations can communicate and co-operate to carry them out, surely the Christian Church, in its arguments and controversies with even the most divergent of antagonists, or the worst of errorists, should insist on doing the same.

Many things could be effected by mutual understandings and agreements within the various bodies and Synods of the Lutheran Church which would compromise none of them, would make neither side a party to any of the errors or heresies imputed to the other, would not even involve Fellowship with them, but which would remove the sin and reproach, now often justly and often unjustly ascribed, from the parties concerned. There should be understandings — to respect each others' common ground, to refuse to allow the less charitable motive to be imputed in a controversy, and to discipline all hatred. Even errorists have rights to be respected, and false doctrine itself has one right none can take away, the right to be dealt with fairly.

There is no part of our Lutheran Church that would compromise herself, as to her more exclusive teachings, by standing with other Lutherans on the common base of mutually accepted teachings, and by acting together on that common lower base, provided that it be definitely understood that there is cordial and earnest disagreement on the narrower and higher base.[1]

IV.

Next in prominence to the issue of Church Unity, among all the general practical religious issues in this land, many persons would mention one in which the Lutheran Church is occasionally

---

[1] A number of practical suggestions as to what might be done along these lines by our Church, in the writer's manuscript as presented to the Conference, are here omitted by him, for the reason that they could not be read, and did not therefore actually become a part of the Proceedings.

drawn into the foreground in a negative way. It is the issue of Moral Reform. The constitutional indisposition and innate slowness of Lutheranism to believe that people can be made better by the imposition of a law from without, just as little as they can be brought into church unity by the adoption of external regulations; together with the disagreement of a large part of the Church in judgment and methods as to that which is to be a subject-matter of reform in our land; possibly has caused her to go to an opposite extreme at times, and to take less interest in necessary and proper reform than she really ought. And, indeed, even in the conspicuous and radical questions of reform, stirred by extreme Puritan agitators, there does not seem to be any widespread and living interest at the present moment. The customary Sabbath-day reform movement, and the agitations against Sunday papers, Sunday trains, Sunday concerts and Sunday amusements, seem to be decadent in radical circles at the present moment. The temperance and the prohibition questions have been put into the background politically by other issues. The peace question has been momentarily forgotten in the excitement of the Spanish war. Nor are there any great social, charity or labor questions sufficiently prominent to absorb the general public mind just at this time. Nevertheless the general situation and conditions are with us always, and new development may spring forth from them again at any day. The attitude of our Church must always be against ecclesiastical participation in such political reform agitations, even where the reforms themselves are both desirable and important.[1]

But there is another side to the question, and one which the Lutheran Church in this land has been slow to recognize and consider. Wherever the Augsburg Confession speaks of the "Imperial Majesty," of "Electors," "Princes and Estates," who are the earthly sources of civil power, as distinct from the magistrates and judges, who are its instruments and organs, there, today, we must read "the American citizen." The same close connection that existed in those days between the individual sources

[1] The writer's MSS. enters into a full discussion of the reasons for this statement.

of civil power and the Christian religion exists to-day between the individual American citizen and the Christian religion. It is not merely the office-bearers, the President, the Governor, the Judge, that the Church obeys, but it is the office creators and controllers in their individual capacity that the Church touches and teaches. Our Church has scarcely opened its eyes to its responsibility in this matter in our land. It has always spoken out boldly of duties to magistrates and office-bearers, but it has failed to realize, that what Luther was to the Elector of Saxony as elector, that the representative of the Church to-day is to be to the American citizen as citizen.

In other words, to speak briefly, *the Christian is the State.* There is to be entire separation between the Church and State, but not between the Christian and the State. The "Let alone" policy which Lutherans are apt to assume and teach with reference to the State is a great mistake. Coming over from the old country, they learn to exercise the elective franchise very quickly as political citizens, but outside of *obedience* to the law, they do not see what it means to be Christian citizens. Trained to obey law, they do not seem to grasp Christian responsibility as to the source of that law. They seem to think the State some outside power which has been constituted from above in a way that does not concern them, and which is to go on by itself, or at least without them as Lutherans. All they ask of it, as Christians, is to be let alone by it, and they feel a right to let it alone as Christians, except when some peculiar interests, language or other, are involved. Such is not their right.[1]

The position just taken in reference to the Church and the State has a direct bearing on what the writer regards as the most important practical "modern American religious issue," viz., the question of Education. This question, including the issues between church and state, between church and American educational influences; between sound and unsound methods and old and new methods in the Church; and including a consideration of what should and could be undertaken in the agencies of cate-

[1] It is impossible to present any more of the argument to be made on this point, in this paper.

chetical instruction and the Sunday-school; and in the placing of parochial instruction on such a permanent and universal footing, as does not exist on the one hand where it is altogether neglected, and on the other hand, where members look on the agency employed largely as a language institution, can be but alluded to; and such other modern religious issues in America, originally treated in the writer's paper, as "Social and Institutional Christianity," "Young People's Movements in American Churches," and "The Woman Suffrage Question," can barely be even alluded to.

But what above all else the writer desires to emphasize by way of conclusion is the fact that the relative prominence of the religious issues before the Church has nothing to do with their relative importance. To the Lutheran Church the most important issues are not matters of worship, howsoever useful these may be; not matters of government, howsoever pressing these may be; not matters of reform, howsoever, urgent these may seem, but matters of teaching. And in matters of teaching the pre-eminent questions are not those commonly discussed; not matters of Origin, whether of Predestination or Creation; not matters of Destiny, whether of Chiliasm or a Future Probation, but matters of Salvation:

First—That we need to be saved. The matter of Sin.

Second—That we have a Saviour. The matter of the Person of Christ.

Third—That we are saved by faith alone. The matter of Justification by Faith, and

Fourth—That Faith comes alone through Word and Sacraments. The matter of the Means of Grace.

THE PROBLEM OF CO-OPERATION,

BY M. W. HAMMA, D.D.,

which is the subject of this paper, is a somewhat new manifestation in modern Lutheran history in this country. Until late years the tendencies were rather to multiply divisions and to perpetuate those already existing. That sooner or later there should come a revulsion against this unhappy state of things, between the brethren of substantially the same faith, should not seem strange, but ought rather to be regarded as the legitimate fruit of divine grace in the hearts of true believers.

In this presence it is not needful to enter into any details as to the disagreements and divisions of the past, now, we hope, happily beginning to disappear. Neither is it necessary to trace the rise of this new movement, called "Practical Co-operation," between three of our general Lutheran bodies, for it is sufficient to say that what has taken place in that direction, is so manifestly a Providential movement, that it demands our most serious and thoughtful attention.

But, as we are yet only upon the threshold of this problem, *it concerns us, first of all, to know what is the scope of its meaning.*

In order to a clear conception of the subject, it is necessary to state the terms of this Basis of Co-operation, as existing between the three bodies having consented thereto.

First, *Home Missions.*—Touching this, the policy was adopted "That wherever one body of the Lutheran Church, hereunto consenting, is in occupation of a field and is shown, in a reasonable degree, able to care for our Lutheran material therein, the other or others shall respect such occupancy, and abstain from any attempt to plant any additional congregation to operate in the same language, and that in case of any disagreement, the Home Mission Boards or Committees of the Bodies concerned shall amicably adjust such differences."

Second, *Foreign Missions.*—The article on this subject is, "That recognizing the intimate relations already existing between the missionaries of the different bodies of the Lutheran Church, where laboring in adjoining foreign fields, we encourage them to promote the upbuilding of the one undivided Lutheran Church, in their christianizing efforts."

Third, *Our Church Papers.*—The action adopted on this item is, "That we deprecate a bitter controversional spirit, wherever found in matters of religion, and that we heartily disapprove of it in any of our Church journals, and that we affectionately and sincerely counsel all who write for, and those who control, our

Lutheran papers and periodicals, to abstain from publishing anything that will tend to foster the spirit of partisan division among the brethren of our Lutheran household, and that we counsel them to seek to exalt those things especially and only, which consistently, with the testimony for the purity of our Lutheran faith, will promote the peace and the unity of our beloved Lutheran Church."

Fourth, *In Conclusion.*—It was ordained "That when these lines of co-operation, or any number of them, shall have been agreed upon by two or more Lutheran Bodies, such action shall be held as a sacred compact between the parties consenting thereto; and that we hereby invoke upon this movement, for the practical unification of our glorious Church, the blessing of Almighty God."

The Fifth Article is explanatory, to the effect, "That the above action is not to be interpreted in such way as to imply a compromise or surrender of the Bodies represented concerning any point of their doctrinal positions."

The following was added to the above basis by subsequent action: "That when any general body has congregations, whatever be the language, the establishment of a congregation of another general body within the territory be not undertaken, unless the Board of Missions occupying the territory, and the officers of the Synod in the field, be first consulted.

"No established congregation shall be hindered by this agreement from changing the language of its worship, or from establishing a mission in another language within its own Parish."

The final court of appeal is a committee of arbitration, composed of three members from each body in the compact, "to whom shall be referred all cases where agreement has not been otherwise obtained," and each general body in this committee shall have one vote only.

While these articles of agreement need no very close analysis to obtain their meaning, yet by some examination, they may be set into the order of a better understanding,

1st. The agreement touching Home Missions is intended to correct that long-standing evil of the unnecessary multiplication of Lutheran congregations in the same locality, ofttimes organized out of an undue zeal rather for party success than for the glory of God. It has not been an uncommon occurrence to build Lutheran Church by the side of Lutheran Church, until, in a community where one organization of the kind would have been ample, two or three divided the field and frittered away an opportunity by jealousies and strifes, and brought defeat and disrepute instead of honor to a noble cause. It was long felt by many that, for those who were practically of the same faith, to give themselves to such methods of work was a scandal too grievous for the Christian name to bear. From the nature of the case, along the line of Home Missions will be found the mutual aggressions, out of which conflicts are likely to grow.

Under the terms of this agreement it is sought to abolish this unchristian and destructive rivalry, and substitute for it a fraternal comity, which will lead all to co-operate for the greatest good of the greatest number.

The congregation of one Lutheran body located in a community that is large enough only to adequately support the one, is to be allowed to hold the field for itself, undivided by the incoming of other Lutheran bodies. And in any territory, where one body has congregations, no other Lutheran body shall enter, unless the Board of Missions occupying the territory, and the officers of the Synod in the field, be first consulted.

This might prove an arbitrary arrangement were it not modified so that a previous consultation is really all that may be necessary to open the door to the congregation seeking entrance.

If a disagreement occurs after consultation, then, as in all other cases, it becomes a matter of arbitration. Under this compact no one body has the power to absolutely close the door of a field against another. Their own consent is not held by the parties in possession as a fixed barrier against those outside; but the courtesy of previous notification and consultation before entrance and work are begun, is named as a condition of good faith.

And it must always be remembered that, after all these negotiations have taken place; first, between the local parties concerned, second, between the Boards, and lastly, in the Committee of Arbitration, between the bodies in interest, the obligation to abide by the final decision, while as strong as moral force can make it, cannot, according to Lutheran polity, be absolutely binding on the losing party, should manifest injustice characterize the decision.

As to the provision, that an established Church shall have the right to change the language of its worship, or to found a mission in another language within its own Parish, those are rights beyond question, when exercised in conformity with the true meaning of the terms in which they are stated.

The article on Foreign Missions, by reason of the remoteness of the work from Home divisions and Home controversies, need but be hospitably entertained, and it will be self-operative in its harmonizing and unifying work.

The fraternal and altogether Christian counsel contained in the paragraph on the conduct of church journals is so far removed from possible objection, and is so thoroughly in the line of the common courtesies of Christianity, that it needs neither apology nor explanation.

From this brief review of the elements which enter into this plan of Co-operation, the purpose of it all may be clearly arrived at, viz., to cultivate a better understanding and to secure such co-operation between the different bodies of Lutherans, along common lines of work, as may be possible and consistent, and as may finally lead to a practically united Lutheran Church.

I use the terms *practically united*, to distinguish from *organically united*, because the latter has never been aimed at as a distinct object of this movement. Indeed, its originators and friends have been so far from seeking organic unity as not only to hold, but to freely express, the belief, that such a consummation, under existing circumstances, would, if even possible, be of very questionable utility.

It is needless to say that if ever such unity comes to pass it will be wrought of the spontaneous influence of the Holy Spirit, and not of man's planning and manufacture.

But it is deemed not only possible, but greatly desirable, for the various Lutheran bodies to come together *into harmonious practical work on common lines,* such as contemplated by this plan of "Co-operation."

But that there are difficulties in the way of the consummation of this problem is a self-evident fact.

One of the first of these obstacles is the diversities of languages and nationalities. The Lutheran is a world-embracing Church, and brings her representatives from all quarters of the globe together into this land, so that the first difficulties that confront any efforts toward a union of these forces in common work are not easy of accomplishment. These obstacles, like the poor, we "have always with us." And while this is, in the main, a permanent condition, yet in every coming generation the work of transformation of many languages and many nationalities into one, as we find them in the Lutheran Church in this country, goes on more easily and more rapidly. It is not safe to say to-day that we cannot work together because we are of different tongues and different lands, for to-morrow, comparatively speaking, we shall be one in language and one in country. While in some parts of the world a certain language is the mummy shroud of *one* religion, or a given nation is the sealed tomb of *another*, in this new world, from the nature of things, it can not be so. The intermingling forces which here so enmesh and environ every path of life are more and more effective in reducing to the minimum linguistic and national obstacles, in the way of the practical unity of the diverse elements present, into a homogeneous people. And it were contradictory of the Divine order if similar influences should not produce similar results in our polyglot Lutheran Church.

Be it far from me to speak lightly of any of the tongues and lands into which our Church is sub-divided. The least of them has a record of immortal honor. Their noble deeds of heroism and martyrs' devotion have added undying lustre to the whole Church of the Reformation. These common bonds of friendship and mutual priceless inheritances are stronger than language ties and national boundaries, and should operate as conjoining influences, in spite of linguistic and national divisions.

These obstacles can never again be as potent in our Church as they have been in the past. They are losing their power of cleavage and their ancient capacity for perpetuating divisions.

Time and the Divine alchemy of God's grace are dissolving these old linguistic difficulties, and will make new combinations of peoples and tongues as we pass along the highway of our unfolding destiny in this new world in which we live.

Again, there is no greater obstacle in the way of "Co-operation" than the real and supposed divergencies of doctrinal interpretations and differences in church practices that exist between disagreeing bodies of Lutherans.

Viewing each other at a distance with the mystifying influences of suspicion and prejudice overhanging, things are not seen in their true form and color. Misconception follows; misjudgment is formed; wrong statements and criticism are given forth; accusation and acrimonious answer succeed each other, and thus crimination and recrimination go on erecting apparently impassable barriers between hostile camps of those who should align shoulder to shoulder against a common enemy.

That there are differences of view is neither right nor prudent to deny. But it may be declared with truth that any dissent from the *fundamental* doctrines of historic Lutheranism existing is confined to the minority within these bodies, a minority, the size of which may be uncertain at times, but that it is an ever-shrinking minority is beyond question.

Nothing can be more certain as a movement in our Church to-day, than that the Lutheranism, not of Calvin or Wesley, but of Luther, is overwhelmingly triumphant in all of the bodies here represented. As to differences which do not touch essentials or fundamentals, these should not count for arguments of disparagement by one party or the other, any more than they did with Luther himself.

Moreover, if Christian charity is to play any part at all in our efforts at co-operation, that sweet angel of God must be allowed here to lead the way to the recognition of an historically orthodox majority, as the body representing, in a sufficient measure, the co-operating party, and to teach Christly forbearance with the dissenting minority. And if there is an extreme minority on the one side or the other opposing the prevailing view, this should not count to prevent the overwhelming majorities from co-operating for mutual good in practical Christian work. It is the majority that represents the true character of a body; it is the majority that writes the platform, that formulates and adopts the creed; it is the majority that sets up the standard of faith and organizes that faith into living, pulsating, miracle-working Christian activities. It is the majority that must lead the high and holy cause, if it is ever to press through the gates of victory and be crowned with universal reigning.

Minorities, by their negations, by their protestations, and by their pessimistic forebodings, elect themselves to lag behind and to count for nothing in the great movements of the controlling body.

When by large majorities three great bodies have severally voted to enter into co-operation with each other, along common lines of Christian work, they have proceeded by the rational, scriptural and providential method for the attainment of the will of God, and the questionings of motives and the misrepresentations of individuals, or small dissatisfied minorities, should not swerve them from their high purpose, else the coming together and the rule of majorities of good men, for the furtherance of noble ends, must be forever abandoned, and individualism with its chaos and destruction, be left to disintegrate the Church and well-ordered Christian society.

Minorities have their rights, which should always be respected and guarded, but it is not one of their rights to rule the majority, when all are upon a line of equality. If the majority would wait for perfect unanimity in matters religious, before taking a forward step, the world would be left either to die of intellectual and spiritual paralysis, or to rot down in its unchecked, inherent corruptions.

Again, at this point it should be observed that the condition of real and supposed difference of view is promoted and greatly aggravated by the vicious system of personal and irresponsible journalism, which so largely prevails in the different bodies of our Church.

Under our system the individual, ambitious of leadership, or desirous of promulgating certain individual views, may install himself in the editor's chair, at the head of a faction, and assume to represent the only true Lutheranism, denouncing all who differ from the views of his self-constituted organ as false to the true faith. Unfortunately, there are many in our own churches who take these irresponsible utterances seriously, simply because these individual sheets are stamped with the Lutheran name. It matters little how extreme, unsound, or un-Lutheran these teachings may be, some will be misled, others will seize upon and attribute them to the whole body, to which the authors may chance to belong, and thus misunderstand and misjudge the whole from an exceptional case. It is largely through the influence of these extreme, factional, irresponsible journals that misjudgment, suspicion, prejudice and divisions are created and fostered in our Lutheran household of faith. At least one of the bodies here represented has entered upon the solution of this difficulty by a concentration of the journals, professedly published in its interest, into one general organ, put forth under the authority of, and responsible to, the governing power of that body.

The increasing excellence of that paper, in every respect, bears ample testimony to the wisdom and success of the policy.

A similar movement in all our general bodies would do a vast deal toward removing misunderstandings, taking down barriers, healing divisions and bringing into closer co-operation Lutheran peoples and interests in this country.

It is altogether likely that the individual organ would still seek to propagate itself through the frailties and perversities of human nature, but its power, as a supposed church organ, would be gone, as over against the authorized journal which stands for the settled faith and polity of the denomination.

And now, in view of all that has been said of the practicability and desirability, on the one hand, and the difficulties in the way of this movement, on the other, what of this "Problem of Co-operation?"

The pessimistic opponent of this cause has already lifted his doleful cry, "Who shall show us any good?"—as if evils that are hoary with age could be cured in a day; as if divisions that have organized themselves into synods and conferences and equipped Christian activities in the interest of specific views and policies could be transformed by a series of resolutions, severally passed, by disagreeing parties. Divisions in churches are not matters of such slight significance, generally, that they can be obliterated by a legislative act. While the original causes of such disagreements are often mere trifles, the accumulated results of agitation and time usually build up a barrier to subsequent union not easily or quickly removed.

This plan of Co-operation has been adopted in its last details by only two of the bodies concerned, at their last conventions, the remaining one having yet to meet and take final action; nevertheless, there are those, who were prophets of evil from the beginning, gainsaying the movement because miracles have not already been wrought in changing the views of other bodies into their own, and because these bodies have not thrown their distinguishing peculiarities to the winds and rushed into the arms of their hitherto objectionable brethren, into a kind of emotional *believe-nothing-in-particular-union*, only to separate the wider when the gush is over. Union comes not by such nineteenth century superficial emotionalism. Continued education, patient waiting and God's Spirit are the only factors that can compose great differences and difficulties, such as have put asunder brethren of the same faith, and bring them again into lasting harmony.

It is along the line of this educational and gracious culture that this conference is held; to this end, these discussions; for this purpose, these fraternal comminglings and free interchange of views, and these and similar influences, if continued, as sure as human minds and hearts are impressible, and as sure as the Truth is omnipotent, must close old chasms and open gates of gold, by and by, for our entering into, not the dream-land, but the reality of Lutheran reunion.

We are already finding that so narrow is the line of separation that we can clasp hands across its bounds, and our hearts that had been so long well-nigh pulseless of sympathy for each other are ready to say, "Is there not a mistake somewhere? Are no these the true brethren? Is not here the self-same faith that was nailed to the Castle Church Door at Wittenberg, that was spoken into immortality at Worms, that was translated from the Bible in Wartburg, and that at Augsburg became the mother of Protestant Christianity in the immortal confession?" Yes, these are the questions that our hearts ask us as we look into each other's faces and hear each other's testimony when we meet on these fraternal terms.

The problem of "Co-operation" will be favorably wrought out, if Patience is permitted "to have her perfect work." There are influences operating in our Church, silent and unseen, chainless as gravitation, and as sure, which are bearing all things toward a common centre before which all these old obstacles will become as the thin air and will some day ensphere and solidify the Lutheran Church now in fragments. Say not, "O dreamer, dispel thy delusions," but look rather toward the gates of the morning; for even now, all the East is red, and the rosy fingers of coming day are turning back the curtains of darkness! And when we shall have gone within the shining gates, may be, ere while, in some way, there will fall on our quickened ear the long-expected message, "They are all one," and the sweet dream of Earth will have been fulfilled, and the waiting heart will say,—"It is enough! It is enough!"

REMARKS.

After the reading of the above papers, Dr. L. E. ALBERT, speaking for the General Synod, made a few closing remarks, giving his impressions of the convention and expressing his hopes for the future. He said: We have listened to a number of first-class essays, and there has been manifest throughout all the discussions a most kindly feeling. What now shall we do to promote the cause of union in the future? We are apt to be enthusiastic while the sessions last and to fall back into the old habits of non-fraternity when they are over. Let us believe that union can be accomplished. Faith is necessary to it. If I were at the head of an army and wanted to find a commander who would take a certain stronghold of the enemy, I should select one who would say, "I believe it can be taken," not one who doubted it. And so, if union of spirit and practice is to come, we must begin with faith in such union. When Spurgeon was a youth, some one placed his hand on his head and said, "You will some day be the greatest preacher in the most influential church in London." Those words may have had much to do with Spurgeon's later success. Great things are possible where there is faith. Hitherto we have been too prone to believe unkind things of each other. Let us henceforth not believe half of what we hear said against each other. Let us rebuke the fault-finding spirit and recognize each other as Christians.

Dr. F. V. N. Painter said: In the South we have great confidence in the possibility of co-operation. According to an old maxim, "Seeing is believing." South of the Potomac we have the same differences that exist north of the Potomac. Some of our ministers cordially accept all the Symbolical Books; others have misgivings about articles in the Augustana. Some use the Common Service in full; others do not use it at all. Some admit only Lutheran communicants to the Lord's table; others welcome all true believers in Christ. Yet there are no parties among us. We feel that the points of agreement are far more numerous and far more vital than the points of difference. Hence, at our Synodical meetings, we shake hands in fraternal greeting, and heartily unite in supporting our mission work, our Orphan Home, and our other Church interests. The existing state of things in the United Synod is not, to be sure, an ideal one. But it shows clearly that earnest Christian men, while differing in non-essential points of faith and practice, can still stand shoulder to shoulder in doing the work to which the Lord has called them.

Dr. Krotel, speaking for the General Council, said: After meeting together here for three days and listening to so many good things, so many sound Lutheran sentiments concerning the Confessions, it is natural we should feel ourselves to be on the verge of enthusiasm and ready to unite in the old hymn, "Blest be the tie that binds." At the Reading Convention in 1866, called for a similar purpose, after a long and harmonious discussion, we united in the well-known hymn, "Now thank we all our God." But we found afterward that we were not so fully agreed as we thought. The harmony was soon disturbed and we drew asunder. We have every reason to congratulate ourselves, and particularly the Committee, on the auspicious beginning made towards a closer union. I confess that at first I had my doubts as to the wisdom of the committee's management;—there seemed to be too many topics and too little time for discussion;—but to my surprise, the Convention was not only largely attended, but the papers and the discussions such as in the fullest measure to justify the Committee's course. I cherish the hope that these Conferences will be repeated in the near future and that such subjects will be selected as will go more to the root of our differences in the triangular house which is here represented. I would suggest that we thank the Committee for its admirable work, and that we take steps to insure another Conference in the near future; that such subjects be selected as ought to be more openly and frankly discussed, subjects not so numerous, so as to allow more time for their consideration on the floor. What we need is discussion, to fight out our differences, if you please, in love; but let us use the Sword of the Spirit in this triangular fight. Our heart's desire is a united Church on the old foundation, a oneness both of faith and practice.

Dr. Owen said: Dr. Krotel hoped that this Committee, or another one, would arrange for a Conference, where the topics would allow a discussion of the differences existing in the General Bodies. He said, "Let us put on the Gospel armor, having our feet shod with the preparation of the Gospel, and let us discuss these questions, meeting argument with argument," etc. I replied that "the Committee had considered that matter very carefully. If brethren would really put on the Gospel Armor, and meet each other, thus panoplied, there would be no danger; but, unfortunately, brethren sometimes put on quite a different armor, and called it the 'Gospel Armor.' The Committee, in arranging the program, selected such topics as would not be likely to call out a discussion of these differences. We did not think it wise to arrange differently for this first Conference. We believed that the time would come when it might be proper to do this, but not now. We gave to the Conference a carefully selected program, and we hoped, and believed, that the brethren would do just what we all expect to do to-night at the reception,—to 'eat what is set before us, asking no questions for conscience sake.'"

THE CHILD CATECHUMENATE.

BY G. U. WENNER, D.D.

It is my purpose to give an account of an institution which was of immense importance in the formative periods of the Church, but which, excepting in the Lutheran Church of the Fatherland, has largely been supplanted by other and inferior methods. Its principles, it is true, are admitted, but, unless I greatly mistake, its practice in this country is almost unknown. The name "catechumen" is sometimes applied to persons who attend a course of catechetical lectures on themes connected with the catechism, or who are engaged in committing to memory a portion of the catechism. Both of these methods have a slender connection with the historical catechumenate, but the connection is in the name rather than in the thing. It is to be feared that the subject is generally ignored in our Practical Theology, and that the students who are graduated from the theological seminaries have but little more than a theoretical knowledge of it.

I desire to make a plea for the restoration of this institution, or at least to raise the question whether some of its features are not among the things which the Church in America greatly needs for its well-being. Some of our churches, notably the English-speaking ones, have departed widely from the methods of our fathers in respect to this matter and have adopted the theories and methods of alien confessions. Others, notably the German-speaking churches, have preserved the forms of an inherited institution, and pride themselves upon possessing it, but its life and real practice have to a large extent been lost. How else can you account for the thousands who are annually confirmed in our city churches after receiving the thinnest possible varnish of religious instruction, and who a few months later inevitably drift into the ranks of the churchless and the worldly? To take children of twelve and thirteen years of age from unchristian households and in six months to prepare them for admission to the Holy Communion, is better than to neglect them altogether, but to be satisfied with such conditions, and to be willing to perpetuate them, is a mark of apathy and decay.

A brief history of the institution will help us to understand its nature. The earliest catechumenate was that of the proselytes. It was based on Christ's command, "Go ye therefore, and make disciples of all the nations, ... teaching them to observe all things whatsoever I commanded you." The Church was a missionary organization, and its aim was to convert people to the Christian view of life. Instruction was thought of as an implantation of the word: "Receive with meekness the implanted word which is able to save your souls." (James 1: 21.) It preceded baptism and was continued afterward under various grades of teachers.

A chief object was to establish Christian usages and to accustom people to them. In later periods, when it became popular to join the Church, the term of probation was extended to several years and a rich liturgical ceremony was prescribed. This was done, partly for the purpose of substituting Christian rites in place of the heathen mysteries, and partly because of the mystagogical or educational value of the forms. There were grades and classes of catechumens, chiefly the *audientes* and the *competentes*. At successive stages of their instruction they were admitted to new glimpses of the Christian doctrine and service. For example, the exact wording of the Creed and the Lord's Prayer was not entrusted to them until the close of their probation. Much of it was simply an ornate ritualism, but the underlying purpose was that the participants might be brought to a personal and heartfelt confession of the Christian faith.

After the middle of the third century, when infant baptism became the rule, the child catechumenate gradually superseded that of the proselytes, and under Gregory the Great it became the rule of the Church. A systematic training of the baptized children was aimed at and to some extent secured through the sponsors, whose duty it was to provide the godchildren with religious instruction until they reached years of discretion and were able to come to their first confession. Among the prescribed subjects were the Creed, the Lord's Prayer and the Gloria. In the ninth century parochial schools were established to assist in the systematic Christian training of the young. The Bible history was largely given in the form of poems, and the plastic representations of the churches of those days aided much in giving the people a definite idea of the story of the Bible.

But not only Christian teaching, Christian *training* also played an important part in the work of the Church at that time. Rules of living and the services of the Church accustomed the people to the Christian view of life. Of special importance was the practice of private confession which began to be transferred from the convent life to the pastoral care of children. It consisted in the recitation of certain church forms, and in instruction on moral distinctions on the basis of Scripture passages. It aimed also to obtain a pastoral view of the state of mind and heart of the child. For the purpose of individualization the Ten Commandments were used as a *speculum peccatorum*. We must not omit to notice that the imposition of penances gradually accustomed the people to the practice of obedience to the Church's demands. The age produced a number of treatises on the method of training catechumens. The most important of them is Gerson's, on the subject of "drawing the little ones to Christ," a work in which the aim of the catechumenate is set forth in a substantially Evangelical manner. These times are sometimes called "the dark ages." But let us not forget that they were periods when the Church converted nations and brought races under the quickening power of Christianity.

The Reformation gave new significance and character to the ancient catechumenate. At first it was not a catechumenate for children, but rather for the whole people. Entire congregations had to be instructed in the fundamentals of religion. As a ripe fruit of his experience in preaching, teaching and the care of souls, Luther published in 1529 his Small Catechism, a book which still holds its place as the fairest fruit of the catechetical literature of all ages. Its arrangement is Decalogue, Creed and Lord's Prayer, that is, Law, Gospel, and the New Life, with supplemental chapters on Baptism and the Lord's Supper. In its form and arrangement, and even in some of its expressions, it did not overlook the best results of the preceding ages. The occasion for its publication was the lamentable condition of the religious instruction of children as he found it during a visitation of the churches in Electoral Saxony. The book at once became exceedingly popular and produced a complete transformation in the religious training of the people.

The example set by Luther was followed by the Reformed, who published their Heidelberg Catechism in 1563, and even by the Romanists who published their Trent Catechism in 1566. The chief fault of Luther's Catechism was that it was too good. So well adapted was it for purposes of instruction, that it became the almost exclusive handbook for ministers, although Luther's own thought in connection with it was that it should be the handbook for parents in the instruction of their children. Each of its chapters is introduced by the words, "In the plain form in which the head of the family should teach them to his household."

The exclusive use of the catechism thus gave to instruction an unduly dogmatic character. But in Spener's time, and that of the Pietists, the religious and pedagogic importance of Bible History came to be understood, and since then this form of imparting religious knowledge has gone hand in hand with the catechism. This remark is true of Germany. In America, and especially in English churches, I am inclined to think we have drifted into the practice of the times before Spener. Only lately have appeared signs of a revival of intelligent Bible study in its application to Christian instruction.

Catechization sympathized thoroughly with all the subsequent intellectual and religious movements. Thus in the days of Rationalism the chief aim was usefulness, not so much the formation of Christian character as the training of useful citizens. Under Pestalozzi the new pedagogical methods were introduced, and the great changes produced a century ago by the titanic leaders in philosophy, art and literature, left their permanent impression upon catechetics as well. It will suffice to characterize the relation of the catechism to present-day movements by saying that Ritschlian catechisms have already begun to appear, and with this statement I may close the historical sketch which I thought it necessary to give.

Two much debated questions are incidentally involved in my subject. The first is the relation of the children to the Church. There are those who believe that the Spirit of God is incapable of influencing the undeveloped spiritual life of a child, and that years of discretion must be attained before we can speak of regenerating influence. Just what the relation of the children to the Church in such a system is, I am unable to discover. They are not Christian, neither are they heathen. They must be in some kind of a Protestant *limbus infantum*. Many of these people retain the practice of infant baptism, but if you question them closely they will admit that they mean nothing by it.

There are those on the other hand who believe that baptism is more than a mere symbol, a pretty form inherited from the past, or a dedication of the child to God on the part of the parents. They believe, in the words of the Westminster Confession, that "by the right use of this ordinance, the grace promised is not only offered, but really exhibited and conferred by the Holy Ghost." Those who thus believe in infant baptism hold, or should hold, that as the Church has baptized the children she is in duty bound to teach them. In Christ's command teaching is correlated with baptism, and the Church is bound to recognize the connection between them.

The second question which suggests itself, not only among ourselves, but especially in our relations to other denominations, is the best method of making Christians. That it is a question, such paragraphs as the following abundantly prove: A Chicago correspondent writes to a certain paper: "A very prominent divine told me a few days ago: 'I am compelled to leave my flock, much against my wishes, not because of lack of appreciation or sympathy on their part, but because of the extreme difficulty I find in interesting outsiders.'"

Henry Drummond speaks of the restlessness that characterizes our modern congregations. "Like the Athenians of old, they are ever seeking after some new thing. There is a hunger and thirst among the people for some new sensation. Yet withal there is an impotence in the pulpit so far as the legitimate results of preaching are concerned."

In our own city numerous pulpits are vacant, because the congregations are anxious to find some great preacher, one who can fill the pews and assure the church treasurer a large and steady income. And for every vacant pulpit in a prominent church there are hundreds of applicants who are willing to sacrifice themselves. And very often they do sacrifice themselves. For a few years later, with broken spirit, they retire to some quiet place where they may rest from the unequal struggle to which they were exposed.

Our present-day forces for the conversion of the world and the edification of the church are:

First and chiefly, the preacher, religious essayist and homilist of the regular pulpit. The *Tribune* recently brought the following notice:

"Next Sunday will be the Rev. Dr. ———'s last appearance for sometime in the pulpit of the ——— Presbyterian Church."

While it is true that a reporter of a daily paper does not always appear to the best advantage in his use of ecclesiastical phraseology, it must be admitted that he is quick to catch the popular conception of a situation.

Then we have secondly the evangelist and revivalist for special seasons and for Carnegie Hall meetings and for other places untainted by the flavor of church associations.

Thirdly, the Sunday school teachers, trained and untrained, upon whom a large part of the responsibility of the religious education of the young rests. If family training might be added to these as an important factor, it would be a delightful surprise.

Supplemental to these forces are the Young People's Societies of Christian Endeavor, Luther Leagues, Kings' Daughters and the like, the great success of which demonstrates a widespread need.

Each of these forces and all combined undoubtedly have a most important place in the economy of the Church, but they cannot take the place of the catechumenate.

What then is the child catechumenate? What is there in it which differentiates it from allied institutions and methods?

It is that institution of Christ and the Church by which children are systematically taught and trained in such a way as to prepare them for a personal participation in the life and privileges of the Christian Church.

That it is an institution of Christ, is argued from the word τηρεῖν, "to observe," in Christ's last command.

Its place in the New Testament is seen from numerous passages, such as Galatians 6:6, "Let the catechumen communicate to him who catechises in all good things." (Literal translation.)

It involves two distinct functions, that of *teaching* and that of *training*.

It has a definite end, that of making mature Christians out of incipient believers.

It pursues a systematic method, leading step by step to the comprehension of that which has been revealed.

And finally, it is an institution *of the church;* that is, the Christian Church itself supplies the organ and ministry by which the work is carried on.

My plea for the restoration of the Child Catechumenate I shall endeavor to enforce by a brief reference, 1, to its principles, and 2, to its practice.

1. PRINCIPLES. The importance of this institution rests chiefly upon the duty which the Church owes to the children which have been entrusted to its care. We acknowledge the claims of the heathen whom we have never seen. But here are the little ones crowding our doors and asking for admission into the kingdom. Then again the trustful nature of the child makes it an unspeakable privilege to guide and an easy task to convert it. While we recognize in them, too, the impress of the fallen nature, there is also that which has been called the *anima naturaliter Christiana.* They respond almost intuitively to the idea of God and immortality. The five-year-old brother of Klopstock was found in the open field during a terrific thunder storm, and when asked what he was doing, he replied, "I am praying to the great God."

The Church is the mother of education. But what a humiliating position we take when we allow secular instruction to be given in the most scientific and effective manner, while the subjects of highest import are entrusted almost wholly to inexpert hands and to methods that stultify rather than edify! A day-school teacher has reason to dread the methods of the religious instruction which take off the sharp edge of intellectual perception on Sunday and unfit the pupil for the best work of Monday.

Again, is it wise to postpone the making of special religious impressions to a time when the mind and heart have long since become preoccupied, and they are far past the time when the germinal purposes of life are formed?

These statements are trite and almost self-evident, and yet to most ministers everything else seems to be of greater importance than that which is of supreme importance in their pastoral relation, the teaching and training of the young. One may go far to see the seminary whose curriculum makes provision for this end, and whose students are graduated with a practical knowledge of its importance.

2. THE PRACTICE. It has been well said that if you wish to train a child properly, you must begin with the grandparents. The importance of this principle is apparent from the fact that during the first five years, the most important of all in the development of the child, the Church can influence the child but very little except through its parents. And yet it is of this age that the Roman Catholic bishop said: " Give us the children for the first six years, and we care not who gets them afterward."

With the sixth year, the child begins to enter into public relation with the Church and its services, and the minister must be prepared to meet this new relation. There will, of course, be different grades and classes. For convenience sake we will assume the following grades: The *primary* class, for children from five to eight years of age; the *secondary* class, for children from eight to twelve; the *preparatorians*, from twelve to thirteen, and the *catechumens* proper, the older children.

I may perhaps be met by the objection that my position implies the necessity of establishing that un-American institution, the parochial school. Whether it is un-American or not is an open question, as well as whether the conditions under which we live render it practicable to establish the parochial school. A little food for thought, however, is afforded by the statement that the parochial school churches of New York City have, during the past decade, sent sixty of their boys into the Lutheran ministry.

But I have not argued in favor of parochial schools, and that question is one that has no necessary connection with the one we are considering.

The grades or classes which I have proposed may be formed, in cities or towns at least, among the children who attend the public schools, by meeting them after school hours, say at four or five o'clock in the afternoon. The younger children might meet once a week, the older ones twice or three times.

The topics or subjects.—For the little ones the Bible Stories, fifteen from the Old Testament and fifteen from the New, may cover the year's curriculum. Add to this a few simple prayers and hymns and you have laid a fair foundation for your work.

For the second grade, extend the work of the first grade in Bible History, and hymns, and lay the foundation of doctrine by introducing explanations of the Ten Commandments and of the Creed.

For the third grade, extend the scheme of the previous grades with the addition of the Church Service and with stories from Church History.

For the fourth grade, amplify the preceding, emphasize the doctrine and introduce the children into some practical forms of Christian work.

It is evident that in order to do this work properly, the minister must be a pedagogue; that is, the instruction should be such as to be intellectually stimulating. But its chief charm and power is derived from the pastoral relation which the instructor holds, and which should make it spiritually quickening. It is true that not every minister is a pedagogue. But he ought to be, and in the Church of the future, as in the Church of the past, pedagogical skill and training ought to be considered a part of the necessary outfit of every minister.

But the principal value of the catechumenate is in the opportunity it affords to *train* the child; that is, to accustom it to the duties and practice of the Christian life. Thus it should be early taught to go to church—at first to the children's services, but as soon as possible to the great congregation. It should be taught the words of the silent prayer when entering the house of God, the significance of the various parts of the service, not excepting the offertory, where the money put on the plate is only an outward expression of the sentiment, "My God, accept my heart this day, and make it always thine." For the purpose of bringing up intelligent hearers I have found it indispensable to require from the two older grades a written report of the sermon. The habit of so listening to a sermon as to fix its chief points and thoughts in the mind, is one that must be cultivated. If you do not believe this, ask some of your most intelligent children next week to give you an outline of the sermon which they last heard.

A chief means of emphasizing and carrying out the principles of Christian training is the private and personal interview with the catechumen. They called it private confession in the olden time, but you may call it by any other name if it will smell sweeter. The essential thing about it is to accustom the child to a confidential and trusting relation to its pastor in spiritual matters. The subjects to be treated are the habit of private prayer, the questions of Christian conduct in its relations to parents, brothers and sisters and other children, and especially in the matter of penitence for sin, faith in a personal Saviour and of the right steps in the new life of obedience.

Those of you who have never tried this method would be amazed at the absence, in many cases, of the most fundamental and primary Christian conceptions, and that, too, among those where you took the Christian view of life for granted. The theology of most of them is, "You must be good if you want to get to heaven." And, "keeping the commandments is the way to be saved." But when in such pastoral intercourse it becomes your privilege to unlock the heart to the gifts of the Gospel, what hearers you will have for the pulpit message! You look down into eyes that respond with grateful eagerness to every word you say.

A word in answer to the objection that will be raised, that one cannot find time for so much additional work. To begin with, drop all those visits of ceremony that go by the name of pastoral calls. Provided it is necessary to do so, but it may not be necessary. The scheme I have presented requires only five afternoon hours each week, and they will be hours of great joy and profit. And while your efforts are directed mainly to the children, you will, at the same time, be binding the parents to you with strong cords of affection and reverence.

But a wise organizer and pastor will readily be able to modify the system in such a way as to distribute the work and make it easy and profitable for all. We need to get rid of many of our hierarchical notions and to introduce a larger diaconate into our church work. Some of us have school teachers and teaching deaconesses who can be entrusted with part of this work. But in all of our churches there are men and women with gifts and graces that would make them excellent helpers in this churchly work of bringing the little ones to Christ and training them up for His service. Chief among these helpers are the parents of the children, especially so far as the home life and the practice of home duties are concerned. But even for the week-day hours at the church, I feel sure that there is much undeveloped material which could be utilized for such work as I have indicated. And what better opportunity than this could be found for bringing into practice those duties which many Lutheran liturgies prescribe for the sponsors, when they direct the minister to exhort those who have presented the child for baptism in the following words: "I now admonish you who have done so charitable a work to this child in its baptism, that ye diligently and faithfully teach it the Ten Commandments, that thereby it may learn to know the will of God; also the Christian Faith, set forth in the Creed, whereby we obtain grace, the forgiveness of sins, and the Holy Ghost; and likewise the Lord's Prayer, that it may call upon God, and find help to withstand the devil, and lead a Christian life, till God shall perfect that which He hath now begun in it, and bring it to life everlasting."

The point to emphasize is that it is a systematic work, conducted by the Church, proceeding from certain acknowledged premises and advancing by approved methods to a certain end. Or, to return to the definition, "*It is an institution of Christ and the Church, by which children are systematically taught and trained in such a way as to prepare them for a personal participation in the life and the privileges of the Christian Church.*"

With the restoration of this institution in a practical way in our churches, the Sunday-school itself would quickly assume a more natural and more important relation to the life of the Church. We should no longer be dependent upon the unsystematic methods of instruction on subjects where only the best methods are barely good enough, and the so-called Sunday-school would become a Children's Service in which the knowledge gained during the week would be fused into sweet experience under the influence of warm-hearted Christian teachers and superintendents.

And a new meaning would also be given to the instruction preparatory to confirmation. Instead of a toilsome drilling into the children of the words and punctuation marks of Luther's Small Catechism and torturing them with undigested material that has to be committed to memory, it would be a simple review of subjects with which the children have long since been made acquainted. The nature of the instruction would therefore be entirely different. It would be a warm, spiritual presentation of the truths of the catechism, would cover a comparatively brief period of time and would have the sole purpose of preparing the children for a proper participation in the privileges of the Lord's Supper. It would be a sort of Lutheran revival season in which others than the children would be glad to take part because of the stimulating and quickening influences that would be sure to accompany such a course of instruction.

This is an age of progress. But it is an age of repristination as well. From many an ecclesiastical wall the modern stucco has been torn off, and the fair lines of its ancient architectural beauty have been restored. A generation has grown up that understands and loves the stately services of our fathers.

All around us voices are heard proclaiming their dissatisfaction with the meagre results of merely Sunday-school methods in building up the Church. Why should we not in this field also return to a system which has stood the test of a decade of Christian centuries?

REGISTER OF NAMES.

The following list of names is a complete register of those clergymen who were present, and of the students and laymen and ladies whose names were handed to the secretaries:

CLERICAL.

ALBERT, CHAS. S., D.D., Phila., Pa.
ALBERT, L. E., D.D., Germantown, Pa.
ALTPETER, PETER, Catawissa, Pa.
ANDRES, W. J., Bath, Pa.
BAUM, WM. M., D.D., Phila., Pa.
BAUM, W. M., JR., Canajoharie, N. Y.
BAUSLIN, PROF. D. H., D.D., Springfield, O.
BELL, E. K., D.D., Mansfield, O.
BERKEMEYER, F., Sellersville, Pa.
BERTOLET, U. S. G., Phila., Pa.
BLOMGREN, C. A., Ph.D., Phila., Pa.
BROWNMILLER, E. S., D.D., Reading, Pa.
CASSADAY, E. R., Phila., Pa.
CLAUSS, C. D., Leacock, Pa.
CONRAD, V. L., Ph.D., D.D., Phila., Pa.
COOPER, C. J., Allentown, Pa.
COOVER, M., Ardmore, Pa.
CRESSMAN, J. J., Kutztown, Pa.
CRIGLER, J. F., Lutherville, Md.
CRITCHLOW, G. W., Pittsburg, Pa.
DELK, E. H., Hagerstown, Md.
DIETTERICH, J. E., Flourtown, Pa.
DIMM, PROF. J. R., D.D, Selinsgrove, Pa.
DIZINGER, J. C., Camden, N. J.
DOERR, F., Wilmington, Del.
DRACH, GEO., Philadelphia, Pa.
DUNBAR, W. H., D.D., Baltimore, Md.
EARHART, D., Philadelphia, Pa
EISENHARDT, G. C., Philadelphia, Pa.
ELLIS, W. J., Philadelphia, Pa.
ELSON, H. W., Ph.D., Philadelphia, Pa
ENDERS, G. W., D.D., York, Pa.

ERDMAN, A. E., Nazareth, Pa.
EVERETT, T. T., D.D., York, Pa.
FABER, GEO. E., Phœnixville, Pa.
FASTNACHT, A. G., York, Pa.
FEGLEY, PROF. H. N., Mechanicsburg, Pa.
FISCHER, C. G., Elizabeth, N. J.
FISHBURN, J., Lebanon, Pa.
FLUCK, J. F. C., Philadelphia, Pa.
FOX, J. B., Slatington, Pa.
FRANCIS, S. A. K., Philadelphia, Pa.
FREAS, WM. S., D.D., Baltimore, Md.
FRY, CHAS. L., Lancaster, Pa.
FRY, FRANK F., Bethlehem, Pa.
FRY, PROF. J., D.D., Mt. Airy, Phila., Pa.
GLADHILL, J. T., Conshohocken, Pa.
GOEDEL, C., Philadelphia, Pa.
GRAHN, E. M., Easton, Pa.
GRAHN, H., D.D., Philadelphia, Pa.
GROFF, J. R., Doylestown, Pa.
HAAS, G. C. F., New York, N. Y.
HAAS, J. A. W., New York, N. Y.
HAFER, L. B., Fort Washington, Pa.
HAMMA, M. W., D.D., Washington, D.C.
HARTMAN, A. S., D.D., Baltimore, Md.
HAY, C. E., D.D., Harrisburg, Pa.
HEILMAN, A. M., Shrewsbury, Pa.
HEILMAN, P. A., Baltimore, Md.
HEINDEL, J. E., Jersey City, N. J.
HEISSLER, J., Trenton, N. J.
HIRZEL, C. J., Philadelphia, Pa.
HOFFMAN, I. C., Chester, Pa.
HOLMAN, S. A., D D., Philadelphia, Pa.

PROCEEDINGS OF GENERAL CONFERENCE. 323

HOPPE, C. F. W., Bethlehem, Pa.
HORN, EDWARD T., D.D., Reading, Pa.
HUDSON, W. G. DE A., Catasauqua, Pa.
HUNTON, W. L., Wilkesbarre, Pa.
HUNTZINGER, F. K., Reading, Pa.
IBACH, W. O., Philadelphia, Pa.
JACOBS, PROF. H. E., D.D., LL.D., Mt. Airy, Phila., Pa.
KAEHLER, F. A., Buffalo, N. Y.
KEEDY, PROF. C. L., M.D., Hagerstown, Md.
KEITER, W. D. C., Bethlehem, Pa.
KELLY, W., Philadelphia, Pa.
KERCHER, G. A., Falls, Phila., Pa.
KILLINGER, E. B., Trenton, N. J.
KLINEFELTER, F., Lionville, Pa.
KLINGLER, PAUL G., Easton, Pa.
KOLLER, J. C., D.D., Hanover, Pa.
KROTEL, G. F., D.D., LL.D., East Orange, N. J.
KUDER, C. F., Siegfried, Pa.
KUHLMAN, L., D.D., Frederick, Md.
KUNZMAN, J. C., Pittsburg, Pa.
LAMBERT, JAS. F., Catasauqua, Pa.
LAMBERT, W. A., Bethlehem, Pa.
LEIBENSPERGER, A. W., Lititz, Pa.
LINDENSTRUTH, L., Mauch Chunk, Pa.
LOOS, GEO. C., Philadelphia, Pa.
LYNCH, R. B., Dublin, Pa.
MCCLANAHAN, G. W., Strasburg, Pa.
MCCONNELL, C. L., Mifflinburg, Pa.
MAIN, J. H., Philadelphia, Pa.
MANHART, F. P., Baltimore, Md.
NEUDEWITZ, E. E., Jersey City, N. J.
NICKEL, W., Applebachsville, Pa.
NICUM, PROF. J., D.D., Rochester, N. Y.
NIEDECKER, J. E., Philadelphia, Pa.
OCHSENFORD, S. E., D.D., Selinsgrove, Pa.
OFFERMANN, F. H., Camden, N. J.
ORT, PROF. S. A., D.D., LL.D., Springfield, O.
OWEN, S. W., D.D., Hagerstown, Md.

PAINTER, PROF. F. V. N., D.D., Salem, Va.
PARSON, W. E., D.D., Washington, D.C.
PASSAVANT, W. A., JR., Pittsburg, Pa.
PATTERSON, R. L., Union Bridge, Md.
PFLUEGER, O. E., Elizabethville, Pa.
RAMER, A. L., Ph.D., Scranton, Pa.
RATH, MYRON O., Allentown, Pa.
REED, D. L., Allegheny, Pa.
REESE, G. C., Chestnut Hill, Pa.
REITER, D. H., Richland Centre, Pa.
RENTZ, W. F., Pottsville, Pa.
REPASS, S. A., D.D., Allentown, Pa.
RICE, J. M., Scioto, Pa.
RICHARDS, H. B., Philadelphia, Pa.
RICKERT, W. H., Philadelphia, Pa.
RITTER, I. B., Emaus, Pa.
RITTER, JER. H., Bath, Pa.
ROEDER, R. D., Norristown, Pa.
SANDT, C. M., Huntingdon, Pa.
SANDT, G. W., Philadelphia, Pa.
SARVER, J., D.D., New Stanton, Pa.
SCHAEFFER, WM. ASHMEAD, D.D., Germantown, Pa.
SCHANTZ, F. J. F., D.D., Myerstown, Pa.
SCHEELE, H. F., St. Joseph, Mo.
SCHEFFER, J. A., Allentown, Pa.
SCHMAUCK, THEODORE E., D.D., Lebanon, Pa.
SCHMIDT, R., Philadelphia, Pa.
SCHMOYER, M. B., East Mauch Chunk, Pa.
SCHOLL, GEO., D.D., Baltimore, Md.
SEIP, PROF. THEO. L., D.D., Allentown, Pa.
SEISS, JOS. A., D.D., LL.D., L.H.D., Philadelphia, Pa.
SHANNON, S. G., Philadelphia, Pa.
SHEELEIGH, M., D.D., Fort Washington, Pa.
SHINDLE, H. C., Philadelphia, Pa.
SIBOLE, E. E., D.D., Philadelphia, Pa.
SIBOLE, J. L., Philadelphia, Pa.

SIEBOTT, H. D. E., Philadelphia, Pa.
SIEGER, P. GEO., Lancaster, Pa.
SINGMASTER, J. A., D.D., Allentown, Pa.
SMITH, L. L., Strasburg, Va.
SMITH, O. P., D.D., Pottstown, Pa.
SNYDER, J. M., Philadelphia, Pa.
SPAETH, PROF. A., D.D., LL.D., Mt. Airy, Phila., Pa.
SPIEKER, PROF. G. F., D.D., Mt. Airy, Phila., Pa.
STALL, S., D.D., Bala, Pa.
STECK, W. H., Coatesville, Pa.
STEINHAEUSER, J., Allentown, Pa.
STOUGH, W. L., Philadelphia, Pa.
STUDEBAKER, A. H., D.D., Baltimore, Md.
STUMP, J., Phillipsburg, N. J.

TATE, M. L., Philadelphia, Pa.
WAIDELICH, J. H., Sellersville, Pa.
WARNER, A. N., Northumberland, Pa.
WASMUND, H. C., Frankford, Phila., Pa.
WEIDLEY, J. E., Pittsburg, Pa.
WEISKOTTEN, C. P., Manayunk, Phila., Pa.
WEISKOTTEN, F. W., Phila., Pa.
WELLER, H. A., Orwigsburg, Pa.
WENNER, G. U., D.D., New York, N. Y.
WHITMORE, F. E., Phila., Pa.
WISCHAN, F., Phila., Pa.
WOLF, PROF. E. J., D.D., Gettysburg, Pa.
YOUNT, A. L., D.D., Greensburg, Pa.
ZIEGENFUSS, S. A., D.D., Germantown. Pa.

STUDENTS OF THEOLOGY.

BARR, W. PENN, Mt. Airy, Phila., Pa.
BAUM, F. J., Gettysburg, Pa.
CARTY, A. C., Mt. Airy, Phila., Pa.
DEAL, JOS. F., Mt. Airy, Phila., Pa.
DOZER, CHAS. E., Mt. Airy, Phila., Pa.
GENSZLER, G. W., Mt. Airy, Phila., Pa.
GLENN, J. O., Mt. Airy, Phila., Pa.
GREISE, G. A., Gettysburg, Pa.
HANKEY, B. F., Mt. Airy, Phila., Pa.
HARTWIG, GEO. H., Mt. Airy, Phila., Pa.
HEROLD, I. S., Mt. Airy, Phila., Pa.
JACOBS, CHAS. M., Mt. Airy, Phila., Pa.
KEEHLEY, JOHN, Mt. Airy, Phila., Pa.
KEMLING, E. J., Mt. Airy, Phila., Pa.
KOPENHAVER, W. M., Mt. Airy, Phila., Pa.
LEHMAN, JOHN J., Mt. Airy, Phila., Pa.
LITTLE, C. H., Mt. Airy, Phila., Pa.

LITTLE, W. H., Mt. Airy, Phila., Pa.
MAMLER, F. L., Mt. Airy, Phila., Pa.
MATTES, JOHN C., Mt. Airy, Phila., Pa.
MATTHEWS, GOMER B., Mt. Airy, Phila., Pa.
MILLER, FRANCIS, Mt. Airy, Phila., Pa.
MOSER, I. O., Gettysburg, Pa.
NELSON, W. I., Mt. Airy, Phila., Pa.
RAHN, CHAS. S., Mt. Airy, Phila., Pa.
REPASS, E. A., Mt. Airy, Phila., Pa.
RICHARDS, H. F., Mt. Airy, Phila., Pa.
STRASSBERGER, H., Mt. Airy, Phila., Pa.
STRODACH, PAUL Z., Mt. Airy, Phila., Pa.
TRABERT, WM., Mt. Airy, Phila., Pa.
WEISKOTTEN, F. F., Mt. Airy, Phila., Pa.
YOUNG, CHAS. J., Mt. Airy, Phila., Pa.

LAYMEN.

ALTVATER, CHAS., Renovo, Pa.
BAETES, HENRY, Phila., Pa.
BENNETT, J. W., Germantown, Pa.
BERKEMEYER, C. M., Sellersville, Pa.
BISHOFF, CHAS., Phila., Pa.
BOXER, HENRY S., Phila., Pa.
BREMER, JOS. A., Phila., Pa.
BURNETT, DR. G. G., San Francisco, Cal.
CAMPBELL, PROF. E. E, Mechanicsburg, Pa.
EBERLY, J. W., Strasburg, Va.
FISCHER, EDW. F., Phila., Pa.
HAGER, C. E., Rigsville, Pa.
HARTRANFT, F. A., ESQ., Phila., Pa.
HEIGHT, GEO. A., Phila., Pa.
HELB, EDWARD, Shrewsbury, Pa.
KELLER, LUTHER P., Phila., Pa.
KUGLER, PAUL J., Ardmore, Pa.

LONG, CHAS., Lebanon, Pa.
MICHELER, GEO., Phila., Pa.
MILLER, E. AUG., ESQ., Phila., Pa.
MILLER, J. WASH., Phila., Pa.
MILLER, WM. J., Phila., Pa.
MOORE, JAS. B., Phila., Pa.
MOSER, J. S., Conshohocken, Pa.
MOYER, H. F., Buffalo, N. Y.
PLITT, PROF. GEO. L., Buffalo, N. Y.
RAUDENBUSH, DR. J. S., Buffalo, N. Y.
SCHLEGELMILCH, G. E., ESQ., Buffalo, N. Y.
SCHLICHTER, J. W., Conshohocken, Pa.
SPAETH, PROF. J. DUNCAN, Phila., Pa.
STAAKE, WM. H., ESQ., Phila., Pa.
STINE, DR. L. D., Phila., Pa.
STOEVER, W. C., ESQ., Phila., Pa.
ULRICH, DR. GEO. R., Phila., Pa.

LADIES.

CHAMBERS, MISS LIZZIE, Phila., Pa.
GROTEVENT, MRS. F. J., Phila., Pa.
HEGEMAN, MRS. G. E., Sellersville, Pa.
HILL, MRS. REUBEN, Mt. Airy, Phila., Pa.
JACOBS, MRS. H. E., Mt. Airy, Phila., Pa.
KUGLER, DR. ANNA S., Ardmore, Pa.

MILLER, MISS K. B., Phila., Pa.
MILLER, MISS M. A., Phila., Pa.
MONROE, MRS. H. E., Phila., Pa.
TATE, MRS. M. L., Phila., Pa.
VOLLERS, MRS. E. P., Staunton, Va.
WELLER, MISS FLORENCE J., Orwigsburg, Pa.

INDEX OF PERSONS.

Albert, C. S., 36, 38, 39, 144, 271.
Albert, J., 54.
Albert, L. E., 35, 39, 90, 307.
Arndt, 197.
Baker, J. C., 47.
Baldwin, 242.

Baum, W. M., 53.
Baum, W. M., Jr., 37.
Bauslin, H. D., 35, 36, 40, 88, 116.
Bell, E. K., 37, 40, 196.
Bengel, 86.
Boltzius, 66.
Braun, A., 71.
Brown, J. A., 52.
Bugenhagen, 68.
Burnett, G. G., 36, 93.
Bushnell, 284.

Channing, 284.
Chemnitz, 233, 236.
Conrad, V. L., 37, 229.

Da Costa, 229.
Darwin, 284.
Deininger, A. G., 54.
Demme, 45.
Dimm, J. R., 38, 237, 250, 269.
Drummond, 314.
Dunbar, W. H., 37, 205, 229.
Dylander, 30.
Earhart, D., 35, 80.
Edwards, J., 284.
Enders, G. W., 38, 248.
Endress, 45.

Fliedner, 217, 218, 219, 221.
Forsyth, 155.
Fox, L. A., 37, 174.
Francke, 197.
Frank, 234, 281.
Freas, Wm. S., 17, 35.
Frederus, 235.
Fritschel, G., 75.
Fry, J., 36, 38, 90, 270.
Fry, Elizabeth, 220.

Gerhard, 233, 236, 241, 242.
Gilbert, D. M., 181.
Goedel, C., 208.
Gordon, 256.
Groff, J. R., 37, 163.
Gronau, 66.
Gunn, W., 46.
Gustavus, Adolphus, 30.

Haas, G. C. F., 37.
Haas, J. A. W., 35, 36, 38, 80, 144, 230, 250.
Hamma, M. W., 39, 297.
Handel, 152.
Harnack, 154, 279.
Hartman, A. S., 38.
Hay, C. A., 47.
Hay, C. E., 36.
Helmuth, J. C. F., 31.
Henkel, P., 42.
Heyer, C. F., 46, 249.
Hodge, 293.
Hoelling, 250.

INDEX OF PERSONS.

Hoffman, J. N., 58.
Hollazius, 236.
Holmes, 284.
Horn, E. T., 35, 38, 39, 80, 81, 90, 249.

Jacobs, H. E., 30, 35, 37, 39, 51, 161, 163, 184, 203, 211, 212.

Kaehler, F. A., 37, 38, 40, 230, 262, 271.
Kaftan, 280.
Keller, B., 47.
Keller, E., 56.
Kliefoth, 158, 184, 236, 250.
Knipstroh, 235.
Koller, J. C., 37, 152.
Krauth, C. P., Sr., 46, 56, 60.
Krauth, C. P., 80, 230.
Krotel, G. F., 35, 36, 38, 39, 40, 89, 132, 271, 308.
Knebel, 230.
Kuhlman, L., 38.
Kunze, J. C., 63, 71, 72, 73 sq., 96, 115.
Kunzman, J. C., 144.
Kurtz, B., 56, 58, 78, 227.
Kurtz, J. N., 67.

La Place, 284.
Lemme, 275.
Lochman, G., 45.
Loche, 90, 250.
Longfellow, 284.
Luckcock, 152.
Luther, 49, 68, 76, 117, 120, 126, 132, 147, 151, 154, 160, 176, 185, 217, 231, 234, 240, 248, 286, 303.

Manhart, F. P., 37, 227.
Mann, W. J., 47.
Martensen, 152, 158.
Matthesius, J., 236.

Mayer, P. F., 17, 58.
Melanchthon, 49, 146, 231, 235.
Miller, R. J., 76.
Miller, W. J., 46.
Morris, J. G., 56.
Morthens, Louise, 219.
Muhlenberg, F. A. C., 71.
Muhlenberg, H. M., 31, 41, 43, 45, 48, 49, 57, 62, 63, 66 sq., 186, 197.
Muhlenberg, W. A., 220.

Nicum, J., 35, 63, 81, 87.

Ochsenford, S. E., 17, 35.
Officer, M., 249.
Origen, 252.
Ort, S. A., 36, 105.
Owen, S. W., 36, 37, 39, 40, 309.

Painter, F. V. N., 36, 37, 38, 39, 40, 94, 308.
Palladius, 236.
Parson, W. E., 38, 250, 271.
Passavant, W. A., 218, 219, 220, 221.
Passavant, W. A., Jr., 37, 38, 40, 216, 230, 270.
Pestalozzi, 313.
Peters, Rich., 70.
Phelps, Elizabeth Stuart, 284.
Philippi, 250.

Quenstedt, 203.
Quitman, 77.

Reichardt, Gertrude, 218.
Reynolds, W. M., 56, 221.
Ritschl, 279.
Rocholl, 278.
Rudman, 30.

Schaeffer, C. F., 50.

Schaeffer, C. W., 47.
Schaff, P., 257.
Schantz, F. J. F., 38, 271.
Scheele, H. F., 35, 36, 37.
Schlatter, M., 69.
Schleiermacher, 274, 280.
Schmauk, T. E., 39, 283.
Schmucker, S. S., 44, 45, 54, 78.
Scholl, Geo., 37, 38, 164, 270.
Seiss, J. A., 17, 36, 37, 38, 115, 184, 247.
Shober, G., 76.
Sibole, E. E., 17, 36.
Smith, C. A., 56.
Smith, L. L., 37, 186.
Spaeth, A., 35, 36, 37, 38, 50, 54, 80, 90, 146, 163, 227.
Spener, 197, 313.
Sprecher, S., 48.
Staake, W. H., 36, 90.
Stedman, 284.
Strebeck, 9, 72, 74.

Torkillus, 64.

Van Buskirk, L., 75.
Vilmar, 231.
Voigt, A. G., 39, 272.

Walther, 231, 250.
Warner, 284.
Weidner, R. F., 38.
Weiss, J., 277.
Wenner, G. U., 39, 309.
Wesley, 198.
Whitefield, 70.
Whittier, 284.
Wichtermann, G. J., 71.
Willard, Frances, 206.
Williams, E. F., 216.
Wolf, E. J., 35, 36, 38, 41, 88, 145, 163, 246.

Zwingli, 77, 278.

INDEX OF SUBJECTS.

Agenda, 50, 55 sq., 57, 63, 77, 81, 185, 235.
Agreement among Lutherans, 175, 308.
Albany, N. Y., 54.
Allentown Case, 53.
Allœosis, 278.
Altar Fellowship, 69, 73.
America, Modern Religious issues in, 283.
Amsterdam, 64.
Antecedents, our common historical, 41 sqq., 63 sqq.
" Common devotional literature, 53 sq., 68 sq.
" " doctrine, 49 sq., 53, 63 sq.
" " heritage, 41, 64 sq., 197, 204.
" " organic form, 41.
" Confessional fidelity, 64 sq., 79, 198.
" Co-operation, 45 sq.
" Discordant elements, 43 sq., 75 sq.
" Divisions, 48 sq.
" Periodical literature, 58 sq.
" Transition from German to English, 61, 74.
Apology, 146, 185, 233.
Apostoli um, 273.
Arbitration, Board of, 30, 34.
Arminians, 199.
Augsburg Confession, 33, 34, 49, 50, 52, 63, 68, 73, 122, 123, 153, 175, 182, 198, 231, 237, 239, 250, 258, 292, 295, 312.
Aversion to intellectual religion, 274.
Barren Hill, 67.
Baptism, 23, 151, 311, 314.
Book of Common Prayer, 178.
Book of Concord. See Symbolical Books.
Cabarrus Co., N. C., 66.
Calenberg K. O., 235.
Call to the ministry, 238, 246, 247.
Calvinism, 77, 198, 256, 284.

INDEX OF SUBJECTS.

Carolinas, 66.
Catechetical instruction, 311 sqq.
Catechism, Luther's, 30, 58, 59, 67, 68, 162, 181, 198, 312.
" Place of in Sunday-school, 192.
Catechumenate, The Child, 309 sqq.
" Advantages, 321.
" Christian training of children, 311.
" Defined, 321.
" Grades in methods of instruction, 317.
" History of, in the early Church, 310 sq.
" History of, in the Reformation period, 312 sq.
" Importance of, 316.
" Its place in the New Testament, 315.
" Object of, 311.
" Objections answered, 319.
" Practice, 317.
" Relation of child to Church, 313 sq.
" Rule of the Church, 311.
" Value of, 318.
Charleston, S. C., 63, 66, 70.
Child Catechumenate, 309, sqq.
Children, Training of, in the spirit of the Church, 190.
Christ, The historical, 278 sq.
Christian activity outside of the Church, 209.
Christianity, Question of genuine. 277.
Church Authority, The Scope and Limitations of, 116 sqq., 132 sqq.
" Defined, 136 sq., 141 sq.
" in Apostolic times, 139.
" in matters of confession, 127 sq., 129.
" in matters of discipline, 144 sq.
" in teaching and worship, 124, 139.
Church Defined, 132, 251.
Church and State, 296.
Church Government, 201.
Church of Apostolic times, 211.
" and Kingdom distinguished, 144.
" Constitution of, 143.
" Congregations, 122, 144.
" Different conceptions of, 118.
" Headship of Christ, 121, 134, 138.
" Liberty, true idea of, 127.
" Limitations of, 125.
" Luther's position, 120.

INDEX OF SUBJECTS. 331

Church Principles involved, 116, 139 sq.
" Protestant conception, 120.
" Romish conception, 119.
" Schools, 69.
" The unity of, 17 sqq.
" " " Definition, 18.
" " " Negative consideration, 18 sq.
" " " Positive side, 19 sq.
" " " What unity demands, 24 sq.
Churland K. O., 185.
Co-education, 99, 103.
Colleges, Lutheran, 96 sq.
Common Book, The, 174 sqq.
" " Definition of the term, 174.
" " Diversity of books in use, 178.
" " Efforts made to secure a, 181.
" " Its contents: Common Service, 182.
　　　　　　　Œcumenical Creeds, etc., 182.
　　　　　　　Orders for ministerial acts, 182.
　　　　　　　Uniformity of Hymnal, 183.
" " Its need, as a bond of union, 174 sq.
　　　　　　　for development of religious life, 179 sq.
　　　　　　　to awaken deeper church love, 180 sq.
" " Uniformity, authorities in favor of, 184.
Common Service, 34, 56, 182, 184 sq.
Communion of Saints, 32.
Confederation of churches, 34.
Conference, General, of Lutherans, 9 sqq., 63, 80.
" Aim of, 16 sq., 31 sq., 309.
" Call of, 12.
" Essays of, 41 sqq.
" Official action with reference to, 9 sq.
" Opening address of, 30 sq.
" Opening service of, 17 sq.
" Preliminary statement concerning, 9 sq.
" Proceedings of, 35 sqq.
" Program of, 13, 35 sq.
" Rules, 14.
Confessional fidelity, 50, 64, 68, 79, 193.
" laxity, 49 sq.
Confirmation, 202.
Congregation, 249.
Constitution of Synods, 71.

Conversion, present-day forces for, 314.
Co-operation, The Problem of, 297 sq., 308.
" Basis of, 298.
" Education, 45.
" Foreign missions, 46.
" Home missions, 47.
" Obstacles in the way, 302.
" differences in practices, 303.
" diversity of language and nationality, 302.
" irresponsible journalism, 304.
" Practicability of present plan, 306, 207, 308.
Creed subscription, 129.
Deaconess, a ministry of mercy, 213, 219.
" Motherhouse, beginning, etc., 216 sqq.
" Work, 205 sqq.
" " Classification of, 228.
" " Early antagonism and difficulties, 220 sq., 227.
" " Enlargement of, 229.
" " in General Synod, 207.
" " Organically connected with Church, 207, 209, 212.
" " Relation to Church, 213.
Deaconesses, Motherhouses of, 205, 208, 209, 214, 216, 219, 221, 223, 225, 227, 230.
" " Adapted to American needs, 226.
" " Beginnings of, 216 sq.
" " Outside the Lutheran Church, 225.
" " Principles of, 222.
" " Relation to Church, 214, 224.
" " Spirit of, 225.
" " Small beginning at Kaiserswerth, 216, 218, 219.
Diaconate, N. T., Female, 206, 211 sq., 213, 217, 223.
" European position not a guide, 208.
" Introduction into this country, 218 sq.
" In its relation to the Church, 210.
" In its greatest usefulness, 210.
" Origin, purpose and authority, 210, 212.
" Protestant Institution in Allegheny Co., 219.
" Scriptural foundation, 223.
" The only safe position, 209, 210.
Diets, 31, 53.
Discipline, 144 sq.
Divisions, 48.
Doctrine and Forms of Prayer, 81 sqq.

Duesseldorf, 217.
Dutch Lutherans, 64.
East Camp, 71.
Eden, Garden of, 284.
Education, Dangerous tendencies, 110.
" Christian, 106, 108 sq.
" Female, 98, 220.
" in the Lutheran Church, 94, 108.
" Needs of, 101 sq., 114.
" Number of institutions, 100, 108.
" Services to the Church, 101, 105, 107 sq.
" Services to the State, 113.
" Spirit of, 98, 112.
" Standard of, 99.
" Standards of Ministerial, 250, 260.
Educational Idea of Lutheran Church, 97 sq.
" Institutions, Our, 94 sqq., 105 sqq.
" Work in this country, 95 sq.
Elders, appointment of, in N. T., 140.
England, 217.
English Lutherans, 200, 204.
Episcopal Church, 74, 75.
"Evangelical Review," 58 sq.
Female Diaconate, 206 sqq.
Female Education in the Lutheran Church, 98, 220.
Foreign Missionary Society, 46.
Foreign Missions, 46.
Foreign Mission Work, Problems in, 164 sqq.
"   "   " Christ's Commission, 164.
"   "   " Denominationalism in, 173.
"   "   " Native Church, 171.
"   "   " Native Ministry, 170.
"   "   " Object of, 172.
"   "   " Requirements, 166 sq.
"   "   " Self-support of native church, 173.
"   "   " The call to labor in, 165.
"   "   " The problem of education, 170.
"   "   " Who shall engage in, 165.
"   "   " Where work is to be done, 168.
Formula Juramenti, 73.
Fort Wayne, Ind., 31, 43, 57.
Franklin College, 46.
Frederick, Md., 45.

General Conference, Proceedings of, 35 sq.
General Council, 31, 32, 33, 41.
General Synod, 31, 32, 33, 42 sq., 47, 48, 80, 255.
" " and Ministerium of Pennsylvania, 41 sq.
Georgia, Lutherans in, 66, 198.
German and English, transition, 61, 75.
German-English Seminary, 86, 115.
German Immigration, 96.
German Lutherans, 65.
German Mass, 185.
Germantown, 30.
Germany, Modern Religious issues, 272.
Gettysburg Theological Seminary, 45, 50, 52, 60, 115.
Gloria Dei Church, 30.
Government of the Church, 201.
Hackensack, N. J., 64, 74.
Hamburg, 65.
Heidelberg Catechism, 312.
Helvetic Confession, 231.
Hildesheim, 235.
"Historical Christ," 278 sq.
Holland, 64, 217.
Home Missionary Society, 47.
Home Missions, 47, 64.
Hoya, 235.
Hymn-Book, Union, 49.
Hymn-Books, 43, 49, 50, 54 sq., 77 sq.
Judicial Oaths, 90 sq.
Justification, spirituality of doctrine, 201.
Kaiserswerth, 216, 218, 219.
Keys, Power of, 124, 144, 239.
Lancaster, Pa., 30.
Laying on of hands, 232, 242, 244.
Lay-workers, 229 sq.
Licensure, 260.
Litany, 85.
Liturgy, 31, 42, 55 sq , 63, 68 sq., 76, 77, 80 sq., 185.
London, 65.
Loonenburg, 65.
Lord's Supper, Spirituality of, 203.
" Place in worship, 154, 160.
" Real Presence, 203.
Lueneburg K. O., 235.

Luther's Small Catechism. See Catechism.
Lutheran Bishops, 201.
" Divisions, 175.
" Estimate of ordination, 230 sqq., 237 sqq.
" Immigration, 96.
" Organizations, 175.
" Polity, weakness of, 176.
" Theology, Sacramental idea in, 146, 152.
" Union, 33, 41.
" University, 104, 115.
" Worship, Sacramental idea in, 146, 152.
Lutheran Church and Modern Religious Issues, 272 sqq., 283 sqq.
" in America, 283 sqq.
" in Germany, 272 sqq.
" Common historical antecedents, 41 sqq., 63 sqq.
" Lack of schools, 95, 199.
Lutheranism and Spirituality, 196 sqq.
" in doctrine and worship, 204.
" Position in America, 205.
" Rightly apprehended, 196.
" Spirituality defined, 196.
" System deeply spiritual, 197, 200, 201, 204.
" versus Romish and Reformed Churches, 203.
Lutherans in America, 205.
" and Reformed, 49, 76.
" Holland, 64.
" New Jersey, 65.
" New York, 64.
" North and South Carolina, 66.
" Philadelphia, 67.
Male Diaconate, 215, 264.
Mary J. Drexel Home, 37, 229.
Mecklenburg K. O., 235.
Ministerium of Pennsylvania. See Synod.
Ministerial Education, Standard of, 250 sqq., 262 sqq.
" " Difficulty to enforce uniformity, 253, 255.
" " Need of primary education, 270.
" " Progress made, 271.
" " Requirements of ministerial office, 251 sq.
" " Standard required and applied, 254, 260 sq., 269
" " The shaping elements, 265, 267.
Ministry, 142, 250, 262.
" Intellectual standing, 271.

Modern Religious Issues, 259, 272, 282.
Moravians, 70.
Motherhouses of Deaconesses, 206 sqq.
Mystical union, 203.
Names, Register of, 322 sqq.
Newberry College, 101.
Newburg, N. Y., 65.
New Jersey, 65.
New Measures, 58, 61.
New Netherland, 128.
New Rhinebeck, 65.
New Testament, Female Diaconate, 216 sq., 213, 216, 217, 223.
" Male Diaconate, 215.
" Sacraments, 151, 153, 162.
New York, 64.
North Carolina, 66.
Old faith and new faith, 278.
Ordination, Lutheran Estimate of, 230 sqq., 237 sqq.
" Call to office, 238, 246, 247.
" Congregation and ministry, 248, 249, 250.
" Doctrine stated, 230, 237, 241 sq.
" Essential import, 243.
" Lutheran position, 237.
" Not a Sacrament, 235.
" Reformed and Lutheran Theologians, 234, 240.
" Scriptural basis, 232 sq., 239 sq.
" Status of the ordained, 245, 246.
" Value of, differently estimated, 230 sqq., 250.
Osnabruock K. O., 235.
Ostfrisian, 235.
Pennsylvania College, 46, 96, 101.
Pennsylvania Liturgy, 31, 50, 55 sq., 68, 77, 80, 81.
Periodical Literature, 58 sq.
Philadelphia, 67, 96, 115.
Platform, The Definite, 78.
Prayer: Its Doctrine and Forms, 81 sqq.
" Definition, 81 sq.
" Family prayer, 90, 93.
" Forms, 83 sq., 88 sq.
" Free prayers, 90.
" Litany, 85.
" Posture in prayer, 90.
" Prayers of the Church, 84, 89.

Prayer: Prayers of lodges, 87.
" Prayer-meetings, 70.
" Prayers to be read, 86, 88, 89.
Promise of Gospel Sealed by Sacraments, 203.
Protestant *versus* Roman countries, 230.
Protestantism arraigned as a failure, 229.
Publication Society, 47.
Pulpit Fellowship, 69.
Quatenus, 130.
Quia, 129, 130.
Rationalism, 200, 313.
Real Presence, 159, 163, 203.
Reformed, 49, 69, 198, 231, 312.
Reformed and Lutheran, 49, 76.
Religious Issues, 259, 272, 283.
" Reverse," 71, 72.
Rhinebeck, 63.
Roanoke College, 101.
Sacramental Idea in Lutheran Theology and Worship, 146 sqq., 152 sqq.
" " and the Sacraments, 161.
" " based on Revelation, 155.
" " errors, 148, 149.
" " inseparable from the Church, 157.
" " involves responsiveness, 158.
" " nature of, in our confessions, 146 sq., 153 sq.
" " other than Lutheran, 152.
" " position of the Lutheran Church, 149, 153, 163.
" " specific meaning of the term, 150.
Sacramental union, nature of, 151.
Sacraments, conception of, 150.
" Distinctive characteristics, 162.
" Essentials in, 163.
" Lutheran position, 152, 158, 159, 163.
" New Testament, 151, 153.
" Spirituality of, 202.
" *versus* Transubstantiation, 160, 163.
Sacramentum *versus* Sacrificium, 146.
Saint John's Church, 17, 31.
" Matthew's Church, 31.
Salzburgers in Georgia, 66, 198.
Savannah, Ga., 63.
Schmid's Dogmatik, 60.
Scientific spirit, 274.

22

Sharon, 65.
Smalcald Articles, 132, 240.
Spirituality and Lutheranism, 196 sqq.
Subjectivism, 274.
Sunday-School, Conception of, 187.
" " Place of Catechism in, 192.
" " Place of Holy Scripture, 191.
" " Service and Church Service, 190.
" " Teaching, 191.
" " Training of children, 190, 191.
Sunday-School Literature, common, 186 sqq.
" " " hindrances to, 194.
" " " kind of Literature needed, 193.
" " " need of common, 195.
Swedes, 64, 187.
Symbolical Books, 41, 50, 53, 58, 59, 60, 63 sq., 73, 76, 78, 123, 173, 232.
Synods, Corpus Evangelicum, 76.
" East Pennsylvania, 45, 47, 51.
" Frankean, 65, 78.
" Maryland and Virginia, 42.
" Ministerium of New York, 42, 49, 54, 55, 57, 63, 67, 71, 77, 222.
" Ministerium of Pennsylvania, 31, 32, 41, 42, 44, 49, 50, 51, 52, 54
57, 61, 63, 66 sq., 71, 77 sq.
North Carolina, 42, 49, 76.
Ohio, Joint Synod, 42, 43, 48, 59.
Pittsburg, 80, 221.
" Tennessee, 48, 51, 59, 178.
" West Pennsylvania, 54, 58.
Synods and Schools, 260, 269 sq.
Synods, Constitution of, 71.
Synods, organization of, 42.
Synods, unity of, 175.
Tarbush, 71.
Transubstantiation, 160, 163.
True Unity of the Church, 17 sqq., 291.
Tulpehocken, 67.
Union Hymn-book, 49.
United Synod of the South, 31, 33, 100 sqq., 308.
Unity of the Church, 17 sqq.
University, a Lutheran, 104, 115.
Virginia Conference, 42.
Wernigerode, 73.
West Camp, 72.

Westminster Confession, 257.
Wittenberg College, 101.
Wittenberg K. O., 235.
Worship, 179.
" Sacramental idea of, 146, 152.
Wuertemberg, 246.
York, Pa., 48.
Zwingli's *Allœosis*, 278.
Zwinglian, 77, 152.

www.ingramcontent.com/pod-product-compliance
Lightning Source LLC
Chambersburg PA
CBHW032047220426
43664CB00008B/900